1990

Series on
Ethical Conflict

The Ethical Contexts for Business Conflicts

Volume I

General Editors

Samuel M. Natale

and

John B. Wilson

UNIVERSITY
PRESS OF
AMERICA

OXFORD
PHILOSOPHY
TRUST

Lanham • New York • London

Copyright © 1990 by

University Press of America®, Inc.

4720 Boston Way
Lanham, MD 20706

3 Henrietta Street
London WC2E 8LU England

Printed in the United States of America

British Cataloging in Publication Information Available

"Chapter 11: A Machiavellian Analysis" copyright 1989 by Arthur Sharplin

"Performance Appraisal: Between Scylla and Charybdis" copyright 1989 by
Charles P. Duffy and Kenneth M. Frawley

Library of Congress Cataloging-in-Publication Data

The Ethical contexts for business conflicts / general editors,
Samuel M. Natale and John B. Wilson.
p.   cm. — (Ethical conflict ; v. 1)
Includes bibliographical references.
1. Business ethics.
I. Natale, Samuel M.   II. Wilson, John, 1928–   .   III. Series.
HF5387.E775   1989   174'.4—dc20   89–22762 CIP

ISBN 0–8191–7597–8 (alk. paper)
ISBN 0–8191–7598–6 (pbk. : alk. paper)

The paper used in this publication meets the minimum requirements of American
National Standard for Information Sciences—Permanence of Paper for Printed Library
Materials, ANSI Z39.48–1984.   ∞

For
Rt. Rev. Walter. F. Sullivan, J.C.D.
Roman Catholic Bishop of Richmond, Virginia
and
Rev. Msgr. James McGrath, J.C.D.
—friends, companions, leaders along the way

Contents

INTRODUCTION

This is the first volume in a series of studies which is aimed at clarifying one of the most vexing and ubiquitous problems of contemporary living—ethics and moral education.

This series is published jointly by the Oxford Philosophy Trust and the University Press of America. The Oxford Philosophy Trust is an independent research and educational unit under the direction of John B. Wilson (UK) and Samuel M. Natale (USA). The work of the trust involves ongoing research into the area of moral education. The goal is to *apply* the results of philosophical thinking by exploring empirical studies to determine precisely how and under what conditions people implement or refuse to implement values they claim are central.

This first volume deals with the area endemic to moral decision making—conflict. This conflict is examined as it appears in corporate living. It is by now axiomatic to say that the corporation has replaced any other organization as the central organization of our time. It is doubtless the most powerful of all structures responsible for the employment of peoples as well as the production of goods desired by them. Power and ubiquity provide, however, no exemption from the tensions inherent in making decisions which effect peoples' lives.

This collection of articles covers a broad array of topics to give the reader a flavor for the kinds of issues which exist in this cognate domain. Within these pages readers will explore everything from the problem of decision making and authority to models of the market which may impact on ethical decisions. Other articles explore some new suggestions for Wall Street as well as studies on the problems and conflicts inherent in personnel assessment and corporate decisions such as declaring bankruptcy. Other authors reflect more systemic concerns such as examining organizational structures for issues involving justice or, in another case, exploring just *how* and *if* values impact on concrete living at all.

These articles should spark both lively discussion as well as considerable distress.

Samuel M. Natale, D. Phil. (Oxon.)
Iona College
New York

Ethics and Decision Making:
Conflict, Authority, and Discipline

Samuel M. Natale, D.Phil. (Oxon.)
Professor, Studies in Corporate Values
Hagan School of Business
Iona College
New Rochelle, New York

and

Visiting Scholar, Mansfield College
University of Oxford
Oxford, England

John B. Wilson, M.A.
Fellow, Mansfield College
University of Oxford
Oxford, England

Barbara Cowell
Research Fellow
Oxford Philosophy Trust
Oxford, England

♦

There is no question but that business ethics has been increasingly of concern since the early 1960s (McElwreath 1987, 9). Even the most superficial familiarity with the literature indicates the three prevalent points of view: an identification of the social responsibility of business; a clarification of the rather specific issues and practices that have a negative effect on the social structure; and finally, an analysis of the social consequences of managerial decisions and styles.

The social responsibility of business has resulted in a predictable controversy between individuals who believe that a business has no social accountability beyond providing a return for its stockholders, and those who believe that a central concern of industry must include stockholder and stakeholder considerations as well as broader global concerns.

Much of the most recent emphasis has been on managerial decision-making styles as well as on consideration of individual behavior of managers within an organization. The whole arena remains clouded, and recognized names such as A. Carr (1970) query whether a business executive can really afford a conscience at all, while authors such as M. Glazer (1983) consider whether managers *should* inform if they note unethical behavior. There is no shortage of authors reflecting on the *context* of business to attempt a determination of the possible structure of an effective and ethical decision-making process.

While there is clear development in the entire area of ethical decision making, we suspect that this may not be the direction of most productive concern. Although increasing emphasis is both sought and mandated in terms of required ethical training and courses in business ethics, the question remains about the actual effectiveness of training in ethics (MacIntyre 1977, 20). MacIntyre has argued that there is really no resolving of ethical problems "either because ethical theory is inadequate or because the individual constructs problems in such a way that the ethical dimension is avoided" (McElwreath 1987, 20).

The central issue, we believe, revolves around a number of other components which include the reality that there appears to be *no systematic business ethical theory* and *no superordinate cultural goals* to which one might appeal. Most of the work emerges rather as a case-by-case analysis which is more akin to the legal case approach to problems, relying on precedent and developed opinion, than to a systematic structure from which secondary and tertiary principles might appropriately be inferred.

The central problems seem to stem from a number of concerns which include diverse and/or opposing cultural assumptions, the nature of the decision-making process itself, the cultural *refusal* to engage in *discipline*, and the hesitancy to make decisions and apply a *prescriptive* weight to them. These trends are easily enough inferable from any analysis of the varied global educational systems as well as anthropological studies.

Although these problems seem far flung, they form a *piece*—that is, they link together in a coherent manner. The dilemma might look something like this: a situation arises, and because of various cultural assumptions and diversity, there is a hesitancy to claim *authority.* As a result, there follows an inability to speak definitively since to utilize authority suggests *power* to judge and *discipline. Tolerance* for diversity, while critical, has increasingly become an over-frequently used escape hatch. It seems necessary that we re-examine the belief that tolerance has no boundary and that moral certainty is not possible in this cognate domain.

In what follows we attempt an examination of the decision-making process, the elements of tolerance, and its relationship to authority and discipline to shed some light by the juxtaposition of what seem to be logically related concepts. Perhaps we might be able at that time to define more adequately the conflicted areas of the on-going debate.

THE PROCESS OF DECIDING

Part of the problem with establishing an ethical frame of reference for decision making lies in the actual process and manner of *how* decisions are made. There appear to be four recurring major concerns.

The first problem is that decision making is anchored on one end by *individual decision processes* and at the other end by *organizational decision processes*. The theory that has concentrated on individual processes emphasizes the way "in which an individual searches for data, values information, and combines prior learning in order to make choices" (McElwreath 1987, 23). An organization is perceived as a data source instead of an integral part of the entire process. On the other hand, organizational decision theorists emphasize the organization's role in establishing the types of decisions which are faced as well as "the context which enables the individual to learn which information is relevant, which cues to attend to, and how choices ought to be valued" (McElwreath 1987, 23.) McElwreath mentions two types of individual process models: those which might be considered as stimulus-response theories and those which are information-processing models. M. Rubenstein (1975) has considered these two models. R. Cyert and J. March (1963) have described the concepts involved in organizational decision models which emphasize the context in which the decision making occurs. It is obvious that any decision process involving the selection and hierarchy of values must involve *both* elements, individual and organizational. The problem is compounded because of the complexity of interaction involved since it appears that individual behavior varies in accordance with organizational norms, goals, and what in general is referred to as "organizational psychology."

The second concern focuses on the existence of *phase theories*. Simply stated, phase theorists assume a sequential series: "the decision maker must complete each preceding phase before passing to the next" (McElwreath 1987, 22). According to this theory, the decision maker proceeds through successive stages until the problem is resolved. H. Mintzberg, D. Raisinghani, and A. Theoret have defined three phases: 1) an identification phase in which a problem is initially recognized; 2) a development phase which includes a search for alternatives to resolve the problem—this phase dominates all others, according to Mintzberg, as it is the phase which furnishes a link between the problem and solution; 3) selection "in which alternatives are matched against decision criteria and the selection of the alternative is made" (Mintzberg, Raisinghani, and Theoret 1976). The problem here is equally obvious. That is, complex decisions often involving multinational corporations require decisions made on limited information and *parts* of the decision process occur *simultaneously*.

The third major issue for our consideration is the extent to which a decision situation has been structured. To state the matter simply, "Structured decisions are those which have routine solutions available, while unstructured decisions are those for which there are no apparent, easily applied solutions" (McElwreath 1987, 22). E. Harrison (1981) has proposed a broad topology which separates decisions into two categories: *programmable* decisions and *nonprogrammable* decisions. Programmable refers to those decision situations that recur in organizations and for which the organization has constructed habit patterns or habitual response patterns (33). However, what is a programmable decision in one organization might be nonprogrammable in another because the firm has never faced the situation previously or has never constructed the problem in such a way previously. Although the problems in this model are equally daunting, some newer research into the area of artificial intelligence has encouraged the decision maker at least to empower him/her to gain vast amounts of data almost instantaneously, thereby, at least theoretically, enabling him/her to construct better hierarchies for deciding. Regrettably, at the moment, the one criteria an AI machine can apply with considerable clarity is the concept of *justice*—this, however, in a very linear manner.

Negotiated decisions are the fourth concern and are of two types that A. Delbecq has defined. "Negotiated decisions are those in which opposing goals are held by various members of the organization who may form a coalition (qtd. in McElwreath 1987, 34). Delbecq's second category of definition is *routine* decisions, those in which group members agree on the goal stated as well as the path to the goal. McElwreath feels there is little difference between this routine category and H. Simon's programmable category. The third type of decisions, for Delbecq are *creative* ones for which there is "no well defined problem and no prior solution set, and which therefore require an innovative solution" (34).

Mintzberg, Raisinghani, and Theoret (1976) first employed the term "structured decision" to refer to a type of decision in which there were no predetermined and explicit set of responses. On the other hand, unstructured decisions are perceived as strategic decisions and are generally resolved at higher levels of the organization. "Structured decisions are described as those which occur in lower levels of an organization and which are handled quite routinely by appropriate operating management."

McElwreath also makes a major distinction between the process of defining a problem and of making a decision. Some research places stress on problem definition and problem finding, while other research emphasized decision making—the act of selecting one alternative from many. He notes that "Newell and Simon describe a problem as a discrepancy between a current and a desired state" (34) and Kepner and Trego define a problem "as the deviation between what is, that is, the current state and a standard of some kind" (36).

Rubinstein (1975) discusses two basic categories of problems: 1) *synthesis* problems in which the distinction between the initial state and the desired state is removed; 2) *analysis* type problems which place emphasis on applying known transformation processes to reach a goal (37). Now, Harrison (1981) is one writer who does not draw a clear difference between problem solving and decision making; for him, "problem structure is perceived as a result of varied input from different external environments" (38). Problem defining occurs as the decision maker imposes or adjusts constraints. In structuring a problem, decision makers who perceive what they feel is an "organizationally correct" response will adopt such a decision as a *constraint*. This constraint is traditionally formulated as corporate *policy*. For our concerns, however, problem solving and decision making are *substantially* different concerns: problem solving may appropriately appeal to pragmatics which do not *necessarily* imply ethical considerations. Problem solving, from our point of view, necessitates ethical considerations as *part of its definition.*

The term *constraint* is employed in describing the effect of goals on decision criteria and problem formulation (Harrison 1981, 39). Simon suggests further that an individual's role is a major determining factor of the premises underlying his/her decisions. W. Pounds draws a further distinction between problem finding and problem structuring: the former being the process of defining differences between an existing situation and a desired situation, the latter being the "process of selecting operators (response sets) that remove the differences" (39).

McElwreath summarizes the decision literature by noting that one needs to address at least the four dimensions raised above: 1) the difference between individual and organizational models of decision making; 2) problem solving and decision making; 3) phase and nonphase approaches; 4) rational and alternative theories.

DISCIPLINE

Few topics are more thorny or evoke such intense emotion than that of discipline. David Hammonds (1984) has adequately summarized the three most frequent ways of examining discipline. First, there is discipline as socialization and character training. School discipline is frequently considered a major aspect of the manner in which children learn to participate in adult society or become socialized. Schools are frequently "regarded as the place where children should be taught the behavioral values of the dominant culture and learn to act accordingly" (18). E. Durkeim perceived school discipline in terms of preparing as a child for the "discipline of society," and felt it was in the interest of public morality for teachers to cultivate their pupils in what he termed the "spirit of discipline" (qtd. in Hammonds 1984, 19). Durkeim emphasized regulating a child's conduct, moderating a child's egocentric desires, and encouraging a child to respect authority. He felt it was essential for a child to perceive school regulations as a reflection of the regulation of society.

D. Ausubel and colleagues argue that discipline is a type of "character training which contributes towards the development of a stable personality" (qtd. in Hammonds 1984, 20). Wilson has argued that children should be taught to obey authority but not in an undifferentiated sense; it is not simply any authority children must be taught to obey but particular authorities in particular situations where to be disobedient could be dangerous and might prevent a task from being achieved.

At the same time, one must avoid educating children into "docility" (Silberman 1973, 9). This also alerts us to the fact that teachers demanding uniform obedience to rigid codes produce anger and disruption rather than discipline (Kohlberg 1964).

Discipline may also be viewed as "control" (Hammonds 1984, 21). Indeed, in most educational literature the term "discipline" is perceived most frequently as meaning the same thing as control. Ausubel et al. feel that discipline is "the imposition of external standards and controls on pupils which if internalized lead to 'self-discipline'" (Ausubel 1978, 13).

Ausubel also discusses "democratic discipline" to describe appropriate ways of controlling children which are not perceived as ends in themselves but as means to successful teaching. "Democratic discipline" means processes which are noncoercive (qtd. in Hammonds 1984, 22). P. Hobson, moreover, addresses a moral issue in noting that coercion can *never* really be an educational method in assisting children to learn what is true.

Control may also be established by the use of principles derived from group dynamics and which are associated with the work of J. Kounin. This technique focuses attention toward the teacher's public demonstration that he/she is cognizant of what is occurring and that he/she is able to facilitate smooth transitions from one activity to another (Harrison 1984, 23). Also, Sanders in 1979 furnished quite practical responses to the matters of establishing and maintaining acceptable behavior through "efficient and sensitive classroom organization and management" (qtd. in Harrison 1984, 24). Whether this can be applied to a corporate structure is highly questionable.

Discipline as *educative* may, however, be more usefully applied. This approach views discipline as *part of* the definition of education. Equally, one might be able to assert legitimately that discipline is *part of* the essential definition of ethical decision making. Such a perspective would appear to be most relevant to moral education generally. Indeed, such authors as Dewey, Piaget, and Kohlberg all consider discipline as educative. Dewey, Piaget and Kohlberg all consider discipline to be the center of moral thought and education. The same appears true in decision making within a corporate structure. Dewey perceives discipline in educational terms and states that "discipline is the form that growth producing learning takes when learning is purposeful and goal directed" (qtd. in Harrison 1984, 25). Piaget (1965) associates discipline with morality in that the foundation of both discipline and morality is a system of rules; further, Piaget believes that "discipline constitutes the essence of morality since discipline is the positive cognitive and active learning of the rules of life" (qtd. in Harrison 1984, 26). Kohlberg amplifies these considerations and suggests that it is in part through the imposition of sensible discipline that a student is encouraged to develop or remain in the same stage of development. This position has significant implications for industry where there is a growing cultural tolerance for "looseness" of decisions. Discipline is rarely imposed for decisions that are considered unethical (unless one identifies illegal with unethical—clearly not our operative point of view). Discipline is then a condition of possibility for ethical and moral development. To refuse judgments and rewards/punishments in the name of some asserted notion of "tolerance" is to eviscerate the possibility of *development* within a moral sphere.

In what we have just argued we distinguish between control and discipline. Control is understood to be of the *manipulative* order while discipline of the *educative* order. The constraining quality of discipline arises not from punitive external forces but from the very values inherent in the activity itself (P. Wilson 1971,22). Our notion of discipline then is that of Wilson who defines discipline as of the "educative order...involved in trying to reach appropriate standards or follow appropriate rules for engaging in valued activity" (79). In short, discipline "should be defined in terms of 'accepting rules' because it brings in the notion of 'obedience'" (79).

These arguments all lead to the clear position that authority, rules, sanctions, or punishment are all *intrinsically involved* in the notion of discipline. Authority is "inseparably connected with a rule-governed form of life and thus presupposes some sort of normative order" (Peters 1966, 239). Peters continues that "authority involves an appeal to an impersonal normative order or value system which regulates behavior basically because of acceptance of it on the part of those who comply" (239).

This line of thinking leads quite clearly to a consideration of normative order as well as authority to judge and reward/punish. In the modern corporate world one is hard pressed to present a unified picture which would submit on first analysis to a "normative order." However, it may be that we simply are avoiding this analysis because the conclusions at which we would arrive would be problematic for industry, unaccepted by people of different motivational systems and finally embarrassing because it simply does not conform to current social attitudes.

Punishment is more focused according to Peters who feels it is appropriate *only* when there has been an infraction of the rules. It may be justified principally on two grounds: 1) when it is a necessary prerequisite to preserve a system of order; 2) by aiding in clarifying "what is right and wrong."

It is impossible to consider moral decision making *if* discipline is not accepted as part of the *educational process*. To invoke discipline suggests in the best of situations that there exists a moral/ethical order. As Wilson argues, "punishment is conceptually related to discipline rather than to control" (P. Wilson 1971, 77).

The *disciplinarian*, however, must be an individual who firmly grasps and properly understands the concepts marked by discipline and who considers discipline to be an important aspect of moral education. There can be no imposition of appropriate discipline unless certain conditions described are present. First there must be a *clear operational description* of the morally (ethically) educated person. Secondly, there needs to be an amplification of this concept into an operational description of the morally educated disciplinarian. Some of the ground work for these tasks have already been undertaken with considerable success.

Sugarman (1973) defines the morally educated person in the following manner:

1. He is someone who has concern for other people such that their feelings, wants and interests count with one and are not lightly overridden for the sake of one's own goals.

2. The morally educated person is competent at social skills, good

at knowing other people's feelings and good at expressing his own.

3. ...is knowledgeable about physical and social worlds.

4. ...is objective and unprejudiced in sizing up situations and unafraid to proceed with the plan of action intended.

5. ...when thinking of what to do in an unfamiliar situation or in passing judgment on action already taken, thinks in terms of universalistic moral principles based on concern for the rights of other people as well as himself. (42-49)

It is a working assumption that the disciplinarian would *be* a morally educated person. Some research has already been done to describe the morally educated disciplinarian (J. Wilson 1981):

1. The morally educated disciplinarian would consider discipline to be an important aspect of moral education and would, therefore, treat discipline as *educative*.

2. ...would have knowledge of the key concepts of discipline—authority, rules, sanctions, rewards, etc. He would thus grasp that discipline has to do with:
a. obedience to legitimate authority
b. the need for rules backed by sanctions
c. the need for the authority's legitimacy and power for educa tional purposes only.

3. ...would demonstrate his knowledge and understanding in his practice of discipline.

4. ...would
a. understand clearly what discipline is required in the project.
b. have the nerve or confidence to act on it.

5. ...would "tolerate being separate," for in acting as an impersonal authority and in preventing people from doing what they wanted to do he would make ... enemies.

6. ...would understand that rational discipline and authority de pend on understanding the point of entitlement, of entrusting certain people with certain delimited powers to do a certain job.

7. ...would understand that "discipline" did not merely mean "control."

8. ...would use his authority and power without "serious feelings of guilt" in the knowledge that people were anxious for adequate methods of control.

9. ...would understand that

a. clear rules and punishments had to be laid down and properly publicized.
b. the punishments had to be effective as deterrents
c. restitutive justice should be enforced by making the offenders pay back in terms of time and effort for the unpleasantness they had inflicted.
d. offenders believed that some person or group of people had to be entrusted with sufficient on the spot power to ensure that this apparatus was actually effective.

10. ...would appreciate that the style of discipline he adopted would have a significant influence, for better or worse, on the moral ethos.... (17-18)

It is clear from the foregoing that ethical decision making *can* be undertaken effectively and that it requires discipline and control which may take the form of punishment in the case of infraction; *however*, it is equally clear that a number of formidable hurdles remain, especially within the corporate world where the basic *assumption* of a "unity of values" is increasingly difficult to make—without, perhaps, heroic virtue. It is our assumption, however, that there exists a unified order from which one might legitimately infer "acceptable" and "unacceptable" actions. To clarify this, we must consider two major issues: values and tolerance. Any decision making must advert to the issue of its value-base as well as to levels of tolerance accepted within corporate policy standards.

THE FRAGMENTATION OF VALUE

In his essay "The Fragmentation of Value" Thomas Nagel (1987) discusses problems "created between the fragmentation of value and the singleness of decision" (174). Nagel feels that there are *five* fundamental types of value that lead to basic conflict, and conflicts can arise within as well as between them, but the latter are especially difficult.

First, there are specific obligations to other people or institutions; i.e., obligations to corporate clients, patients, to family, to hospital or university at which one works, etc. Such obligations must be undertaken, whether by deliberate undertaking or by some special relation to the individual or institution in question. In any case their existence is contingent on a subject's relation to others, even if the relation does not need to be voluntary.

A second category is "constraints on action deriving from general rights that everyone has, either to do certain things or not to be treated in certain ways" (175). Rights to liberty of certain kinds are not contingent on specific obligations that others have incurred, not to interfere, assault, etc. Rather, rights are quite general and possibly restrict what others might do to their possessor; therefore a doctor has rather specific obligations to patients and also general duties to treat anyone in certain ways.

Third, we have what might be termed utility: the consideration that weighs the effects of what one does on everyone's welfare—"Whether or not the components of that welfare are connected to special obligations or general rights" (175). Utility involves all aspects of benefit and harm for all people, not just for those for whom the agent has a special relation.

A fourth category is one of perfectionist ends or values, by which Nagel means the "intrinsic value of certain achievements or creations, apart from their value to individuals who experience or use them" (176). Examples would be the intrinsic value of scientific discovery or space exploration or artistic creation; such pursuits do not really serve the interests of the individuals who are directly involved in them and of some spectators. The pursuit of such ends is not solely justified in terms of interests, but they are considered, according to Nagel, to have an intrinsic value.

A fifth or final category for Nagel is one of *commitment* to one's own projects or undertakings, a value in addition to whatever reasons may have led to them initially. Whatever one has set out to undertake, then "the further pursuit of that project, once begun, acquires remarkable importance" (176). In part, it is a desire to be the type of individual who finishes what he begins. However, such commitments must not be confused with self-interest since self-interest directs itself at "the integrated fulfillment over time of all one's interests and desires (or at least those desires one does not wish to eliminate)" (176). Nagel believes that obligations, rights, utility, private commitments all are *values* which enter constantly into our decisions, and conflicts among them arise in many arenas—not the least of which is corporate decision making. A simpler moral conception might allow "a solution in terms of a short list of clear prohibitions and injunctions, with the balance of decision left to personal preference or discretion, but that will not work with so mixed a collection" (177).

Nagel's general point is that formal differences among types of reason reflect differences of a fundamental nature in their sources, and that this rules out a certain kind of solution to conflicts among these types. Obviously, human beings are subject to moral and other motivational claims of quite different kinds.

Further, Nagel asks whether basic practical conflicts have any solution. We always have to do something, even if it is nothing. Nagel contends that there can be good judgment without total justification, whether explicit or implicit. "The fact that one cannot say why a certain decision is the correct one, given a particular balance of conflicting reasons, does not mean that the claim to correctness is meaningless" (180). If one indeed has taken the process of practical justification as far as it will go in the course of arriving at the conflict, one might well be able to proceed both without further justification and also without irrationality. What makes this possible is *judgment*. This concept has been singularly thorny in the area of corporate ethics since "judgments" as described above can be undertaken in severely distorted ways dependent on the motivation of the judge.

Now to search for a single theory of how to decide the correct thing to do is similar to searching for a single theory of how to decide what one must believe. One should employ exact principles and methods to deal with the aspects of a problem for which they are available, but at times there are also other aspects, and one must resist the temptation either to ignore them or to treat them by methods to which they might not be susceptible (181).

Nagel notes that we are quite familiar with the fragmentation of understanding and method when it come to belief, but we are curiously prone to resist it in the case of decision. Nagel does not feel that ethics is a science but that the relation between ethical theory and practical decisions is similar to a relation between scientific theory and beliefs about singular events in the world.

Progress in certain areas of ethics and value theory do not need to wait for the discovery of a general foundation; John Rawls, Nagel notes, claims not only "that the pursuit of substantive moral theory, for example the theory of justice, can proceed independently of views about the foundation of ethics, but that until substantive theory is further developed, the search for foundations may be premature" (183).

Nagel does not believe that all value rests on a single foundation nor is able to be combined into a unified system: different types of values illustrate the development and articulation of different points of view, all combining to produce decisions. Ethics is not like physics, representing one point of view, but "ethics is more like understanding or knowledge in general that it is like physics" (183). As our world understanding involves various points of view, so values derive from several viewpoints.

For Nagel, the fragmentation of effort and results has great implications for the type of strategy to be employed in applying results to practical decisions, particularly questions of public policy. A lacking of a general theory of value should not act as an obstacle to employing the areas of understanding that *do exist*. What we need most, according to Nagel, "is a method of breaking up and analyzing problems to say what evaluative principles apply, and how" (184). This is not really a decision method—although in special cases it would yield a decision—but ordinarily it indicates the *junctures at which different types of ethical considerations needed to be introduced* in order to furnish the basis for an intelligent, responsible decision. We also need, according to Nagel, a "consensus about what important ethical and evaluative questions have to be considered if a policy decision is to be made responsibly" (185). However, this is not equivalent to a consensus in ethics; what it does mean is that there are certain aspects of any problem which most individuals who work in ethics and value theory would agree should be contemplated in such a manner that *whoever makes the decision will be exposed to the currently available relevant ideas*. Nagel does not recommend ethics as a decision procedure but as "an essential resource for making decisions, just as physics, economics, and demography are" (186). For most questions that require a decision, ethical considerations are truly many, complex, and confused with others. Nagel concludes by observing that ethical considerations need to contemplated in a systematic way; however, in most instances a reasonable decision can be attained solely by sound judgment which is also informed by the most solid arguments that any relevant discipline can offer.

It appears that the formation of individuals to make ethical decisions may be a more broadly based task and involve the informing of judgment rather than simple decision making. This suggest, of course, that *other* significant variables need to be included in the equation. Some of these issues include considerations of empathy, justice, and respect—items which are more difficult to define than to recognize when encountered.

Given the pluralism that exists in culture, is a neutral or objective vantage point possible? In short, is an *objective* ethic possible?

Traditionally, one hears that no objective position is possible because of personal and cultural relativism. The supporters of this position argue that based on the semi-infinite variety in different cultures, no universal ethic appears possible. This is evident in the cultural attitudes toward women for example. In some cultures women are paid less, treated as inferior, etc., while in other cultures, more acceptable standards are applied. Although one can look at the data of various cultural experiences, there are also *universal* criteria which are being ignored. For example, women need to be viewed as human *persons* and when this is done, the criteria shift considerably, allowing for the consideration of their rights and entitlements that flow from personhood rather than gender. Gender is clearly an inferior criteria for analysis than personhood.

This fragmentation of value may never be fully escaped; however it can be unified a bit. For example, very often individuals making decisions lack the necessary data (facts) on which to base their decisions. In addition to this, there is a confusion of terms and definitional inadequacy. Finally, one can use examples of various moral situations and analyze these in terms of "position-counterposition." A final attempt at clarification can be made by careful *logical* analysis of situations and examination of basic assumptions proper to the agent and the object *as well as* the transaction under investigation. These criteria have been reasonably well attested to.

All the above having been said, it must also be added that human nature seems to have a built-in defensive system (more or less adequately analyzed by the various schools of psychology) which shows that people have a highly defensive and vested interest in *maintaining* their biases and distortions. It may be necessary to engage in an educational process *first* which aims at reduction of negative defenses *before* actually beginning the ethical/moral education under discussion here.

TOLERATION

In another article entitled "The Limits of Toleration" Brenda Almond (1987) notes that against the virtue of respect for freedom of conscience must be set the voice of tolerating the intolerable. She observes that "the toleration principle itself has an ethical, a social and a politico-legal form" (43). She raises the question of whether the notion of toleration needs to be reappraised. Are both, for example, political left and right to be discovered with a clearer perception of utilitarian necessity, if not of truth and virtue, than the old liberal advocates of the open society?

First, it is necessary to perceive and comprehend the function of some ambiguities in the notion of *tolerance of opinion*. Expressing an opinion may be passive or aggressive, and it may be influenced by education or propaganda or mass advertising (46). If opinion is not unchangeable, then the protection of a right to an opinion may not be distinguished from the protection of a right to its expression. Almond believes there is a sense in which opinion itself cannot truly be tolerated—the reason being if one shares the opinion, then it makes no real sense to discuss tolerating it, and if one disagrees with the opinion, then one is truly committed to its repudiation (46-47).

Most of the beliefs which we deem as important are really beliefs *about* action; therefore, if we assume the standard case for toleration, religious belief, "it is only at the most superficial level that it can be taken as a case of abstract and metaphysical belief without consequences in the real world" (49). Toleration of belief might be separated from a question of practice at least with respect to searching for scientific truth. The notion of pure opinion might be set aside for a more sophisticated awareness and acceptance of the role which opinion performs in human affairs.

Almond observes that those who oppose toleration might do so because where truth can be attained, there really can be no actual case for tolerating untruth. Historically, especially within the context of burning of heretics and religious wars in Europe, it might well be possible to discover people who give expression to a multitude of differing arguments about toleration. The first argument Almond labels as *religious truth is a development*—"a graduate evolution in which people over generations come closer to truth without ever arriving at a position of final unarguable dogma" (50). A second argument may be stated as *falsehood is harmless* because truth will always win. A third position may be indicated as "In practice truth cannot be imposed by force" (50); in other words, one cannot simply sanction the burning of heretics. Fourth, reason is always preferable to revelation, even if such entails skepticism concerning the ability of human beings to attain certainty or truth. Finally, liberty in general is impossible without liberty of conscience.

Further, Almond observes that any real commitment to truth or principle involves a prerequisite unwillingness to concede error. It is difficult to avoid being indifferent when one tolerates differences, and it may appear that any choices which are posed with respect to toleration "are either to abandon conviction and thus concede the case for toleration on the grounds of uncertainty, or to retain one's convictions at the expense of toleration" (51). However, the toleration question involves whether it is possible to be committed to the ideas that truth is attainable and others must be protected in their mistakes.

Almond discusses Herbert Marcuse's attack on toleration, and indeed Marcuse has become so much the representative of this viewpoint and any political movements which express it that it is difficult to remember that Marcuse was born less than 40 years after the publication of J.S. Mill's "On Liberty." Perhaps Marcuse is a reminder "of the close connection between the ideal of tolerance and the ideal of pluralism" (52). Also, as Almond observes, if a plurality of views is able to flourish, it is almost necessary that falsity be represented in addition to truth. A major function of toleration is to protect reason and conscience as agents in searching for truth. As P. King has said, "the toleration principle is directly put in question at any time it is supposed that there is a truth, that it can be known, and that it enjoys some highest priority or supreme value" (qtd. in Almond 1987, 53).

However, although truth, whether an abstraction or whatever, may be a disputable concept, the basic fact is that opinions may be closer to or further from the truth, as well as better or worse in an ethical sense. Even a muted belief in ethical objectivity might combine with awareness of what humans do believe "to justify our unease when forced to tread the borders of toleration" (53).

Almond concludes by observing that in the contemporary world both a state-sanctioned torturer and a revolutionary bomber attempt—as did heretic burners in the past—to destroy an opinion by destroying a person. Simultaneously, psychiatric treatment of someone for "deviant opinions" illustrates an ultimate personality invasion and rejection of the ideal of toleration. The phrase "a fair hearing" means tolerating an expression of opinion, "stopping short, however, of action and incitement to action at that point where the principle of protection of the defenseless must take priority" (55). It is through this point on the "toleration continuum"—one that extends from opinion through expressing opinion, to inciting to action, and to action itself —"where the line must be drawn marking off the limits of toleration" (55).

In making concrete *business* decisions, this line of toleration must be accurately and *sensibly* drawn with respect for the goals and objectives of business. Certainly, one of the goals of business is to make a profit and any discussion of decisions must take this into consideration. There is considerable work needed here in the area of distinguishing elements of profit which vary from economic to humane. This continuum *requires* that an operational line be drawn.

Nor is it sufficient, as suggested by many authorities, that the pluralism of modern corporate societies requires that no "condition of possibility" can be designated. Certainly, one must tolerate a broad spectrum of approaches *but* this toleration can never be allowed to degenerate into a vacuous position which is equivalent to some corporate credo of "whatever you need to do to make a profit, as long as it is legal is acceptable." It is *not* legal nor is it acceptable to argue that decisions can be predicted on purely profit-oriented concerns. One needs to argue more adequately that while profit-making corporate concerns are certainly *part of the consideration*, even these can be overruled under conditions requiring assessment of the "common good"— most broadly defined.

The argument has been put most accurately by Douglas Sturm (1985) who argues that:

> The primary ethical question...is not what is predictable. Nor is it what is possible. Nor is it what will enable the human species merely to survive. It is rather what will conduce to the common good. Human life is intrinsically relational. It is lived in a set of contexts—a biosphere (the relationship between self and nature), a sociosphere (the relationship between self and other) and a psychosphere (the relationship between self and self). The common good is that texture of relationships in which the life of all is enhanced by the actions and dispositions of each one. Its common name is sympathy. Its profound meaning is love. Its ordinary, everyday demand is justice. Its grounding is ultimately ontological. That is, the common good is not an abstract principle imposed upon the reality of the world. It is a quality that derives from the structure of experience. It is the deepest impulse and profoundest need of all being. The suffering and misery that result from its violation are themselves witness to its presence.
>
> Thus, to assess the full significance of the culture of the corporation, to interpret the meaning of the world that it manifests within itself..., the world that it produces through its agency... and the world that it tends to promote for the future even if it should itself disappear..., it must be measured by its conformity to the common good. The ultimate judgment of the corporation and its culture, like the ultimate judgment of all life, is whether and to what degree within the ongoing passage of history, it bodies forth some creative advance within the community of being.
>
> In sum, the corporation, like the Sabbath, was not made for its own survival. Its legitimacy depends on whether its meaning it truly representative of the meaning of life itself. (158)

While it is clear that this demand places constraints on decision makers, it is equally clear that these constraints can be operationalized by consideration of what we have discussed previously. For example, while tolerating a considerable divergence of opinions and points of view even within a broad cultural foundation with a clear disunity of value structures, there still remain definite considerations which the corporation must attend to. For example, no matter how analyzed, the corporate response of Union Carbide to the Bhopal, India, incident *must* be judged seriously deficient. One might argue degrees of accountability; however, there can be no serious disagreement that the corporation made serious errors in ethical judgment in their control responsibilities regarding the lives of workers, industry safety, corporate image, and the common good. No matter how formulated, tolerance and fragmentation of value notwithstanding, the corporation acted inappropriately and unethically.

AUTHORITY AND DISCIPLINE

It seems then that the problems discussed above are not insoluble, though they remain clearly difficult. Rather, it may be that there is a growing cultural phobia to the entire notion of authority and discipline.

In a series of publications we have attempted to clarify the philosophy of moral education. We believe, however, that whether or not any rational basis will actually be put to educational use depends upon our attitude toward certain basic concepts, especially that of authority. How in fact *do* we think or feel about authority?

It is important to realize that there are major differences between individuals and groups and to appreciate what the differences are. We can identify and distinguish two types of reactions. The first involves *identification* with authority: here the individual (or corporation/society as a whole) views himself/herself as the unquestionable representative of a corpus of truths and values. Such a representative possesses the right answers and sees his/her job consisting of passing on these answers to individuals so that they might end up believing them and acting in accordance with them. The individual welcomes the power, authority, sanctions, and disciplinary measures deemed necessary to put it into practice.

The second involves *rejection* of authority: the individual is in a state of reaction against whatever one takes to be current authorities and does not regard his/her own beliefs and values as having priority over others, or as forming a firm and secure basis for education. A type of relativistic position might be adopted in which the objectivity of truth and value in itself is called into question or even denied.

Now it is fairly easy to perceive how each of these reactions strays from the concept of appropriate education and in the case of our concern, *ethical education.* On the other hand, the notion of education—and indeed of learning itself—is connected within the logically basic notion of a rational stance towards the world. Right answers cannot be the starting point of education since their rightness can only be a function of the criteria of reason which justify them as right. This is perhaps most obvious in the case of moral/ethical education, where it is clear that no first-order set of values—no specific *moral content*—can be taken for granted. For the latter type of education, we must rely on initiating individuals in corporations into a grasp of the rational procedures which they can use to generate their own values.

On the other hand, to dismantle or reject authority in general, to fall into any kind of relativism, to react against the whole concept of "right answers," is equally to stray from education since the notions of reason, learning, knowledge, truth, and education itself are connected to that concept. Rational procedures do have authority, and educators and decision makers can and must have authority insofar as they act as representatives of the procedures; further, ethical decision makers as well as educators need the practical or social authority necessary to transmit these procedures to their subordinates; that is, the authority and power necessary to enforce whatever discipline is required for education.

The second reaction is the more complex one and deserves our more immediate attention. Characteristic symptoms of it *include* the following general ideas: 1) that education and authoritative/ethical decision making is a contestable concept without any fixed definition and is therefore fundamentally an ideological notion; 2) that rules and punishment should be reduced to a minimum; 3) that anger, aggression, violence, etc., are bad; 4) that decision makers should not have *impersonal* authority; 5) that there are no things existing in their own right called "subjects," "discipline," or "forms of thought" with their own rules and standards; 6) that there are no objective and demonstrably correct values.

One basic matter to mention here is the natural resentment which anyone feels at being in the power of someone else. It seems to the subordinate to be deeply and dangerously unfair, though the nature of society demands that under specific conditions dependence on others in positions of power are necessary. Previous research (Natale 1973) has indicated that this response may be modified by an *empathic* and *identification* process. That is, the decision maker not only identifies with the "objects" of his/her decision but also is empathic to these individuals' needs, wants, and aspirations.

Feelings of guilt may also arise, especially if an individual has to assume an authoritative position or exercise power, and even more so if one has profited from institutions connected with privilege. The question of what *authority* an executive, priest, social worker, or whatever is supposed to have—what expertise he/she possesses which justifies his/her professional work—is rarely raised at all because the reply might well be, in certain instances, no authority at all. Decision makers must become more reasonable if education of subordinates is to proceed well, not merely just to accept dictation from outside. Education *must* remain largely in the hands of educators who alone—like parents—are on sufficiently intimate terms with their pupils to have any hope of making the right decisions.

We can certainly detect tendencies to extremism which we must carefully watch; we need to understand the roots of our feelings more deeply and in more detail. Therefore, we and some colleagues interviewed several hundred people in business and other professions to discover what and how they thought about discipline and authority in corporation as well as in schools, where the foundation is laid for these attitudes. We focused primarily on discipline since we felt this was the way in which the idea of authority impinged on them most directly. We divided our respondents into six groups: 1) pupils of secondary school age; 2) parents of pupils at secondary schools; 3) teachers at secondary schools; 4) educational theorists and administrators;

5) corporate executives responsible for policy decisions; 6) first line managers responsible for implementing policy decisions. We compiled a list of 20 questions based on what appeared to be the most relevant features of discipline and authority; these questions were divided into three groups: conceptual clarity, empirical fact, and suggestions for improvement. The result(s) of the responses and the most interesting thing about these responses was that pupils and parents (with some exceptions) seemed to be more closely in touch with a proper understanding of discipline and authority than were educational theorists, teachers, or corporate decision makers.

The research done was at least sufficient for us to take seriously the question of just why, psychologically speaking, there appeared to be a good deal of opposition to the properly understood notions of discipline and authority. A basic problem, we feel, is the *toleration of being separate*. Exercising authority and imposing sanctions involve *distancing* oneself from the person in obvious ways. First, one is acting not as an equal or a friend but as an impersonal authority and in a sense not a person at all, though one still remains a person when exercising this authority. Second, one is acting contrary to the desires of the other; that is, preventing him/her from doing what he/she wants, perhaps making him/her suffer in fairly clear-cut ways.

Clearly, it is impossible to sustain an orderly life without the apparatus of discipline and rules. It is evident also that we must trust people with authority and power in order to get certain jobs done efficiently or done at all. The actual delegation of power, however, depends on the existence of some kind of trust, which in turn may be seen as dependent on being able to tolerate filling some place or position in a hierarchy or structured system. To fill the place and allow other people to fill their places is thus ultimately dependent on the tolerance of separation.

While this ability to tolerate separation may appear problematic in educational circles, etc., corporate life is *de facto* based on it. A strict day-to-day hierarchy of procedures is maintained and some corporations even separate dining facilities. Further, status is observable throughout the entire corporate system. Perhaps the ethical decision maker is confronted here not only by the fear of separation but also by the sense of *isolation* that would accrue to his/her actions as a result of taking a stand which was unpopular, even if correct. The corporate structure might not tolerate decisions *beyond* a certain level *even if they are morally appropriate* because the corporation has its own survival and development as a superseding concern. This is not as easily surmounted as one might assume. For example, a large United States multinational corporation refused either to sell or repair their product when they became aware that South Africa was using the product to track dissident blacks. The company's refusal was appropriate and noble. However, the "gap" in product was immediately filled by two other countries. The moral repugnance of their action notwithstanding, one might legitimately ask: How many noble actions can a corporation engage in and survive?

Plato and a long line of later thinkers believed that it was possible and desirable to impose authority from above and to make such imposition permanently effective. Could this problem described above be adjudicated by a moral agreement/consideration that would *prohibit* other corporations from filling the gap created by the first corporation's refusal to provide further materials to South Africa, for example? What we are asking baldly is something like this: Are there situations which are universally repugnant— local culture, principle of toleration, and fragmentation of values not-withstanding—such that there can be universal agreement that to provide help to a repressive regime is *categorically* wrong? In short, can we say *anything* of significance that cannot be gainsaid by the argument that there are differing values? Perhaps we would suggest there are (admittedly few) universal principles which can be logically and legitimately inferred from the general principle that all people have certain rights which inhere in their existence and may not be removed by any kind of law, etc.

We are not arguing for an Orwellian society with mindless rules imposed without consideration, but we *are* saying that it is necessary—in fact, it is the only way forward—that we must begin to establish a greater *understanding* of discipline and authority; from this comes the emotional and practical acceptance of them.

It is as if most of us still thought of authority in the way that members of a very primitive society or very young children might think of it—not as a necessary piece of equipment to get certain things done but in a semimagical way. In reference to authority in our survey, there was clearly a feeling that teachers either should or should not be invested with some sort of numinous power calling for "respect," if not awe. Rather like priests or CEOs, they were seen as either having this power or as pretenders. It is intriguing that the responses *split* completely with virtually *no nuanced understanding* of a continuum of authority that might reside in person A under condition B. This split suggests that more intrapsychic conditions are providing the engine. These intrapsychic conditions, of course, are driven by organizational norms, etc.

Respect for all visible holders of authority has declined over the past decades. However, it has *not* been replaced by respect for rational authority— this is too sophisticated a concept for the ordinary intelligence to grasp or rather too impersonal a practice for our feelings to accept wholeheartedly.

Given people as they are—apparently incapable of firmly grasping and using the notion of rational authority—should we attempt to *educate* them so that they can obtain such a grasp or give rational authority up as a bad job and reinforce some kind of nonrational authority such as "profit at all costs"? It is a regrettable symptom of our own intellectual incompetence that the words "discipline" and "authority" have come to be associated— wrongly we feel—almost exclusively with dictatorship. There must be at least *some* people who have a proper grasp of concepts—some educated class or some set of individuals who will be able to transmit their understanding to others. The desirability of more education about discipline is clear enough. Even if only in order to be able to educate people in discipline, our schools and society must be reasonably trouble free. We must have order and obedience in our corporations if even our most liberal aims are to be fulfilled. Moreover, there will always be some people who cannot or will not grasp the necessary concepts; not everything can be achieved by education.

Corporate managers are in a peculiar place, not unlike teachers, for they have the dual role of education and keeping order. The research is legion which confirms that values conform not from the grass roots up but rather from the top *down*. In terms of day-to-day corporate living, discipline cannot be separated from the notion of obedience in authority in a task-like situation and stand perhaps for what might be meant by self-discipline. However, it is entirely clear that managers, at least, must be clear about authority, for they are the people with the task of educating the coming managers who will influence corporate politics.

What would the first step consist of? Initially we might want to say that mangers and teachers need to be educated into a broader understanding of the moral accountability that flows from their decisions. They need to engage in some hard thinking *and* acting to measure their ability to implement decisions that are based on universally accepted values. We are aware that this is a daunting venture indeed, and no attempt is made to suggest that this can be done fully now or lightly. *However*, it is about time that we, the community of business ethicists, either fold our tents and admit that we do little more than present case studies and situational ethics *or* begin to develop some universal principles from which real-world action might be inferred with relative accuracy. There will never be a unified world view, we agree, but this does not logically preclude central principles of value which supersede *under all conditions* other goals such as success or profit.

References

Almond, Brenda. 1987 *Moral Concerns*. Atlantic Highlands: Humanities Press International.

Behrman, I. 1981. *Discourses on Ethics and Business*. Cambridge: Gunn and Hain.

Carr, A. 1970. "Can an Executive Afford a Conscience?" *Harvard Business Review:* 58-64.

Cyert, R., and J. March. 1963. *A Behavioral Theory of the Firm*. Englewood Cliffs: Prentice-Hall.

Delbecq, A. 1967. "The Management of Decision Making Within the Firm: Three Strategies for Three Types of Decision Making." *Academy of Management Journal*: 329-339.

Friedman, M. 1962. *Capitalism and Freedom.* Chicago: U of Chicago P.

Glazer, M. 1983. "Ten Whistleblowers and How They Fared." *The Hastings Center Report.* Hastings on Hudson.

Hammonds, David G. 1984. "Discipline: Authority, Rules, and Sanctions." *A Case Study of Three Primary Schools.* Oxford University.

Harrison, E. 1981. *The Managerial Decision Making Process.* Boston: Houghton Mifflin.

Kohlberg, Lawrence. 1964. "Development of Moral Character." *Review of Child Development Research.* Ed. L. Hoffman and L. W. Hoffman. New York: Russel Sage.

MacIntyre, A. 1977. "Why Are the Problems of Business Ethics Insoluable?" *Proceedings of the First National Conference on Business Ethics.* Ed. W. Hoffman. Waltham: Center for Business Ethics at Bentley College. 99-107.

―――. 1982. *After Virtue.* Notre Dame: U of Notre Dame P.

McElwreath, Daniel Arthur. 1987. *How Managers Build An Ethical Component into Their Business Decision Process: The Functional Influence.* Fairleigh Dickinson University.

Mintzberg, H., D. Raisinghani, and A. Theoret. 1976. "The Structure of Unstructured Decision Processes." *Administrative Science Quarterly* 21: 246-75.

Nagel, Thomas. 1987. "The Fragmentation of Value." *Moral Dilemmas.* Ed. Christopher W. Gowans. New York: Oxford UP.

Natale, Samuel M. 1987. *Ethics and Morals in Business.* 2nd ed. Birmingham: Religious Education Press.

Pounds, W. 1969. "The Process of Problem Finding." *Industrial Management Review*: 1-19.

Rubinstein, M. 1975. *Patterns of Problem Solving.* Englewood Cliffs: Prentice-Hall.

Silberman, C. 1973. *Crisis in the Classroom: The Remaking of American Education.* London: Wildwood House.

Sturm, Douglas. 1985. "Corporate Culture and the Common Good." *Thought* (Ed. S. Natale) 40: 141-60.

Wilson, John B., Barbara Cowell, Samuel M. Natale. "The Psychological Background To Moral Education." Unpublished paper.

Wilson, P. 1971. *Interest in Discipline and Education.* London: Routledge and Kegan Paul.

Chapter 11: A Machiavellian Analysis

Arthur Sharplin, Ph.D.
Distinguished Professor of Management
McNeese State University
Lake Charles, Louisiana

◆

Machiavelli's little book *The Prince* is given much credit for having influenced managers through the ages. In essence the author told his prince how to use others to serve his own interest—without concern for morality. So "Machiavellian" has come to suggest cunning, duplicity, or bad faith. *The Prince*, although the book purports to be a *pre*scription for leader behavior, may only be a *de*scription of the darker side of such behavior. Of course, one can argue that Machiavelli gave aid, in the form of effective strategies and tactics, and comfort, in the form of implied absolution, to those who would coerce and control others for personal gain.

This essay describes Chapter 11 reorganization and details bankruptcy strategies which may empower and otherwise benefit managers. Some of these "Machiavellian" strategies may fall within a particular manager's range of acceptable behavior and be considered worthy of adoption. Others, though clearly unethical by usual standards, should be understood for the threat they represent to creditors and others caught in Chapter 11's web. In any case no absolution is offered.

HOW CHAPTER 11 WORKS

Chapter 11 of the U.S. Bankruptcy Code became effective October 1, 1979 and was amended in 1984 and 1986. This law replaced various business reorganization provisions in earlier law. A premise of Chapter 11 is the pleasing idea that most businesses are worth at least as much as going concerns as in liquidation.[1] If this is true, stockholders and creditors may get more out of a troubled company by allowing it to continue operating than by liquidating it. A claimed societal benefit is that employees keep their jobs and the community keeps the tax base and economic and social activity related to the debtor firm. Practically any company or individual may seek Chapter 11 protection. Insolvency is not a requirement.

Administration of the Debtor Firm

Because U.S. bankruptcy judges do not have the lifetime tenures and salary protection of other federal judges, they are limited to ruling on "non-controversial" matters. But many of the issues in bankruptcy are, in fact, highly controversial. So each bankruptcy court operates under the supervision of a federal district court. A U.S. trustee helps in the administration of cases under the bankruptcy court's jurisdiction.

A bankruptcy court assumes oversight of any firm which desires to "reorganize" under Chapter 11. Upon filing, the firm becomes the "debtor in possession" (DIP) with the powers and obligations of a trustee in bankruptcy. The prefiling managers continue to operate the company in "the ordinary course of business" while a plan to emerge from court protection is being formulated, approved, and confirmed.

A committee of unsecured creditors is appointed by the U.S. trustee. A committee of equity security holders may also be appointed and usually is. Other committees or advocates may be established if necessary to represent interests which diverge from those of shareholders and unsecured creditors. In the Manville Corporation case, for example, a committee was set up for present asbestos tort claimants, and an individual was appointed as an advocate for future claimants. In the A.H. Robins case a committee was formed to represent women who had used the company's Dalkon Shield intrauterine device. The committees were charged with representing their respective claimant groups and participating in the formulation of a plan of reorganization.

For the first 120 days after filing only the DIP can submit a reorganization plan. If a plan is not submitted within 120 days and accepted by "impaired" claimant groups within 180 days, any party in interest, even an individual shareholder or creditor, may file a plan. Both time limits may be extended or shortened for cause by the bankruptcy court. For example, Manville Corporation was given more than four years to prepare its plan and seek approval of it. On the other hand, Worlds of Wonder, Inc. filed for Chapter 11 protection in December 1987. The company's banks and unsecured creditors were allowed to submit a plan which was approved by the bankruptcy court in March 1988.

The bankruptcy judge is authorized to confirm a plan if the following requirements, among others, are met. The plan must be proposed in good faith and the proponent must disclose certain specified information. Each holder of a claim or interest who has not accepted the plan must be allowed at least as much value, as of the plan's effective date, as Chapter 7 liquidation would provide. Each class of claims or interests which is "impaired" under the plan must have accepted the plan—unless the judge rules the plan does not discriminate unfairly and is fair and equitable with respect to the class.[2] Finally, confirmation of the plan must not be likely to be followed by the need for further financial reorganization or liquidation.

While the plan is being negotiated, approved, and confirmed, all prefiling claims are automatically stayed, and executory contracts may be unilaterally canceled by the debtor. The court has authority to lift the automatic stay with regard to particular claims. Also, the cancellation of executory contracts may create allowable claims against the debtor estate.

Ideally, the plan will provide that the value of the going concern as of the effective date of the plan will be allocated first to the administrative costs of the proceeding and any postfiling obligations of the debtor and then to the claimant groups in order of their "absolute priority in liquidation." Thus, the allowed prefiling claims on the debtor estate may be satisfied in this sequence: 1) secured debt (up to the value of respective collateral as of the effective date of the plan); 2) unsecured debt (including nominally secured debt above the value of respective collateral); and 3) equity claims in order of preference (e.g., preferred, then common). The "value" may be in the form of cash, securities, or other real or personal property and should be at least equivalent to what each party would have gotten if the company had been liquidated. Any claim not provided for in the final reorganization plan is discharged.

Managerial Incentives in Chapter 11

After filing for reorganization, management is bombarded with powerful conflicting demands. Employees want their jobs assured at the same or higher pay levels. Stockholders want share price to be propped up and dividends to be reinstated at the earliest possible time. Creditors demand payment or special considerations such as extra collateral or higher interest rates. The typical bankruptcy judge wants decorum and consensus to prevail and rapid progress to be made toward consummation of a workable plan.

Managers are forestalled from their traditional role of representing only shareholder interests. Shareholders normally have a committee to look out for them and putting management on their side would prejudice the interests of other claimants. Besides, little or no shareholder equity may be left in the debtor firm, so the court may rule there is no shareholder interest to protect. To prevent shareholders from extracting undue consideration from managers or voting in new ones, shareholders may be disenfranchised during the reorganization process. For example, the judge in the five-years-long Manville case turned down several petitions to require management to conduct annual and special stockholder meetings. He even disbanded the shareholders' committee in the bankruptcy court.

Unlike most fiduciaries, management of a Chapter 11 debtor has strong financial interests in its truster—depending upon it for income and employment. So burdened with profound self-interest and faced with an ambiguous charter, managers may seek to turn the reorganization process to personal ends. A common premise is that filing for Chapter 11 protection stigmatizes management.[3] The Machiavellian will not worry about such stigma, per se. But the belief that the stigma exists can lead the executive to feel, "If I am going to have the onus, I may as well take the bonus." The potential benefits Chapter 11 can provide managers are many. As compared to outright liquidation or austere survival without court protection, bankruptcy reorganization can lead to improved pay and benefits, lengthened careers, lowered job demands, and heightened respectability for the managers. The remainder of this article addresses strategies for accomplishing these objectives.

135,399

PREFILING STRATEGIES

Long before any prospective filing date, management can begin to prepare for Chapter 11 reorganization. If reorganization is to be of maximum benefit to management, managers must keep close counsel and treat reorganization as a strategy. These ideas are discussed in the first two subsections below. The remaining six subsections show how advance preparation can assure a unified Chapter 11 team, a favorable bankruptcy court, adequate cash, control of unmortgaged assets, an appropriate organization structure, and favorable executive salaries and incentives.

Keeping Close Counsel

Machiavelli wrote, "Every one admits how praiseworthy it is in a prince to keep faith, and to live with integrity and not with craft. Nevertheless our experience has been that those princes who have done great things have held good faith of little account." He encouraged his prince "to appear merciful, faithful, humane, religious, upright, and to be so, but with a mind so framed that should you require not to be so, you may be able and know how to change to the opposite" (Ch. 18).

Senior managers who would succeed personally while in Chapter 11 must keep in mind that the reorganization process is largely one of negotiation. Moreover, the negotiators involved tend to be sophisticated advocates of powerful vested interests. In such a situation openness becomes a liability. Negotiating strategies and true objectives, for example, can hardly be revealed to opposing parties. So top managers usually keep close counsel. Planned means and ends may be known only to the chief executive and the small cadre of manager/directors who typically govern the corporation.

The need for secrecy often begins when bankruptcy is first remotely contemplated. Even in the Braniff Airlines case, featured in a Harvard Business School case on "bankruptcy ethics," it was deemed necessary to keep preparations for filing secret (Whiteside 1984, 1). And Manville Corporation directors held an unannounced meeting during the afternoon of August 25, 1982, to approve a Chapter 11 petition prepared for filing the next day. Whether by design or not, Manville's strategies from 1978 on prepared the company well for bankruptcy, although company executives disclaim any thought of Chapter 11 before 1982.[4]

Crafty managers can devise many ways to avoid confessing preparation for bankruptcy. For example, they might keep discussion of bankruptcy to a minimum. Any unavoidable interchanges may be had with or through attorneys and others who can cite "privileged communication." Unavoidable discussions among managers themselves can be informal and disjointed. Bringing up a prospective Chapter 11 filing at a board of directors meeting, for example, might cause later actions to be construed as being taken "in anticipation of bankruptcy."

Treating Reorganization as a Strategy

Howard Putnam, chief executive of Braniff when the company filed for bankruptcy reorganization, said, "We used Chapter 11 as a last resort, not as a strategy." The distinction is not merely semantic. By treating bankruptcy reorganization as a last resort, Braniff management may have assured that the company would not survive as a major competitor. Putnam revealed that efforts to avoid bankruptcy sapped the energies of executives, depleted company resources, and virtually destroyed Braniff's customer base (Putnam 1986).

In contrast, Sanford Sigoloff, chief executive of Wickes Corporation, took over six months in advance of that company's bankruptcy filing, made thorough preparations, and, by all accounts, managed a successful reorganization. In fact, Sigoloff developed a formal presentation on the management of reorganization, complete with sophisticated slides and handouts (Sigoloff 1983).

Braniff chief Putnam and his financial assistant Phil Guthrie received their agreed-upon compensation and left Braniff to form their own small investment company. Sigoloff and his team divided $18 million in bonuses and continued to manage their revitalized corporation. In 1988 Sigoloff put together an offer to buy the company.

Assuring a Unified Management Team

When management confronts the other powerful interests in the bankruptcy court, squabbling among the managers themselves, except perhaps for "show," may be extremely detrimental. Also, a coherent strategy must be followed if the managers are to serve themselves at the expense of other parties—and the strategy cannot be openly discussed. So the managers must understand one another's motives and incentives. Further, the motives and incentives of top managers must be similar, or at least compatible, for the best results. Managers or directors who do not meet this requirement may be encouraged, or forced, to leave.

Such management solidarity can be illustrated by two examples. Sanford Sigoloff brought a number of trusted lieutenants with him to Wickes Corporation to assure his control of that company's Chapter 11 strategy. They were placed throughout the organization, not just in a top few posts.

Manville Corporation provides an even better example of management harmony in bankruptcy. After the firm began to lose asbestos tort lawsuits in the 1970s, Richard Goodwin, an outsider who had been brought in as president, was removed and replaced with John McKinney, an attorney who had been with the firm since 1950. Top management continuity was maintained thereafter, especially after the company began its rapid decline in 1978. The five most highly paid managers shown on Manville's 1982 proxy statement, issued only months before the Chapter 11 filing, each had about 30 years tenure. Eight of the 11 directors had been with the company since the fifties and sixties, when Manville was denying its earlier knowledge of asbestos dangers. One senior executive, who vehemently disagreed with the prospective decision to file a bankruptcy petition, resigned. At the time of the filing, five directors, including McKinney, were attorneys.

Judge Shopping

In general, a company may file its Chapter 11 petition wherever it has substantial operations. Certainly the decision of where to file is an important strategic one, and one management can often make unilaterally.[5] Top bankruptcy attorneys can advise which bankruptcy courts tend to be more favorable to management. But more is to be considered. Among the criteria for choosing a court may be 1) the frequency with which managements of debtor companies in the court are replaced with trustees,[6] 2) access to top lawyers and consultants respected by the court,[7] 3) management comfort with the usual process of the court,[8] and 4) the workload the court is experiencing—an overburdened judge may be more inclined to look aside as management overpowers other parties at interest and to depend upon management to maintain progress and order. The need to have operations in a favorable bankruptcy district might conceivably be a factor in office or plant location decisions long before any actual bankruptcy filing.

Coveting Cash

Machiavelli wrote of the need for princes to be able to support themselves with their own resources, "either by an abundance of men or money" (Ch. 10). Managers of Chapter 11 firms will have more power and easier jobs if they control as much cash as possible after the filing. Cash can be saved, for example, by deferring maintenance on fixed assets, extending terms or delaying payment of accounts payable and other debt, and cutting dividend on stock. Any excess funds which can be accumulated before the intended—but still secret—filing date can be invested in inventories or other semiliquid assets. Holding cash before filing may later lead to charges of bad faith in the bankruptcy court.

In most Chapter 11 cases large money balances are a source of influence rather than a means of survival. Adequate cash to pay attorneys and other expenses after filing is normally not a problem. The DIP is forestalled from paying prefiling debt, such as accounts payable, and receivables flow in as cash. Within months after Manville Corporation's August 1982 filing date the company had over $200 million in liquid assets, up from only $27 million at midyear. By 1986 the firm's cash and marketable securities totaled $445 million.

Maximizing Lien-Free Assets

Machiavellian managers who plan a Chapter 11 filing may seek to control as many unmortgaged assets as possible by the filing date. Then, lien-free items can be sold or kept, at management's option, although court approval may be required for major asset sales. In fact items, facilities, or whole divisions may even be bought out of the bankruptcy by managers themselves, if and when they choose to leave the company.[9] The need for cash to consummate a prospective plan can justify such sales.

Effective prefiling strategies to free assets of liens may include selling debentures or stock to pay off secured revolving credit or to refund mortgage bonds; stock and debt offerings may be enhanced with convertibility and repurchase provisions.[10] Also, as many new assets as possible can be purchased with proceeds of unsecured loans. The negotiation of the release of liens may be possible with some creditors and other ways may be found to convert secured debt to unsecured. All this must be done well in advance of filing—and at least ostensibly before filing is contemplated—if management is to avoid accusations that the transactions were carried out "in anticipation of bankruptcy." Of course, managers may have—or fabricate—a good "business reason" other than preparation for bankruptcy for each major action taken prior to filing.

Reorganizing for Bankruptcy

Corporate reorganizations and restructurings can be accomplished before filing to lighten the management load and increase flexibility under Chapter 11. For example, separate divisions may be set up for a company's best operations. And operations subject to tort claims, oppressive labor contracts, or other contingencies can be similarly isolated. Then, those divisions may file their own Chapter 11 petitions—and emerge from reorganization as the managers choose. The best and safest divisions may be favored through interdivisional subsidies, such as low-transfer pricing, loan guarantees by other units, and so forth. Not only can such favored divisions provide a source of cash if sold but they may be a safe haven for managers who might have found themselves at some risk in the consolidated company.[11]

Improving Manager Pay and Benefits

The managers' golden parachutes, incentive plans, salaries, and benefits may be improved before a Chapter 11 filing is "contemplated." The need to keep excellent managers during hard times can be used to justify such moves. Then, the prefiling obligations to managers can simply be reaffirmed after the firm enters bankruptcy. In fact prefiling benefit levels may form a base for further enhancement after filing.[12] Improving major benefit programs may require bankruptcy court approval, not usually too difficult to obtain.[13] Simply reaffirming prefiling obligations may be deemed "in the ordinary course of business" and thus within management's clear authority. Actually, reaffirmation is probably unnecessary. These obligations may be deemed "executory contracts," which remain in effect unless specifically rejected by management.

POSTFILING STRATEGIES

In *Management and Machiavelli* (1968) Anthony Jay likened the management of modern corporations to that of a medieval political state. But Jay's analogy understates the power of corporate managers who enter the Chapter 11 process having made such preparations as those discussed above. As mentioned earlier, Chapter 11 management has the powers of a bankruptcy trustee—but a burden of self-interest prohibited to other fiduciaries. Shareholders can usually be disenfranchised, so that check on management power is often inconsequential. The outside directors on a typical corporate board owe their positions to top management and depend upon the inside directors to do most substantive work. Even if inclined to dissent from management strategies, outside directors are usually fully employed elsewhere and are hardly in a position to manage a bankrupt firm actively. As will be argued below, other parties at interest—creditors, contingent claimants, and so forth—are especially subject to sabotage by Machiavellian managers.[14] In particular, management's control of a large "slush fund" and its ability to facilitate or hinder payments to all parties in interest provide extraordinary power.

The overburdened bankruptcy judge,[15] though charged with assuring equity, lacks the power of other federal judges and is dependent upon DIPs to maintain order and progress in Chapter 11 cases. Bankruptcy judges often go to great extremes to assure consensus among parties in interest concerning prospective decisions. A well-known tactic, for example, is to tell opposing attorneys to "Go out in the hall and work it out," when conflict is evident. Whoever the clashing parties, DIPs are uniquely empowered to mediate the needed consensus. To borrow from Machiavelli himself, the judge is like the King of France in the Middle Ages, who "is placed in the midst of an ancient body of lords [who] have their own prerogatives, nor can the king take these away except at his peril" (Ch. 4).

Retain the Best Legal and Consulting Talent

By hiring the top bankruptcy lawyers and investment bankers and most respected financial consultants who normally practice in the chosen court, management can strengthen its own hand and deny this talent to other parties in interest as well. Only a few reasonable choices exist in each category, at least for major firms. A study of the consultants and counsel used in the leading strategic bankruptcies—Manville, Wickes, A. H. Robins, Texaco, etc.—will reveal who those individuals are. At worst, the cost of such talent is practically irrelevent, simply reducing expected payments to creditors. At best, management profligacy in this area encourages payees to be enthusiastic in representing their benefactors and flexible about any ethical concerns. Also, insuring bankruptcy "camp followers"—on every side—profit from a Chapter 11 helps assure management will have allies if it wishes to prolong the journey or make questionable moves.

Be Patient

It is a well established fact that complex bankruptcies can be extended for years. The Wickes Corporation Chapter 11 case took nearly three years. Manville had already been in bankruptcy over five years when 1988 began.

Executives of Chapter 11 firms may have many reasons to prefer delay. Some may need additional tenure to retirement. Others may want time to set themselves up in jobs in favored divisions. All can gain from added years at inflated pay and benefit levels and from the competitive advantages Chapter 11 provides.

Among the typical parties in interest in a bankruptcy case, management alone usually benefits from delay. Stockholders typically receive no dividends during the pendency of a case. Unsecured creditors may helplessly watch as their collateral is depreciated through use.[16] All claimants may see the bankruptcy estate depleted through administrative costs, increasing obligations to managers, isolation of assets from certain claims, and lack of management attention to the firm's business.

Despite the advantages of delay, some senior managers will decide to leave the company. Others will become expendable or even harmful to the Chapter 11 strategy. Departees may be accorded maximum severance, pension, and other benefits—to set a precedent for later departures and to prevent turncoating. In fact certain managers may contrive to offend other parties in interest so that the managers can leave under pressure, negotiating special severance arrangements.[17]

Taking Advantage of Conflicts of Interest in the Court

As DIP, management has extraordinary power to determine how much money participants in the case get and how hard they have to work for it. Most participants in major bankruptcy cases are "hired guns," attorneys and consultants who work for money. They are typically paid by management upon approval of billings by the bankruptcy judge. In its capacity as trustee the DIP may challenge any billing. Persons who cooperate with management may be permitted to charge the estate high hourly rates for a wide range of activities, ostensibly—or actually—related to representation of particular parties in interest.

Those who do not cooperate with a Machiavellian DIP may find themselves challenged at every turn. The experience of the asbestos victims' committee in the Manville bankruptcy is a case in point. That committee consisted of 19 contingent-fee attorneys and one asbestos victim. Until early 1984, the committee aggressively confronted Manville management. For example, during September 1983 through January 1984, the committee asked the bankruptcy court to dismiss the bankruptcy filing ("Committee of Asbestos" 1983), rejected management's proposed reorganization plan ("Asbestos Claimants" 1983), requested that Manville's top management be replaced with a trustee ("Asbestos-Related" 1984), and even petitioned the court to cut the managers' salaries ("Committee of Asbestos" 1984). But in January 1984 Manville obtained a hearing date on a motion to void the A-H attorneys' contingent-fee agreements, which generally gave the attorneys one-third of any settlement or judgment proceeds ("Hearing Set" 1984). Manville had called the fee arrangements "completely unconscionable" ("Johns-Manville Asks" 1983). In March 1984 the A-H committee withdrew its motion to decrease management salaries ("Committee of Asbestos" 1984). For the ensuing two years the *Asbestos Litigation Reporter*, which reported legal news and filings in asbestos cases,[18] revealed no actions by the A-H committee to contest the authority or benefits of Manville management or to remove the company from bankruptcy court protection ("In re Johns-Manville" 1987).

Bankruptcy practice can be remunerative indeed for those who obtain management's favor. In general, individual parties in interest have little incentive, and questionable authority, to complain about what representatives of other parties in interest are paid. And the bankruptcy judge may be unlikely to reject a billing unless someone objects to it.

Using Bankruptcy to Strengthen the Firm's Business

If prefiling management plans to stay with the reorganized firm, they may benefit by maintaining or improving its competitiveness. Also, growth, or at least stability, may be important. Over the long haul, paying high management salaries requires profitability, but company size is the main determinant of how high those salaries might be. A Chapter 11 filing provides several opportunities for accomplishing these objectives.

Labor costs can be stabilized or reduced. Worker expectations regarding pay and benefits are lowered and labor contracts may be rejected if certain conditions are met. It may even be possible for management to cultivate a "save the company" culture of hard work and self-sacrifice by workers.

Capital costs may be cut. Interest on prefiling unsecured debt is suspended and no payments have to be made on such debt during the pendency of the proceeding. The debt itself may eventually be discharged, reducing financial leverage. New borrowings, if required, may be given preference by the bankruptcy court, resulting in lower interest rates.[19]

Pricing flexibility may be improved. Not only may costs be lower for the bankrupt company, as indicated above, but there is typically no necessity for profits. In fact high earnings before a plan is negotiated with the claimant committees may weaken management's negotiating position. So management may focus on preparing the company for postplan performance. For example, prices may be set wherever necessary to maintain, or improve, market share. Where industry structure discourages price competition, management can shower customers with costly services, including liberal return policies.[20]

Chapter 11 offers an opportunity to strip off unproductive assets. Small items may be sold "in the ordinary course of business." Selling larger units, plants or divisions, for example, usually requires court approval. However, such approval is often given routinely. For example, Wickes Corporation sold off 13 divisions while under court protection. And Manville Corporation sold dozens of plants and facilities, including several whole divisions. It is a rare court which will substitute its judgment for that of management in such matters.

Keeping Control of Information

An often-cited disadvantage of pursuing Chapter 11 as a strategy is the "glass bowl" nature of the proceeding. Many imagine parties in interest have free access to information from the debtor. However, such need not be the case. Bankruptcy courts routinely allow DIPs to limit regular financial reporting to standard annual and quarterly reports. When parties request more information, they can be provided partial, or even misleading, information. Or the requesters may be required to go through the bankruptcy court. There, they can be forced to justify specifically any need for information they claim to have. Practically any information useful to a party in interest would also be potentially helpful to a competitor. Management usually has the right to withhold such material from unfriendly hands.

CONCLUSION

If, as Lord Acton said, "Power tends to corrupt and absolute power corrupts absolutely" (qtd. in Himmelfarb 1952, 239), Chapter 11 managers can hardly be expected to avoid yielding, at least to some degree. So, as scandalous as the strategies described here may appear, they are predictable. In fact the listings here at best only summarize and perhaps barely suggest the range of disingenuous Chapter 11 strategies Machiavellian managers can use.

Machiavelli wrote, "Those who by valorous ways become princes... acquire a principality with difficulty, but they keep it with ease.... Those who solely by good fortune become princes from being private citizens have little trouble in rising, but much in keeping atop" (Ch. 6, 7). Managers who wait until fortune—or misfortune—forces them into Chapter 11, instead of treating it as a strategy to be skillfully executed, will find the work hard and the benefits few. This was apparently true of Braniff, though not of Wickes or Manville.

Among the principalities of medieval Europe, Machievelli found examples of a third category of princes, those who "have obtained principality by wickedness" (Ch. 8). Similarly, there may be companies with wicked backgrounds among the great bankrupt corporations of the 1980s. For them, Machiavelli offered this advice:

> Some may wonder how it can happen that Agathocles, and his like, after infinite treacheries and cruelties, should live for long secure in this country.... I believe that this follows from severities being badly or properly used. Those may be called properly used, if of evil it is lawful to speak well, that are applied at one blow and are necessary to one's security, and that are not persisted in

afterwards unless they can be turned to the advantage of the subjects.(Ch. 8)

The efforts by Manville to stave off the asbestos-health claimants and the to crush them *en masse* with a six-years-long automatic stay of their claims seem consistent with this counsel. The company's ability to rejoin respectable corporate America as it prepared to emerge from bankruptcy in 1988 indicates the managers knew how to "properly use" severities.

All parties at interest in bankruptcy cases, including judges, claimants, and managers, have much to gain from a careful application of Machiavelli to the bankruptcy experience. I hope the resulting understanding will lead to more ethical behavior by everyone involved.

Endnotes

[1] The popularity of "leveraged buyouts" and takeovers, after which acquisitions are dismembered and sold, suggests this may not be an entirely valid assumption.

[2] A class of claims or interests is unimpaired if reinstated and the holders compensated for damages or if paid in cash. Acceptance of a plan by a creditor class requires approval by over half in number and at least two-thirds in amount of allowed claims in the class. Classes of interests, such as shareholders, must approve by at least two-thirds in amount of such interests.

[3] See, for example, Sutton and Callahan 1987.

[4] The Manville story is told in detail in Sharplin 1985, 207-223. Also see Altman 1983 and Sharplin 1988.

[5] There are exceptions. Federal district judge Barefoot Sanders, of Dallas, ordered the famous Hunt brothers and their companies back to the bankruptcy court in his district after they tried to file their Chapter 11 petitions in New Orleans.

[6] Bankruptcy judges in major cases tend to leave management in place. For example, bankruptcy judge Robert Merhige, Jr., of Richmond, Virginia, held A. H. Robins in contempt for making unauthorized payments and accused Robins executives of "subterfuge" after they later made another $150,000 of other such payments. Yet, Merhige stopped short of replacing management with a trustee.

[7] For example, Manville Corporation filed its petition in New York City, home of leading investment banker Morgan Stanley and Company and top law firm Davis Polk Wardwell, with which Manville had strong relationships

going back to the thirties. Concurrently with its Chapter 11 filing, Manville was able to place these firms on retainer.

[8] Some bankruptcy judges actively try to impose "equity" while others seek consensus, expecting parties to "go out into the hall and work things out." Since Machiavellian managers are likely to seek results fair only to themselves, they may tend to prefer the latter approach.

[9] For example, a former Manville president left the company in 1986 and formed a corporation which purchased several Manville plants, with court approval. See "3 Manville Manufacturing Plants Sold to Former President Hulce" 1988. Management-led groups are likely to be successful in bidding for assets they covet because of their inside knowledge and because contacts within the debtor corporation can enhance the value of the assets after sale. For example, Manville Corporation managers might pay more than competitive prices for the output from the plants sold to their former colleague Hulce.

[10] When Manville Corporation bought Olinkraft Corporation in 1978, half the purchase price was represented by a $300 million issue of preferred stock. A mandatory sinking-fund provision required repurchase of the stock at par beginning in 1987, several years after the provision was nullified under Chapter 11.

[11] For example, Manville's forest products division (MFP) emerged from Chapter 11 protection in 1983, long before its parent Manville Corporation was prepared to do so. MFP had been acquired in 1978 and had never been involved in asbestos production. Manville's main asbestos divisions were sold to a group headed by company executives in 1983 and emerged from bankruptcy, shielded by the bankruptcy court from most asbestos liabilities.

[12] A year before the Manville bankruptcy filing in 1982, management set up munificent "Special Termination Agreements" for top managers. Then, the golden parachutes were enhanced in 1985. See "Key Manville Officers Allowed Severance in Event of Termination by Trustee" 1986. A new executive bonus plan adopted in 1987 provided for bonuses as high as 97.1 percent of annual salaries for senior managers who stayed. See "New Bonus Plan for Executives Approved by Court" 1987.

[13] For example, in 1988 Public Service Company of New Hampshire, which had been pushed into Chapter 11 by nuclear plant investment, obtained bankruptcy court approval to enhance employee benefits to assure they would remain with the company during reorganization.

[14] In an early analysis of the 1978 law the director of the Executive Office for United States Trustees wrongly concluded it empowered creditors more than debtors. See Levine and Sherman 1980.

[14]In an early analysis of the 1978 law the director of the Executive Office for United States Trustees wrongly concluded it empowered creditors more than debtors. See Levine and Sherman 1980.

[15]For example, during the year ended June 30, 1986, there were 477,856 bankruptcy filings in the nation's 93 bankruptcy courts, up from 364,536 in the year earlier period. Of these, 21,175 and 18,866, respectively, were business Chapter 11 filings. Data from *Annual Report of the Administrative Office of the U.S. Courts* 1986, 328, and 1985, 464.

[16]Bankruptcy courts have traditionally protected secured creditors whose collateral was deemed insufficient by requiring interest payments on their debt before plan confirmation. In 1987, however, the U.S. Supreme Court ruled this was not mandated by the bankruptcy code.

[17]Examples of offense if not contrivance include former Manville president John Hulce, who left in 1986 under pressure from asbestos victims but with a large severance package, and Donald Kingsborough who resigned as chief executive of Worlds of Wonder, Inc. in 1988 at the request of creditors. The offended creditors agreed to payments to Kingsborough including $212,000 for "emotional distress."

[18]Published by Andrew Publications, Edgemont, PA 19028.

[19]An excellent discussion of capital costs for a Chapter 11 firm is provided in Eisenberg 1987.

[20]See Miller and Newlin 1987. They write, weak businesses "can be at a competitive disadvantage to a Chapter 11 company that is rejecting expensive executory contracts and building cash reserves under the automatic stay" (37).

References

Annual Report of the Administrative Office of the U.S. Courts. 1985. 1986.

Altman, Edward I. 1983. "Exploring the Road to Bankruptcy." *Journal of Business Strategy* 4.2 (Fall): 36-41.

"Asbestos Claimants Committee Rejects Plan." 1983. *Asbestos Litigation Reporter* Nov. 25: 7416.

"Asbestos-Related Litigants Move to Have Bankruptcy Court Appoint Trustee." 1984. *Asbestos Litigation Reporter* Jan. 6: 7625.

"Committee of Asbestos Related Litigants Again Asks Bankruptcy Court to Dismiss Johns-Manville Bankruptcy." 1983. *Asbestos Litigation Reporter* Sept. 23: 7148.

"Committee of Asbestos-Related Litigants and/or Creditors Withdraws Its Motion to Reduce Salaries of Manville Officers." 1984. *Asbestos Litigation Reporter* Mar. 16: 7999.

Eisenberg, Theodore. 1987. "Bankruptcy in the Administrative State." *Law and Contemporary Problems* 50.2 (Spring): 15-20.

"Hearing Set on Replacement for Plaintiff Contingency Fee Arrangements." 1984. *Asbestos Litigation Reporter* Feb. 3: 7785.

Himmelfarb, Gertrude. 1952. *Lord Acton: A Study in Conscience and Politics*. Chicago: U of Chicago P.

"In re Johns-Manville Corp." 1987. *Asbestos Litigation Reporter: Eight-Year Cumulative Index, February 1979-July 1987*. Edgemont: Andrews, August. 37-38.

Jay, Anthony. 1968. *Management and Machiavelli*. New York: Holt, Rinehart and Winston.

"Johns-Manville Asks Court to Avoid Asbestos-Claimants Attorney Fees." 1983. *Asbestos Litigation Reporter* Nov. 25: 7411.

"Key Manville Officers Allowed Severance in Event of Termination by Trustee." 1986. *Stockholders and Creditors News Service Re. Johns-Manville, et al.* Apr. 7: 4995.

Levine, Richard, L., and H. David Sherman. 1980. "Trade-Offs in the New Bankruptcy Law." *Harvard Business Review* Mar.-Apr.: 46-52.

Machiavelli, Nicolo. *The Prince*. Trans. W. K. Marriott. Chicago: Encyclopedia Brittanica.

Miller, John A., and Terrance W. Newlin. 1987. "Managing a Successful Chapter 11 Reorganization." *Management Review* 76 (May): 35-39.

"New Bonus Plan for Executors Approved by Court." 1987. *Stockholders and Creditors News Service Re. Johns-Manville, et al.* Aug. 10: 6778-79.

Putnam, Howard. 1986. "Bankruptcy Ethics." Symposium of the Cambridge Forum. Cambridge, MA, Oct. 10.

Sharplin, Arthur. 1988. "Manville's Search for the Ring of Gyges." *The Ethics of Organizational Transformation: Mergers, Takeovers and Corporate Restructuring*. Westport: Quorum.

————. 1985. *Strategic Management*. New York: McGraw Hill.

Sigoloff, Sanford. 1983. "The Wickes Reorganization." Presented at "Bankruptcy Proceedings: The Effect on Product Liability." Andrews Publications. Miami, FL, Mar.

Sutton, Robert I., and Anita L. Callahan. 1987. "The Stigma of Bankruptcy: Spoiled Organizational Image and Its Management." *Academy of Management Journal* 3: 405-36.

"3 Manville Manufacturing Plants Sold to Former President Hulce." 1988. *Stockholders and Creditors News Service Re. Johns-Manville Corp., et al.* Jan. 11: 7 +.

Whiteside, David E. 1984. "Braniff International: The Ethics of Bankruptcy." Harvard Business School. Case No. 5-384-182.

Ethics on Wall Street

David P. Schmidt, Ph.D.
Trinity Center for Ethics and Corporate Policy
New York, New York
♦

In recent years many Americans have grown increasingly wary of the financial markets and the securities industry as symbolized by Wall Street. Following the stock market crash of October 1987, individual investors fled the financial markets, believing them rigged in favor of arbitrageurs and program traders. Audiences across America accepted the depiction of Boesky-like greed in the popular movie *Wall Street* as typical of what goes on in investment banks. Even citizens who did not support Jesse Jackson were irked when the populist candidate for the 1988 Democratic presidential ticket was openly jeered on the floor of the New York Stock Exchange. From small towns to Capitol Hill, many question whether there are any ethics on Wall Street.

My objective is to develop an answer to this question. My strategy is not first to reply with examples of ethical conduct on the Street. That strategy will not work without an account of ethics that everyone will accept, which we can then apply to Wall Street. Wall Street needs a compelling vision of what its ethics should be. I take the position that the Street should broaden and update its understanding of ethics. When Wall Street attains a clear understanding of ethics that makes sense for the nature of its business and satisfies the rest of society, then it will be able to marshall evidence that it is ethical.

I will propose for Wall Street a relational ethics of responsibility. This is a fruitful approach for an industry the operations of which depend so heavily on relations of trust and confidence. I don't argue that this particular approach to ethics, which is but one of several possibilities, solves all of Wall Street's problems. However, I do believe that a relational ethics of responsibility is generally superior to the other approaches to ethics that Wall Street usually takes.

I write for the concerns of people in business. Thus the following discussion is only as philosophically rigorous as is necessary to put forward some basic points about the practical relevance of a relational ethics of responsibility. (I hope that my exposition is coherent and persuasive, even if a more complete defense of its underlying concepts is deferred for now.) Wall Street has a vested interest in the following discussion for at least two reasons: first, if it fails to maintain a minimum ethical posture, the government will intervene more than it already has; second, a relational ethics of responsibility is part of what constitutes good business judgment.

First, I will name some dominant features of business on Wall Street that any account of ethics needs to reckon with. Second, I will note two conventional approaches to ethics on Wall Street and their shortcomings for the current situation. Third, I will propose a relational ethics of responsibility and indicate briefly some ways in which this approach to ethics can make a positive, pragmatic difference for business. This approach to ethics also helps us isolate the biggest challenge for Wall Street's ethical credibility before the rest of society, and I will conclude with a comment for what Wall Street needs to do in order to maintain the public's trust and confidence.

THE CURRENT SITUATION

A full description of the rapid and sweeping changes taking place in the securities industry lies beyond the scope and purposes of the present discussion, which will not duplicate the historical summaries and overviews of the industry that are available (Auerbach and Hayes 1986; Brooks 1973; Brooks 1987; Sobel 1982; Sobel 1987; Williamson 1988). I will note only two of the most significant features of the current situation on Wall Street that challenge any account of ethics for that industry. These two features are the changes that are taking place 1) in the external environment and 2) in the industry's participants and their products. These features are not mutually exclusive, though they can be distinguished in terms of the somewhat different challenges they pose to ethics.

First to note are important changes in Wall Street's environment. The most visible changes have to do with rapidly developing technology and communications. Also of critical importance are regulatory changes, such as shelf registration and the end of fixed commissions, which have made Wall Street more competitive and, some would argue, more volatile and short term in outlook. In addition, we should note ongoing changes in such areas as monetary policy which contribute to interest rate volatility and other forms of uncertainty. Any ethics on Wall Street will have to be able to deal with a business that has become risky, fast paced, and extremely competitive.

Related to these environmental changes are important developments within Wall Street in terms of the industry's participants, products, and services. Because of the changes in public policy, such as the crumbling of the Glass-Steagall Act, commercial banks and companies in real estate and insurance are entering the traditional business of the securities industry. The growth of the conglomerate and institutional funds has brought sophisticated and powerful clients to Wall Street. Global financial markets now include foreign banks that dwarf their American counterparts in size and capital resources. And in association with all these developments, there is unprecedented innovation. The Street continues to spew out esoteric products and imaginative services that generate new, potentially profitable markets. The traditional underwriting and trading/distribution functions of Wall Street rise and fall relative to each other in profitability and importance, while new functions threaten to take their place. Any ethics on Wall Street will have to reckon with an industry the very nature and purpose of which is becoming increasingly harder to grasp.

The profound changes in these two features of Wall Street can be summarized succinctly, if inadequately, by saying the securities industry is now principally concerned with managing the flow of a prodigious amount of information in very short periods of time. The heart of the business is not *product*, though one might come to this conclusion from observing the legions of young MBAs scrambling to invent the next major financial innovation that, like securitization of credit, will transform the boundaries of the industry and open new vistas of profit. I would argue to the contrary that the heart of the business now is the flow of information. Over time the successful securities firm will be the one that is superior in its capacity to absorb, understand, and act quickly on the torrential outpouring of information. "Today, investment bankers care even more about being in the center of the 'information flow' than in the center of 'capital flow'" (Williamson 1988, 55). Any account of ethics for Wall Street must be able to speak to this development.

THE CONVENTIONAL APPROACHES TO ETHICS

Wall Street typically displays two conventional approaches to ethics: compliance with regulations and nostalgia for traditional values. Both have played an important role in maintaining an ethical posture on Wall Street, and both will continue to do so. However, the following account of these two approaches will argue that they are limited in their ability to deal effectively with the current challenges facing Wall Street.

Wall Street's concern with regulations dates back to the imposition of new public policy after the stock market crash of 1929. No longer confident in the financial market's ability to police itself, Congress passed legislation that began a history of growing regulatory supervision of the financial markets. This history includes direct governmental regulation, controls by the exchanges, and the self-policing of securities firms.

Even with the growing deregulation of the financial markets in recent years, Wall Street is still strongly conditioned to use a rules or regulatory approach to deal with wrongful behavior. For example, the most common response to insider trading in most securities firms is in-house regulations (Chinese Walls) that restrict the flow of certain information between the arbitrage and investment banking functions. Members of the industry must attest periodically, often by signing their firm's ethics statement, that they have not broken securities laws. Wall Street's most natural response to the question of ethics takes the form of compliance with rules and regulations.

Important though regulations may be for establishing a relatively level playing field, an ethics of rules has significant shortcomings for Wall Street's current situation. It is difficult to frame regulations that are sufficiently detailed *and* flexible to cope with the variability on Wall Street. Sobel argues that the securities act of 1934 was designed as a "corrective mechanism for an unchanging securities district..." (1982, 167). Thus it is fair to ask whether the fast tempo of today's Wall Street can be controlled adequately by rules. For instance, some argue we should not develop a statutory definition of insider trading, because that would lock the industry into a rigid notion of wrongdoing that could be easily circumvented.

Perhaps a more important limitation of a rules approach to ethics is its tendency to minimalism and conservatism. An ethics of rules tends to dwell at the level of staying out of trouble. But what the industry now needs to function well and to maintain the public trust is precisely a move toward doing business in an exemplary fashion that goes beyond the letter of the law. In a word, Wall Street needs rules, but it needs more than rules if it is to claim seriously that it has an ethic adequate to its dynamic and increasingly "gray" areas of its business.

Other than compliance with regulation, the concern for ethics on Wall Street usually appears in the form of nostalgia for the values of a bygone era. For many people today, the Wall Street of the previous generation represents a more humane period when the business was conducted among gentlemen who subscribed to a powerful, self-regulating culture.

Several features separate that era on Wall Street from the current situation. First, the securities industry of that day possessed a small, stable, homogeneous work force. Wall Street drew from but a few of the best schools and even then accepted only those with the correct family background and social bearing. Second, the business of Wall Street was fairly circumscribed, consisting primarily of traditional underwriting and advisory services. The industry's established functions, stable products, and neat divisions of labor were maintained by time-honored practices and customs that bespoke a cohesive ethos. Perhaps central to that milieu was the sacred faith in long-term, exclusive client relations. In a word, the business had a clearly understood mission or purpose. Not everyone liked it, particularly those who could not break in to the white shoe Wall Street crowd. But no one doubted its existence or failed to understand what its values were.

Tradition is an important part of ethics, but an ethics of nostalgia encounters significant practical obstacles on today's Wall Street. First of all, this type of ethics is most meaningful only for the more mature segment of the industry's workforce, a dwindling minority, that has been on the Street since at least before the "go go years" of the 1960s. Furthermore, it is not possible to turn back the clock. The most attractive aspect of the Wall Street of yesteryear—its clear, traditional mission—is precisely what is now at issue. An ethics based on the fulfillment of a purpose or telos is only possible when everyone agrees about their purposes. But we have entered a time on Wall Street where the basic purposes and directions of the industry are increasingly in flux. Wall Street is searching for a deeper sense of mission to give direction to its increasingly transactional and commodity-like businesses. The loss of purpose accounts for the growing public sentiment that Wall Street today is concerned only with its own greed. Many on the Street are uncomfortable with the public's view but do not know fully how to counter it, because they are unsure of their own vision of what their business is about.

An ethics of nostalgia is tempting but not possible. Wall Street must move forward and chart a new direction that makes sense for today. I want to examine whether a relational ethics of responsibility can help to clarify Wall Street's values and sense of direction.

A RELATIONAL ETHICS OF RESPONSIBILITY

Wall Street's need for something like a relational ethics of responsibility is indicated by the special management of securities firms. The study of management issues specific to Wall Street is a comparatively recent development (Rappaport 1988). Robert B. Eccles and Dwight B. Crane provide helpful insights on this subject in their article "Managing Though Networks in Investment Banking" (1987). A summary of their main points will help identify issues that an ethics on Wall Street should take into account.

Eccles and Crane note that most investment banks are organized differently than industrial corporations, which usually are structured vertically as hierarchies that clearly map out their individual members' spans of responsibility and authority, as well as the key linkages to maintain in order to do business. In contrast, Wall Street firms consist of dynamic and flexible networks that maintain the firm's complex webs of relationships with customers and competitors.

Firms that are structured according to dynamic, flexible networks will disperse authority. These firms value horizontal organizational relations and *ad hoc*, functional teams over established, vertical hierarchies. When a securities firm operates according to dynamic networks, its members will work in informal relationships with others throughout the firm. To function effectively, a network-oriented firm will value flexible cooperation and the free exchange of information, not the building of empires. It will replace the "star system" of *prima donnas* with team players.

The concept of dynamic and flexible networks, which helps to illuminate securities firms' management needs, draws our attention to particular issues that prompt ethical concern. These issues stem principally from the ambiguity that inevitably accompanies flexible organizational roles and overlapping responsibilities. Team work in a network of people often requires them to make trade-offs and compromises. This process inevitably creates conflicts of interest and challenges trust and mutual confidence within the firm and between the firm and its clients. Though an excellent way to nurture adaptability, the dynamic and flexible network creates "gray" situations that call for a relational ethics of responsibility.

The Christian moral philosopher H. Richard Niebuhr was a leading American contributor to the idea of a relational ethics of responsibility (1963; 1970). His work was shaped by his view of *persons as responders*, an image of human agency that draws deeply from the social and interactive aspects of our experience. "No person is an island," and our values emerge most vividly and honestly in our responses to others, particularly in times of emergencies or other unexpected occasions when we respond uninhibitedly. The responsive character of human life is perhaps most evident in the varied uses of language in conversation. Says Niebuhr, "To be engaged in dialogue, to answer questions addressed to us, to defend ourselves against attacks, to reply to injunctions, to meet challenges—this is common experience" (1970). Persons are responders when they act in response to their interpretation of others' actions upon them and when they act in expectation of others' responses to their own actions. His account of how these responses can also be responsible provides the clue for understanding the full magnitude of the ethical challenge facing Wall Street today.

The image of the responder functions like a lens that lets us isolate and examine aspects of the moral life that are especially pertinent to Wall Street today. I think that this image illuminates the emphatically relational nature of work in the securities industry and is more helpful for this purpose than other images of human agency that have underwritten more traditional approaches to ethics (for example, "person as citizen" and deontology, which emphasizes living under the law, or "person as maker" and teleology, which emphasizes working toward a recognized goal). With the image of the responder as our starting point, we are positioned to address several key issues on Wall Street that prompt ethical concern. Specifically, I will sketch some aspects of a relational ethics of responsibility in terms of the following three topics: The Meaning of Value, The Fitting Response, and Trust.

The Meaning of Value

We use the idea of value to indicate that which has significance for us. Accounts of value run through many discussions of ethics, although moral thinkers have argued endlessly about exactly what value is. Niebuhr's account of value steers a course between objectivism, which says that value has some sort of independent status in the real world, and subjectivism, which says that value is nothing more than individuals' feelings and preferences. Lying somewhere between these extremes is the relational perspective of the responder image, which says that value exists only in relations between persons. Viewed relationally, value is objective in the sense that value relations are independent of the feelings of any one person; but value is not objective in the sense that value itself is an independent, objective part of reality. Seen this way, we must always speak of value as "value for something" because nothing is valuable in and of itself; something is valuable specifically for this or for that, in terms of particular relations.

This relational account does not avoid all the philosophical puzzles about the meaning of value. But we don't need now to deal with all those problems in order to glimpse the constructive possibilities of this relational way of thinking for concerns on Wall Street. The securities business is committed to providing value for clients. But there is uncertainty about what this really means. For example, a common expression on the Street is "We add value to this deal." (By implication, "We add more value than our competitors, so you should do business with us, not them.") But what is this value that is added to a deal? Do people mean the speed of executing a transaction, or its cost, or both? Do people mean imaginative approaches to meeting financial needs? If so, how do we know whether one approach is more valuable than another? Is value determined by how much profit is realized? To define value strictly in terms of financial profit only raises more questions: Profit in the short or long term? What about all the intangibles that distinguish one provider of financial services from another? Does the industry know how to price the value of the various factors that contribute to successful transactions and healthy client relations?

A relational account of value points us in the right direction for dealing with these questions by reminding us there is a close connection between "We add value to a deal" and another Wall Street slogan, "We serve the client." There is no value on Wall Street apart from relationships between providers of financial services and users of those services. Some firms seem to forget this simple but essential fact. In their rush to anticipate client needs they risk running ahead of the client, making decisions for the client, and concocting products or services that don't really matter to anyone. These firms end up in the dubious position of having to create demand for their hot ideas. This aggressive, insensitive approach to business often does not create real value, only the fiction of it.

The Fitting Response

When value is present in a relation, Niebuhr says that it is a "fitting" relation (1979, 103). Following the image of the responder, we can say in an abstract way that the fitting response is one that fits harmoniously or appropriately within the ongoing process of interpretation, action, and anticipation of further response.

The idea of a fitting response has roots in the pragmatic tradition in American thought. It was William James who explored the idea of "the fitting" as something that starts with direct sense experience: when shoes fit too tightly, we know it; the right key opens the lock. More complex situations call for a more intricate process of discernment and judgment, but the notion of "the fitting" still applies. A composer knows when the notes of a musical score fit together in the right way to make harmonious music. A builder knows how to make blocks fit together to form a sound structure. In a similar vein we might say that an investment banker knows when the various components of a transaction are in place so that the deal will work. These examples show that fittingness, the value of a relation, is closely tied to the usefulness of the relation. When things fit together in the right way, they produce the desired effect. William James said that something like this was at work in the pleasure of discovering the right piece for a particular hole in a jigsaw puzzle (1983, 553).

There is an important aesthetic or perceptual dimension to the fitting response. Before we can judge what is the fitting thing to do, we must be able to describe accurately what the situation requires. The fitting response requires discernment and interpretation, not blind action. Much of contemporary ethical theory is written in ways that emphasize making tough choices in the face of quandaries (Pincoffs 1986). Although decisions are necessary, ethics is not only about making decisions. Before we can decide, we must know how to describe what is going on. The fitting response is possible when we first have an honest, accurate account of the relevant circumstances.

The fitting response poses significant challenges to Wall Street, where the pace is so quick that decisions and actions often must be made without much time for reflection. In complex business situations the judgment of whether the response was fitting must wait until sometime later. The problem is that the fitting response is not something that can be specified in advance by following a checklist or set of rules. Discerning the fitting response is an art that cannot be boiled down to a procedure. Becoming skilled in this art is like learning a craft, a complex set of practical skills. In essence the fitting response is part of what constitutes a sound business judgment.

A relational ethic of responsibility, with its emphasis on the fitting response, points to a serious issue for Wall Street. More than any other industry, Wall Street looks to its youngest members for innovations that will drive the business. Talent counts, not seniority, and often the tangible rewards go to the sheer technical expertise of the industry's newcomers, the newly minted MBAs armed with the latest financial techniques from our leading business schools. Even people who have been in the business only five or six years have to work hard to keep up with the technical brilliance of their firms' recent recruits.

The abilities and intelligence of Wall Street's newcomers should not be underestimated. At the same time it is vital to recognize their shortcomings in experience and training. The notion of the fitting response helps us to see that a person can bring advanced skills to a situation but fail to discern the appropriate application of those skills. For example, knowing the arcane variations of interest rate swaps is not the same as understanding when it is appropriate to use them. Being able to compute accurately the amount of leverage a deal requires is not the same as judging whether the risk exposure is warranted.

People with more seniority have the experience and maturity necessary to make a determination about what is the fitting response. But the high degree of specialization that the industry requires makes it difficult to coordinate their more seasoned perspectives with the highly technical expertise of individuals working on the details of particular transactions. The dynamic and flexible network is one management tool for bringing together these views and abilities. The notion of the fitting response underscores the ethical and pragmatic urgency for developing ways to bring together these views and abilities for the creation of real value.

Trust

Niebuhr maintains that everyone lives on the basis of faith, which is a fundamental attitude of confidence in whatever gives value to their lives. Life takes its meaning from having a loyalty to some cause or purpose (1970, 16-24). Although human faith is universal, the objects of faith will vary.

Some people place their ultimate confidence in their nation, others in God, others in success or wealth, and so on. Niebuhr views trust as an important part of human faith: trust is the confidence we have in that which gives us value.

A relational ethics of responsibility can help us understand what trust is and how it can occur in business organizations (Herman 1987). Its starting point is that we are responsive beings, constantly interpreting the intentions and actions of others toward us. The ways that others interact with us indicate how they value us. We trust them if we consent to the valuation they place upon us. If we disagree with their valuation, we mistrust them. Mutual trust exists when two people consent to the value which each attaches to the other.

Compensation is an explicit form of valuing. For instance, one reason I am committed to my securities firm is that I am confident that I will be compensated fairly for my work. If the salary and bonus I receive matches my assessment of what my work is worth, I will be loyal to the firm and trust is affirmed. If my compensation is lower than what I honestly feel I am worth, I will lose confidence in the firm's valuation of me and trust will suffer. Of course, people constantly value each other, usually in ways that are more subtle than this example of financial compensation. In every relation there is valuation and with it the creation or destruction of trust.

Under what conditions does trust flourish? Niebuhr's relational theory says that genuine trust is possible only when the particular values people place on each other are ordered in relation to some broader value (1970, 100-13). Just as ships refer to the stars in order to navigate and to determine their positions *vis-á-vis* each other, people require a common point of reference to help them relate their individual values. Using theological language, Niebuhr identified God as the ultimate center of value that orders all other values. Trust among people is "integrative" when they value each other as God does.

Niebuhr's theory challenges business people to consider how they can promote "integrative" trust among members of their organizations. Wall Street lacks a general value or standard to order the individual valuations of its people. Business organizations usually operate on an exchange model of relationships, in which employees value each other as discrete, independent centers of value, quite apart from any comprehensive center of value. Thus when individuals dispute their particular valuations of each other, they have no recourse to a more general, shared value that can order their conflicts. As a consequence, it is difficult to generate and sustain trust within business organizations. A securities firm, which operates according to dynamic and flexible networks, is particularly vulnerable to the disintegrative effects of lacking a common value or purpose that can order the valuing activities of its members.

There is much talk on Wall Street about trust and its importance for the orderly functioning of the financial markets. Phrases like "Our word is our bond" abound. But Niebuhr's requirement for creating and building trust shows how much more can be done to nurture this intangible, yet essential, quality of trust among Wall Streeters. It is not enough for firms to publish advertisements asserting their trustworthiness as many have done recently. The industry's public assertions of trustworthiness must be backed up by a thoughtful, rigorous examination of the values that are reflected in the daily business decisions and actions of its members. Only when individuals and organizations are aware of their values can they begin the hard but vital process of identifying some shared, more comprehensive values that can join them together in trust.

THE PUBLIC CONFIDENCE

I began with the position that Wall Street needs an understanding of ethics that makes sense for the nature of its business and satisfies the rest of society. Noting the industry's current circumstances that call for management through dynamic, flexible networks, I proposed a relational ethics of responsibility as an approach especially suited to Wall Street. While not ending the need for regulations on proper conduct, this relational account of ethics suggests ways for Wall Street to take more positive action on its ethics. Still left unanswered, however, is the question of whether a relational ethics of responsibility on Wall Street will satisfy the rest of society.

Wall Street's biggest challenge is to maintain the trust and confidence of the American people. Its failure to do so keeps investors away from the markets and invites additional governmental intervention. The relational account of the conditions for trust isolates the most critical component of maintaining the public confidence: for there to be trust between Wall Street and the rest of society, there must be a more comprehensive, ultimate value which both share and which can order the valuations each has of the other. Such a comprehensive center of value is now missing from our public life. We have a pluralism in which people across society follow many individual "gods." It is not surprising, therefore, to find such mistrust between Wall and Main Street when it is so difficult to name any general value that harmonizes their separate, often competing interests.

An ethics of nostalgia yearns for a simpler era when people agreed on their values. It is doubtful that any such era actually existed, and in any case I have indicated why this approach is not adequate for the volatile and ambiguous circumstances of today's markets. Alternatively, many are tempted to use the law of the land to impose a national consensus. But while we need rules and regulations to maintain a level playing field, an ethics of rules cannot tell us what game we should play. The relational ethics of responsibility identifies the need for a center of value more comprehensive than the valuations within particular relationships. But it leaves us with the question of how to name that comprehensive center of value.

Wall Street's challenge to maintain the public confidence is a theological issue, for it raises the question of what are our ultimate values. Business usually sidesteps this kind of question, preferring to operate at the pragmatic level of getting things done, leaving the "big picture" questions for theologians and philosophers. However, Wall Street cannot afford to wait for theologians and philosophers to answer these questions. To restore the public confidence, Wall Street must lead in building more fitting relations with its clients and society through which we can identify and understand better the values that unite us in trust.

References

Auerbach, Joseph, and Samuel L. Hayes, III. 1986. *Investment Banking and Diligence: What Price Deregulation?* Boston: Harvard Business School Press.

Brooks, John. 1973. *The Go-Go Years*. New York: Truman Talley Books.

———. 1987. *The Takeover Game*. New York: Truman Talley Books.

Eccles, Robert G., and Dwight B. Crane. 1987. "Managing Through Networks in Investment Banking." *California Management Review* Fall: 176-95.

Herman, Stewart W. 1987. "Exchange-Based Trust and Integrative Trust in the Relationship Between Employee and Organization." Unpublished paper given at the National Conference of the American Academy of Religion, Boston, December 7, 1987.

James, William. 1983. *The Principles of Psychology*. Cambridge: Harvard UP.

Niebuhr, H. Richard. 1963. *The Responsible Self*. New York: Harper and Row.

———. 1970. *Radical Monotheism and Western Culture*. New York: Harper and Row.

Pincoffs, Edmund L. 1986. *Quandaries and Virtues*. Lawrence: U of Kansas P.

Rappaport, Stephen P. 1988. *Management on Wall Street: Making Securities Firms Work*. Homewood: Dow Jones-Irwin.

Sobel, Robert. 1982. *Inside Wall Street*. New York: W. W. Norton.

———. 1987. *The New Game on Wall Street*. New York: John Wiley & Sons.

Williamson, J. Peter, ed. 1988. *Investment Banking Handbook*. New York: John Wiley & Sons.

Option Pricing and Market Manipulation

Vincent Calluzzo, Ph.D.
Assistant Professor
Hagan School of Business
Iona College
New Rochelle, New York

♦

Since the market crash of October 19, 1987, much has been said and written about index arbitrage and perception of market manipulation by large institutional investors. Index arbitrage is the practice of buying or selling an index option and selling or buying the corresponding future contract or the underlying assets to exploit price discrepancies. This paper will examine the effect a well-capitalized investor may have on the market by following a simpler plan of exploiting inefficient pricing of index options. This paper will survey option pricing models, test one of the models on the Standard and Poor 100 Index Option (OEX), and discuss the implications of using option pricing models to manipulate the market.

DEFINITION OF TERMS

Included in this discussion of option pricing techniques must be a definition of key terms. In finance two vehicles that can be used to transfer risk are the futures contract and the option.

Futures Contracts

The futures contract guarantees the buyer the delivery of a good on a future fixed date (expiration date) at a fixed price (exercise price). The buyer of the contract has limited risk—the price of the contract. The seller of the contract has unlimited risk because the seller must provide the goods on the expiration date of the contract regardless of the price of the goods on that day.

Options

There are two types of options, calls and puts. A call gives the buyer of the option the right to buy and a put gives the buyer of the option the right to sell a good at a fixed price (exercise price) on a fixed date (expiration date). The option contract differs from a futures contract in that the buyer of the option is not required to consummate the agreement on the expiration date. For this right, the buyer of the option contract pays the seller an agreed upon amount of money (premium).

The buyer of the option is at risk for the premium, which is usually a fraction of the amount of money paid for a comparable futures contract. The risk for the seller of the option is the same as the risk experienced by the seller of the futures contract less the premium paid for the option.

In addition, options can be classified as *in the money, at the money,* and *out of the money. In the money* means that the exercise price is less than the current price of the underlying asset. *At the money* refers to options whose exercise price is the equal to the price of the underlying asset. If the exercise price of an option is greater than the price of the underlying asset, then the option is said to be *out of the money.*

Options are said to be derivative of assets because their underlying value is a function of some other asset. Some examples: the price of a stock option is dependent on the stock, while an index option premium is dependent on the basket of assets that comprise the index.

In addition to the premium the writer (seller) of a financial option has the additional benefit of reduced transaction costs. When a futures contract is settled, the individual who has written the contract must transfer the underlying asset. If it is stock, the writer must transfer the stock. There is a transaction cost associated with both buying and transferring the stock. If the writer of a futures contract has written an option instead and the option had been exercised, the transaction cost would be saved because financial options have cash settlements. The settlement for an option is the difference between the exercise price and the price of the underlying asset, not the underlying asset itself.

OPTIONS: A BRIEF HISTORY

Options were first traded during the Great Bulb Market in Holland in the 1600s. At that time tulip bulbs were traded, and the price of a bulb was comparable to an ounce of gold today. To hedge against the rising price of bulbs, people traded options on the bulbs.

At the onset of this century the area of mathematical analysis called stochastic processes was developed. A stochastic processes is the study of random events over time. This type of analysis has been applied to the examination of the spread of contagious diseases in the population, the outcome of games of chance, the motion of a drunkard, or the motion of an atomic particle. Some of these techniques have been quite successfully applied to the pricing of options on stocks.

One of the first to model the price of options on stocks was the French mathematician Bachelier. However, the model he created was a failure for a number of reasons. In not restricting the value of the stock to nonnegative values, the model assumes unlimited liability to the investor. He overlooked the effect of interest rates and risk aversion. Lastly, the formula for a call option increases without bound as expiration time increases. This is inconsistent. The price of a call should be less than or equal to the price of the underlying asset.

In 1964 Sprenkel developed a model which assumes that the price of stock follows a log-normal distribution. This eliminated the possibility of negative stock prices which plagued the Bachelier model. The model also assumes that the mean expected price change is zero thereby allowing for both positive interest rates and risk aversion. The major difficulty encountered with this analysis is found in the final formula for the option price. There is a parameter for risk aversion which cannot be measured directly or empirically.

Boness in 1964 made the following assumptions:

1. The market is competitive in the sense that the equilibrium price of all stocks of the same risk class imply the same expected yield. For convenience and in light of imperfect information, all stocks are defined to be of the same class.
2. The probability distribution of expected percentage changes of any stock is log-normal.
3. Variance of returns is directly proportional to time.
4. Investors are indifferent to risk.

This model is an improvement over Sprenkle in that it takes into account the time value of money, but it fails to consider the levels of risk for both the stock and the option.

Samuelson (1965) assumed that stock prices follow Geometric Brownian Motion with positive drift g, that options grow at the rate k, and that stock prices have a log-normal distribution. While this model does derive an expression for the price of an option, it is unable to estimate the parameter k.

Thorp-Kassouf (1967) developed an option-pricing model using curve-fitting techniques to historical option-pricing data. They use the option-pricing model to create a riskless hedge. This hedging technique was later used by Black and Scholes to create their model.

Shelton (1967) conducted statistical study of warrants. Warrants are similar to options but have a life span of a few years as opposed to a few months for options. Using step-wise regression he found three significant factors—lost dividends, length of time until expiration, and the difference between warrants being traded on an exchange vs. over-the-counter trades. Furthermore, he found that the trading price of the warrant as well as the past trend and past volatility of the stock were insignificant.

Black and Scholes developed a model to price options in 1973. Included in this model are the following assumption:

1) Stock prices have a log-normal probability distribution with constant variance
2) Stock prices follow a random walk in continuous time
3) There is no penalty for short sales
4) The riskless interest rate is constant
5) The stocks pay no dividends or other distributions
6) The investor can borrow any fraction of the price of the security to buy it or hold it at the short term interest rate
7) The option is European, that is it cannot be exercised prior to the expiration date.

To develop the model, Black and Scholes created a hedged position using the stocks and the options on the stock. They then showed that the hedge is riskless and therefore earns the riskless rate. The expression for the value of the hedge is a partial differential equation that can be transformed into the classic heat equation of physics. This equation has a closed form solution which is a function of five measurable observable variables. The variables are the price of the stock, the riskless rate, the exercise price of the option, the time until expiration of the option, and the variance of the stock price. The formula is

$$C + SN(d_1) - e^{-rt} XN(d_2)$$

where
S is the stock price
r is the riskless rate
t is the time until the expiration of the option
X is the exercise price of the option
N is the normal distribution
$d_1 = (\ln(S/X) - [r + 1/2\sigma^2 T])/\sigma T^{1/2}$
$d_2 = (\ln(S/X) + [r-1/2\sigma^2 T])/\sigma T^{1/2}$
ln is the natural logarithm
σ is the variance of the stock price

All of the variables are observable, except for 0, which can be estimated.

R. C. Merton (1973) developed a rational-pricing theory for options. In his rational-pricing theory he derived bounds for the price of the option and adjusted the price model to protect them from payouts on the stock (splits and dividends).

He derived an option-pricing model for American Options and derived the Black-Scholes Model assuming only the Capital Asset Pricing Model. Finally, he proceeded to extend the Black-Scholes Model. He relaxed many Black-Scholes assumptions. He assumed interest rates, that the price dynamics are not stationary, and that investors do not have homogenous expectations. He also extended the formula to include unprotected options; that is, options on stocks that have payouts over the life of the option.

In 1976 Cox and Ross in their paper "Valuation of Options for Alternate Stochastic Processes" examined a number of stochastic processes that can be used to describe the movement of stock prices in continuous time as well as developed option-pricing models based upon the respective stochastic processes. Among the processes studied were the log-normal diffusion process, the jump process.

Cox, Ross, and Rubinstein (1979) continued the work begun by Cox and Ross (1976). The authors assumed that stock prices follow a binomial process and by using arbitrage arguments, developed a simplified approach to option pricing. The final result, the Binomial Option Pricing Formula, is independent of the investors' feelings regarding the expected movement of the market. It is not dependent on the investors' attitude toward risk. The only assumption made here is that the investor prefers more wealth to less and therefore has an incentive to take advantage of riskless arbitrage opportunities. The only random variable in the formula is the price of the stock.

PRICING OPTIONS

This section of the paper will compare the price of an option on the Standard and Poor 100 Index to that derived from the Black-Scholes model. In addition, use of the Black-Scholes model to forecast the price of the OEX option for the next trading day will be included. An evaluation will be performed to determine if the model successfully anticipates the market. The analysis will be done on 486 OEX options, starting from the first date of trading of the January calls, Oct. 21, 1985, until expiration on January 18, 1986.

To evaluate the Black-Scholes Model, we need the values of five parameters: the value of the index, the exercise price, the time until expiration, the riskless rate, and the variance of the rate of return on the underlying asset.

We use the closing price of the OEX. The Monday auction of United States Treasury Bills with maturity dates as close to the expiration date of the option are used to determine the riskless rate. Both values can be found in either the *New York Times* or the *Wall Street Journal*. The variance of the rate of the rate of return is estimated by assuming that the option that closes closest to *at the money* is properly priced, and use it to calculate an implied variance.

In table 1 the results of evaluating the Black-Scholes model is presented. In addition to the value of the Model, we include the closing premium, the closing value of the index, the number of days until expiration, the closing premium of the option on the next day the option is traded, the Black-Scholes values for the next trading day.

We assume that the model values the option correctly. If the difference between the premium of the option and the Black-Scholes price is positive, the option is said to be over priced, and the investor would be wise to sell the option. If the difference is negative, the investor should buy the option.

In table 1 the likely actions of the investor based upon the Black-Scholes price is given. Taking a conservative approach, our investment decision will require that each model recommendation be the same; otherwise no investment will is made.

In table 2-4 three trading strategies are examined. In table 2 the strategy is trading every day. If both recommendations are to buy, the investor buys. If both recommendations are to sell, the investor sells the option; otherwise, no investment is made. Following this strategy the investor would realize a profit of $17.625.

Table 3 examines the trader who trades every day except on Fridays. This investor would feel that using the Black-Scholes model to forecast three days out is not good practice. Following this strategy the investor would realize a profit of $20.015.

Finally, in table 4 there is an examination of the profitability of trading only if there is a trading day on the following day. The investor who follows this strategy would realize a profit of $20.177.

All three strategies are profitable, but the investors who limit their trading seem to be somewhat more profitable.

A summary of the profitability of each strategy is given in table 5.

Table 5

	Profit on Writing	Profit on Buying	Total Profit	Profit on Buying and Selling Each Day
strategy 1	-11.125	28.750	17.625	13.875
strategy 2	-18.010	38.625	20.615	20.823
strategy 3	- 7.323	27.500	20.177	43.385

The profits shown in table 5 do not include transaction costs, the cost of money, nor taxes.

Contrary to a number of studies that have been conducted, these results seem to indicate that writing the OEX Options is not profitable. One reason might be the unprecedented bull market of 1982-1987. The data is from late 1986 to early 1987. Another reason might be because of the underlying model. Black-Scholes was used because of the general knowledge of the model, ease of collecting the data required by the model, and ease of evaluating the model.

It is only required that the model shows that the option is consistently underpriced or overpriced; the well-capitalized investor then has the ability to manipulate or exploit the market to his/her advantage.

Consider the following simple strategy. Suppose the model shows that an option is overpriced. The prudent investor would sell option contracts. The theory of an efficient market suggests that the market will react and the price will fall. When the price falls the investor can then buy calls of the same options to cover the call he had written call. In the process the investor will make a profit on the difference in price between the price at which he sells the option, plus the time use of the money from the sale, minus the price he pays to purchase the option and the transaction cost.

$$\text{profit} = C_1 (1 + e^{rt}) - (c_1 + T)$$

where

C_1 = the premium on the option the investor sells

r = riskless rate of return

t = the time until the position is unwound

c_1 = the premium on the option the investor buys to close out his position

T = the transaction cost for the round trip.

To be profitable,

$$c_1 > C_1(1 + e^{rt}) - T.$$

It can be argued that the individual will not make a profit on this price differential due to the high cost of trading the option, but as the number of options traded increases, the transaction cost decreases sharply. And the transaction cost becomes significantly less costly.

Next, suppose the option is underpriced according to the model, then the investor should buy an option contract. Again, the theory is that the market will react to the underpricing and the price will rise. When the market rises, the investor then writes the same option, receiving the difference in price minus transaction costs as his profit.

$$\text{profit} = C_1 - (c_1 + T + e^{rt})$$

For this position to be profitable,

$$C_1 > c_1 + T + e^{rt}.$$

The expression e^{rt} is the cost of the money while the position is held. In order for this position to be profitable, the spread between c_1 and C_1 must be larger than in the prior scenario offset the cost of money while the position is held.

In the theory of an efficient market all investors who have the same information as such will know that an option is under and overpriced. Assuming that the option is overpriced, there should be a large number of investors willing to sell the option, yet few willing to buy it. The large supply of investors willing to write the option and the short supply of investors willing to buy the option should therefore cause the premium on the option to drop to its correct market price. Given the fact that the actual market is not a perfect market, and there is a time lag involved in disseminating information, some investors could make large profits because of the price discrepancy. A similar argument can be made for options that are underpriced.

Again it can be argued that the market is relatively efficient and any price discrepancy will be short lived making it difficult for an investor to see a profit given transaction costs. In fact theoretically, the expected value of profits made from exploiting the market inefficiencies is zero. But a case can be made that the market can be manipulated by large investors.

Suppose the investor has a model that anticipates the market by a few days. He uses the same simple strategy of selling overpriced options and buying underpriced options. In a somewhat efficient market the opportunity to make profits on mispriced assets is short lived. If an investor sees an inefficiently priced option, the act of trying to capitalize on the inefficiency itself will cause the price to correct itself. This is due to the added supply of buyers or sellers of options. If the investor is wrong, then the investor will be at risk for a large sum of money.

If the investor expects a movement up or down in the short term, then the investor could time the buy or sell orders. Consequently, the market could absorb the orders without having a major impact on the price of the option. Executing the buy or sell order in this fashion, the investor will probably not realize all of the theoretical profit that would have been obtained if the order could have been executed at one time, since market would have more time to absorb and adjust to the impact of the buy/sell orders. In this scenario the argument can be made that the cumulative effect of the size of the order itself would have an impact on the market. If the investment was sufficiently large and the market responded in a favorable way to the investor, this action must lead to the following question. Did the investor anticipate the action market or conversely did the investor's action with this substantial investment manipulate the market, affecting the market change?

From a purely mathematical standpoint, the model price is the correct price for the asset with the discrepancy explained by stating that the market is pricing the asset incorrectly. Yet there seems to be some inherent basic flaw with the claim when applied to the action of people. Do the actions of people follow a stochastic partial differential equation? We are only now discovering the mathematical equation to describe that behavior. Or do we use mathematical analysis to analyze the activities of man? If there is a difference, the truth lies with the activities of man and the error with the mathematical analysis which does not include the full breadth of the human experience.

References

Bachelier, L. 1900; 1964. "Theory of Speculation" (English translation). *The Random Character of Stock Market Prices*. Ed. P. Cootner. Cambridge: MIT Press. 17-78.

Black, F., and M. Scholes. 1972. "The Valuation of Options Contracts and a Test of Market Efficiency." *Journal of Finance* 27.2: 399-417.

————. 1973. "The Pricing of Options and Corporate Liabilities." *Journal of Political Economy* 81: 637-59.

Boness, A. J. 1964. "Elements of a Theory of Stock-Option Value." *Journal of Political Economy* 72.2: 163-75.

Cootner, P. H. ed. 1964. *The Random Character of Stock Market Prices*. Cambridge: MIT Press.

Cox, J., and S. Ross 1976. "The Valuation of Options for Alternate Stochastic Processes." *Journal of Financial Economics* 3: 145-66.

Cox, J., S. Ross, and M. Rubinstein. 1979. "Options Pricing: A Simplified Approach." *Journal of Financial Economics* 7: 229-63.

Geske, R., and R. Roll. 1984. "On Valuing American Call Options With the Black-Scholes European Formula." *Journal of Finance* 39.2: 443-55.

Giguere, G. 1958. "Warrants, A Mathematical Method of Evaluation." *Analysts Journal* 14: 17-25.

Kassouf, S. T. 1968. "Warrant Price Behavior—1945 to 1964." *Financial Analysts Journal* 27: 123-26.

Macbeth, J. D., and L. J. Merville. 1979. "An Empirical Examination of the Black-Scholes Call Option Pricing Model." *Journal of Finance* 34.5: 1173-86.

————. 1980. "Tests of the Black-Scholes and Cox Call Option Valuation Models." *Journal of Finance* 35.2: 285-303.

Merton, R. C. 1973. "The Theory of Rational Option Pricing." *Bell Journal of Economics* Fall: 141-83.

————. 1976. "Option Pricing When Underlying Stock Returns are Discontinuous." *Journal of Financial Economics* 3.1: 125-44.

Samuelson, P. A. 1965. "Rational Theory of Warrant Pricing." *Industrial Management Review* 6: 13-31.

Shelton, J. P. 1967a. "The Relation on the Pricing of a Warrant to the Price of Its Associated Stock, Part I." *Financial Analysts Journal* 23: 143-51.

————. 1967b. "The Relation on the Pricing of a Warrant to the Price of Its Associated Stock, Part II." *Financial Analysts Journal* 24: 84-99.

Smith, C. W. 1976. "Option Pricing: A Review." *Journal of Financial Economics* 3: 3-51.

Sprenkle, C. M. 1964. "Warrant Prices as Indicators of Expectations and Preferences." *The Random Character of Stock Prices*. Ed. P. Cootner. Cambridge: MIT Press. 412-74.

Sterk, W. 1982. "Tests of Two Models for Valuing Call Options on Stocks with Dividends." *Journal of Finance* 37: 1229-37.

Theil, H. 1966. *Applied Economic Forecasting*. Amsterdam: Holland Publishing; Chicago: Rand McNally.

Thorp, E. O., and S. T. Kassouf. 1967. *Beat the Market* New York: Random House.

Trennepohl, G. 1981. "A Comparison of Listed Option Premiums and Black and Scholes Model Prices: 1973-1979." *Journal of Financial Research* 4.1: 11-20.

Whaley, R. E. 1981. "On Valuation of American Call Options on Stocks with Known Dividends." *Journal of Financial Economics* 9: 207-11.

————. 1982. "Valuation of American Call Options on Dividend-Paying Stocks—Empirical Tests." *Journal of Financial Economics* 10: 29-58.

Table 1.1

Closing Premiums	Closing Index	Exercise Price	Days until Expiration	Next trading Day Closing Premiums	Black Scholes Price For Trading Day	Difference Actual - Black Scholes	Likely Action	Black Scholes Price For Next Trading Day	Difference Today's premium Tomorrow's Black Scholes Price	Likely Action	Decision
7.7500	180.99	175	89	8.1250	9.2589	-1.5089	Buy	6.022	1.7282	Sell	No Action
4.3750	180.99	180	89	4.8750	4.3522	0.0228	Sell	1.029	3.3461	Sell	Sell
2.1875	180.99	185	89	2.5000	0.0445	2.1430	Sell	0.000	2.1875	Sell	Sell
0.9375	180.99	190	89	1.0000	0.0000	0.9375	Sell	0.000	0.9375	Buy	Buy
12.0000	182.14	170	88	13.1250	15.2801	-3.2801	Buy	12.171	-0.1706	Buy	No Action
8.1250	182.14	175	88	9.1250	10.3725	-2.2475	Buy	7.171	0.9535	Sell	No Action
4.8750	182.14	180	88	5.5000	5.4648	-0.5898	Buy	2.172	2.7026	Sell	Sell
2.5000	182.14	185	88	2.8750	0.5572	1.9428	Sell	0.000	2.5000	Sell	Sell
1.0000	182.14	190	88	1.1875	0.0000	1.0000	Sell	0.000	1.0000	Sell	Sell
13.1250	183.04	170	87	13.0000	16.1448	-3.0197	Buy	13.070	0.0548	Sell	No Action
9.1250	183.04	175	87	9.0000	11.2361	-2.1111	Buy	8.071	1.0539	Sell	No Action
5.5000	183.04	180	87	4.7500	6.3274	-0.8274	Buy	3.072	2.4280	Sell	No Action
2.8750	183.04	185	87	2.4375	1.4187	1.4563	Sell	0.000	2.8750	Sell	Sell
1.1875	183.04	190	87	1.0000	0.0000	1.1875	Sell	0.000	1.1875	Sell	Sell
13.0000	181.96	170	86	11.0000	15.0294	-2.0294	Buy	11.990	1.0101	Sell	No Action
9.0000	181.96	175	86	7.2500	10.1197	-1.1197	Buy	6.991	2.0093	Sell	No Action
4.7500	181.96	180	86	4.0000	5.2099	-0.4599	Buy	1.992	2.7584	Sell	No Action
2.4375	181.96	185	86	2.0000	0.3002	2.1373	Sell	0.000	2.4375	Sell	Sell
1.0000	181.96	190	86	0.8125	0.0000	1.0000	Sell	0.000	1.0000	Sell	Sell
11.0000	180.83	170	85	11.2500	13.8640	-2.8640	Buy	10.859	0.1412	Buy	No Action
7.2500	180.83	175	85	7.6250	8.9532	-1.7032	Buy	5.860	1.3903	Sell	No Action
4.0000	180.83	180	85	4.3750	4.0425	-0.0425	Buy	0.860	3.1395	Sell	No Action
2.0000	180.83	185	85	2.0000	0.0000	2.0000	Sell	0.000	2.0000	Sell	Sell
0.8125	180.83	190	85	0.8125	0.0000	0.8125	Sell	0.000	0.8125	Sell	Sell
11.2500	181.19	170	82	13.0000	14.1433	-2.8933	Buy	17.218	0.0315	Buy	No Action
7.6250	181.19	175	82	8.8750	9.2302	-1.6052	Buy	6.219	1.4057	Sell	No Action
4.3750	181.19	180	82	5.0000	4.3170	0.0580	Sell	1.220	3.1549	Sell	Sell
2.0000	181.19	185	82	2.4375	0.0000	2.0000	Sell	0.000	2.0000	Sell	Sell
0.8125	181.19	190	82	1.0000	0.0000	0.8125	Sell	0.000	0.8125	Sell	Sell
13.0000	182.63	170	81	13.2500	15.5476	-2.5476	Buy	12.658	0.3419	Buy	No Action
8.8750	182.63	175	81	8.8750	10.6334	-1.7584	Buy	7.659	1.2161	Sell	No Action
5.0000	182.63	180	81	5.3750	5.7192	-0.7192	Buy	2.660	2.3402	Sell	No Action
2.4375	182.63	185	81	2.6875	0.8051	1.6324	Sell	0.000	2.4375	Sell	Sell
1.0000	182.63	190	81	1.1250	0.0000	1.0000	Sell	0.000	1.0000	Sell	Sell
13.2500	183.50	170	80	13.2500	16.3819	-3.2569	Buy	13.528	-0.4027	Buy	No Action
8.8750	183.50	175	80	8.7500	11.4667	-2.5917	Buy	8.529	0.3464	Buy	No Action
5.3750	183.50	180	80	5.1250	6.5514	-1.1764	Buy	3.529	1.8456	Sell	No Action
2.6875	183.50	185	80	2.5000	1.6362	1.0513	Sell	0.000	2.6875	Sell	Sell
1.1250	183.50	190	80	1.0625	0.0000	1.1250	Sell	0.000	1.1250	Sell	Sell
13.2500	183.17	170	79	14.2500	16.0162	-2.7662	Buy	13.197	0.0526	Buy	No Action
8.7500	183.17	175	79	10.2500	10.9999	-2.3499	Buy	8.198	0.5518	Buy	No Action
5.1250	183.17	180	79	6.0000	6.1836	-1.0586	Buy	3.199	1.9260	Sell	No Action
2.5000	183.17	185	79	3.2500	1.2673	1.2327	Sell	0.000	2.5000	Sell	Sell
0.0000	183.17	190	79	1.2500	0.0000	1.0625	Sell	0.000	1.0625	Sell	Sell

Table 1.2

Closing Premiums	Closing Index	Exercise Price	Days until Expiration	Next trading Day Closing Premiums	Black Scholes Price For Trading Day	Difference Actual - Black Scholes	Likely Action	Black Scholes Price For Next Trading Day	Difference Today's premium Tomorrow's Black Scholes Price	Likely Action	Decision
14.2500	184.81	170	78	14.3750	17.6205	-3.3705	Buy	14.836	-0.5863	Buy	Buy
10.2500	184.81	175	78	9.7500	12.7031	-2.4531	Buy	9.837	0.4129	Sell	No Action
6.0000	184.81	180	78	6.0000	7.7858	-1.7858	Buy	4.838	1.1621	Sell	No Action
3.2500	184.81	185	78	3.1250	2.8684	0.3816	Sell	0.000	3.2500	Sell	Sell
1.2500	184.81	190	78	1.2500	0.0000	1.2500	Sell	0.000	1.2500	Sell	Sell
14.3750	184.92	170	75	15.5000	17.6118	-3.2368	Buy	14.946	-0.5710	Buy	Buy
9.7500	184.92	175	75	10.3750	12.6910	-2.9410	Buy	9.947	-0.1968	Buy	Buy
6.0000	184.92	180	75	6.6250	7.7702	-1.7702	Buy	4.948	1.0525	Sell	No Action
3.1250	184.92	185	75	3.5000	2.8493	0.2757	Sell	0.002	3.1234	Sell	Sell
1.2500	184.92	190	75	1.4375	0.0000	1.2500	Sell	0.000	1.2500	Sell	Sell
15.5000	185.89	170	74	15.7500	18.5462	-3.0462	Buy	15.916	-0.4156	Buy	Buy
10.3750	185.89	175	74	10.2500	13.6243	-3.2493	Buy	10.916	-0.5440	Buy	Buy
6.6250	185.89	180	74	6.6250	8.7025	-2.0775	Buy	5.917	0.7079	Sell	No Action
3.5000	185.89	185	74	3.5000	3.7806	-0.2806	Buy	0.918	2.5821	Sell	No Action
1.5000	185.89	190	74	1.3750	0.0000	1.5000	Sell	0.000	1.5000	Sell	Sell
1.5000	185.89	195	74	0.4375	0.0000	1.5000	Sell	0.000	1.5000	Sell	Sell
15.7500	185.86	170	73	15.0000	18.4806	-2.7306	Buy	15.885	-0.1350	Buy	Buy
10.7500	185.86	175	73	10.7500	13.5577	-2.8077	Buy	10.886	-0.1360	Buy	Buy
6.6250	185.86	180	73	6.5000	8.6348	-2.0098	Buy	5.887	0.7382	Sell	No Action
3.5000	185.86	185	73	3.3750	3.7118	-0.2118	Buy	0.888	2.6125	Sell	No Action
1.3750	185.86	190	73	1.3125	0.0000	1.3750	Sell	0.000	1.3750	Sell	Sell
0.4375	185.86	195	73	0.3750	0.0000	0.4375	Sell	0.000	0.4375	Sell	Sell
15.0000	185.55	170	72	16.1250	18.1350	-3.1350	Buy	15.575	-0.5750	Buy	Buy
10.7500	185.55	175	72	12.0000	13.2110	-2.4610	Buy	10.576	0.1743	Sell	No Action
6.5000	185.55	180	72	7.8760	8.2870	-1.7870	Buy	5.576	0.9236	Sell	No Action
3.3750	185.55	185	72	4.2500	3.3631	0.0119	Sell	0.577	2.7979	Sell	Sell
1.3125	185.55	190	72	1.7500	0.0000	1.3125	Sell	0.000	1.3125	Sell	Sell
0.3750	185.55	195	72	0.6250	0.0000	0.3750	Sell	0.000	0.3750	Sell	Sell
16.1250	186.37	170	71	14.5000	18.9193	-2.7943	Buy	16.394	-0.2689	Buy	Buy
12.0000	186.37	175	71	10.5000	13.9943	-1.9943	Buy	11.395	0.6054	Sell	No Action
7.8750	186.37	180	71	6.2500	9.0693	-1.1943	Buy	6.395	1.4797	Sell	No Action
4.2500	186.37	185	71	3.0000	4.1443	0.1057	Sell	1.396	2.8540	Sell	Sell
1.7500	186.37	190	71	1.2500	0.0000	1.7500	Sell	0.000	1.7500	Sell	Sell
0.6250	186.37	195	71	0.6250	0.0000	0.6250	Sell	0.000	0.6250	Sell	Sell
14.5000	189.82	175	68	16.0000	17.3342	-2.8342	Buy	14.844	-0.3442	Buy	Buy
10.5000	189.82	180	68	11.5000	12.4061	-1.9061	Buy	9.845	0.6551	Sell	No Action
6.2500	189.82	185	68	7.3760	7.4779	-1.2279	Buy	4.846	1.4044	Sell	No Action
3.0000	189.82	190	68	4.2500	2.5497	0.4503	Sell	0.000	3.0000	Sell	Sell
1.2500	189.82	195	68	2.0000	0.0000	1.2500	Sell	0.000	1.2500	Sell	Sell
20.5000	190.90	170	67	15.5000	23.3067	-2.8067	Buy	20.923	-0.4232	Buy	Buy
16.0000	190.90	175	67	11.0000	18.3775	-2.3775	Buy	15.924	0.0761	Sell	No Action
11.5000	190.90	180	67	6.6250	13.4483	-1.9483	Buy	10.925	0.5755	Sell	No Action
7.3750	190.90	185	67	3.6250	8.5191	-1.1441	Buy	5.925	1.4498	Sell	No Action
4.2500	190.90	190	67	1.7500	3.5899	0.6601	Sell	0.926	3.3241	Sell	Sell
2.0000	190.90	195	67	0.0000	0.0000	2.0000	Sell	0.000	2.0000	Sell	Sell

Table 1.3

Closing Premiums	Closing Index	Exercise Price	Days until Expiration	Next trading Day Closing Premiums	Black Scholes Price For Trading Day	Difference Actual - Black Scholes	Likely Action	Black Scholes Price For Next Trading Day	Difference Today's premium Tomorrow's Black Scholes Price	Likely Action	Decision
15.5000	190.04	175	66	17.5000	17.4808	-1.9808	Buy	15.063	0.4365	Sell	No Action
10.1250	190.04	180	66	12.6250	12.5505	-2.4255	Buy	10.064	0.0600	Sell	No Action
6.6250	190.04	185	66	8.3780	7.6205	-0.9963	Buy	5.065	1.5602	Sell	No Action
3.6250	190.04	190	66	4.7500	2.6900	0.9360	Sell	0.068	3.5569	Sell	Sell
1.7500	190.04	195	66	2.5000	0.0000	1.7500	Sell	0.000	1.7500	Sell	Sell
0.6875	190.04	200	66	1.0000	0.0000	0.6875	Sell	0.000	0.6875	Buy	Buy
22.0000	192.08	170	65	22.0000	24.4154	-2.4154	Buy	22.102	-0.1025	Buy	No Action
17.5000	192.08	175	65	18.0000	19.4841	-1.9841	Buy	17.103	0.3969	Sell	No Action
12.6250	192.08	180	65	12.0000	14.5528	-1.9278	Buy	12.104	0.5212	Sell	No Action
8.3750	192.08	185	65	7.6250	9.6214	-1.2464	Buy	7.104	1.2705	Sell	No Action
4.7500	192.08	190	65	4.3750	4.6901	0.0599	Sell	2.105	2.6449	Sell	Sell
2.5000	192.08	195	65	2.1250	0.0000	2.5000	Sell	0.000	2.5000	Sell	Sell
1.0000	192.08	200	65	0.9375	0.0000	1.0000	Sell	0.000	1.0000	Sell	Sell
22.0000	190.98	170	64	22.0000	23.2297	-1.2797	Buy	21.001	0.9986	Sell	No Action
18.0000	190.98	175	64	17.0000	18.3473	-0.3473	Buy	16.002	1.9979	Sell	No Action
12.0000	190.98	180	64	12.5000	13.4150	-1.4150	Buy	11.003	0.9973	Sell	No Action
7.6250	190.98	185	64	8.2500	8.4826	-0.8576	Buy	6.003	1.6217	Sell	No Action
4.3750	190.98	190	64	4.7500	3.5803	0.8247	Sell	1.004	3.3711	Sell	Sell
2.1250	190.98	195	64	2.2500	0.0000	2.1250	Sell	0.000	2.1250	Sell	Sell
0.9375	190.98	200	64	1.0000	0.0000	0.9375	Sell	0.000	0.9375	Sell	Sell
22.0000	192.08	170	61	22.7500	24.2819	-2.2819	Buy	22.101	-0.1011	Buy	Buy
17.0000	192.08	175	61	17.0000	19.3467	-2.3467	Buy	17.102	-0.1017	Buy	Buy
12.5000	192.08	180	61	12.5000	14.4114	-1.9114	Buy	12.102	0.3977	Sell	No Action
8.2500	192.08	185	61	8.1250	9.4762	-1.2262	Buy	7.103	1.1471	Sell	No Action
4.7500	192.08	190	61	4.5000	4.5410	0.2090	Sell	2.104	2.6464	Sell	Sell
2.2500	192.08	195	61	2.1875	0.0000	2.2500	Sell	0.000	2.2500	Sell	Sell
1.0000	192.08	200	61	0.8125	0.0000	1.0000	Sell	0.000	1.0000	Sell	Sell
0.2500	192.08	205	61	0.2500	0.0000	0.2500	Sell	0.000	0.2500	Sell	Sell
22.7500	192.08	170	60	18.2500	24.2461	-1.4961	Buy	22.101	0.6493	Buy	Buy
17.0000	192.08	175	60	13.0000	19.3098	-2.3098	Buy	17.101	-0.1013	Buy	Buy
12.5000	192.08	180	60	8.7500	14.3735	-1.8735	Buy	12.102	0.3981	Sell	No Action
8.1250	192.08	185	60	5.0000	9.4372	-1.3122	Buy	7.103	1.0224	Sell	No Action
4.5000	192.08	190	60	2.4375	4.5009	-0.0009	Sell	2.103	2.3968	Sell	Sell
2.1875	192.08	195	60	0.9375	0.0000	2.1875	Sell	0.000	2.1875	Sell	Sell
0.8125	192.08	200	60	0.3125	0.0000	0.8125	Sell	0.000	0.8125	Sell	Sell
0.2500	192.08	205	60	0.0000	0.0000	0.2500	Sell	0.000	0.2500	Sell	Sell
18.2500	192.62	175	59	19.7500	19.8128	-1.5628	Buy	17.641	0.6090	Buy	Buy
13.0000	192.62	180	59	15.0000	14.8755	-1.8755	Buy	12.642	0.3584	Sell	No Action
8.7500	192.62	185	59	11.0000	9.9381	-1.1881	Buy	7.642	1.0778	Sell	No Action
5.0000	192.62	190	59	6.6250	5.0008	-0.0008	Sell	2.643	2.3672	Sell	Sell
2.4375	192.62	195	59	3.6250	0.0661	2.3714	Sell	0.000	2.4375	Sell	Sell
0.9375	192.62	200	59	1.5000	0.0000	0.9375	Sell	0.000	0.9375	Sell	Sell
0.3125	192.62	205	59	0.5625	0.0000	0.3125	Sell	0.000	0.3125	Sell	Sell

Table 1.4

Closing Premiums	Closing Index	Exercise Price	Days until Expiration	Next trading Day Closing Premiums	Black Scholes Price For Trading Day	Difference Actual - Black Scholes	Likely Action	Black Scholes Price For Next Trading Day	Likely Action	Difference Today's premium Tomorrow's Black Scholes Price	Likely Action	Decision
19.7500	194.98	175	58	20.3750	22.1359	-2.3859	Buy	20.001	Buy	-0.2506	Buy	Buy
15.5000	194.98	180	58	15.1250	17.1975	-1.6975	Buy	15.001	Sell	0.4908	Sell	No Action
11.0000	194.98	185	58	10.7500	12.2591	-1.2591	Buy	10.002	Sell	0.9982	Sell	No Action
6.6250	194.98	190	58	6.5000	7.3207	-0.6957	Buy	5.002	Sell	1.6226	Sell	No Action
3.6250	194.98	195	58	3.5000	2.3823	1.2427	Sell	0.023	Sell	3.6015	Sell	Sell
1.5000	194.98	200	58	1.5000	0.0000	1.5000	Sell	0.000	Sell	1.5000	Sell	Sell
0.5625	194.98	205	58	0.5625	0.0000	0.5625	Sell	0.000	Sell	0.5625	Sell	Sell
25.7500	194.79	170	57	24.5000	26.8484	-1.0984	Buy	24.809	Buy	0.9410	Sell	No Action
20.3750	194.79	175	57	19.7500	21.9089	-1.5339	Buy	19.810	Buy	0.5656	Sell	No Action
15.1250	194.79	180	57	14.5000	16.9695	-1.8445	Buy	14.810	Buy	0.3349	Sell	No Action
10.7500	194.79	185	57	9.8750	12.0300	-1.2800	Buy	9.811	Buy	0.9394	Sell	No Action
6.500	194.79	190	57	5.8750	7.0906	-0.5906	Buy	4.811	Buy	1.6888	Sell	No Action
3.5000	194.79	195	57	3.0000	2.1511	1.3489	Sell	0.000	Sell	3.5000	Sell	Sell
1.5000	194.79	200	57	1.3825	0.0000	1.5000	Sell	0.000	Sell	1.5000	Sell	Sell
0.5625	194.79	205	57	0.5000	0.0000	0.5625	Sell	0.000	Sell	0.5625	Sell	Sell
19.7500	193.69	175	54	20.0000	20.6718	-0.9218	Buy	18.709	Buy	1.0408	Sell	No Action
14.5000	193.69	180	54	15.1250	15.7284	-1.2284	Buy	13.710	Buy	0.7903	Sell	No Action
9.8750	193.69	185	54	10.2500	10.7851	-0.9101	Buy	8.710	Buy	1.1647	Sell	No Action
5.8750	193.69	190	54	6.2500	5.8417	0.0333	Sell	3.711	Sell	2.1642	Sell	Sell
3.0000	193.69	195	54	3.2500	0.8983	2.1017	Sell	0.000	Sell	3.0000	Sell	Sell
1.3125	193.69	200	54	1.3750	0.0000	1.3125	Sell	0.000	Sell	1.3125	Sell	Sell
0.5000	193.69	205	54	0.5000	0.0000	0.5000	Sell	0.000	Sell	0.5000	Sell	Sell
24.2500	194.30	170	53	24.5000	26.1897	-1.9397	Buy	24.318	Buy	-0.0683	Buy	Buy
20.0000	194.30	175	53	21.7500	21.2453	-1.2453	Buy	19.319	Buy	0.6822	Sell	No Action
15.1250	191.30	180	53	17.3750	16.3009	-1.1759	Buy	14.319	Buy	0.8057	Sell	No Action
10.2500	194.30	185	53	12.5000	11.3565	-1.1065	Buy	9.320	Buy	0.9301	Sell	No Action
6.2500	194.30	190	53	8.0000	6.4121	-0.1621	Buy	4.320	Buy	1.9296	Sell	No Action
3.2500	194.30	195	53	4.5000	1.4676	1.7824	Sell	0.000	Sell	3.2500	Sell	Sell
1.3750	194.30	200	53	2.1250	0.0000	1.3750	Sell	0.000	Sell	1.3750	Sell	Sell
0.5000	194.30	205	53	0.9375	0.0000	0.5000	Sell	0.000	Sell	0.5000	Sell	Sell
24.5000	196.42	170	52	24.0000	28.2743	-3.7743	Buy	26.438	Buy	-1.9376	Buy	Buy
21.7500	196.42	175	52	21.2500	23.3288	-1.5788	Buy	21.438	Buy	0.3129	Sell	No Action
17.3750	196.42	180	52	16.3750	18.3854	-1.0084	Buy	16.439	Buy	0.9364	Sell	No Action
12.5000	196.42	185	52	11.7500	13.4379	-0.9379	Buy	11.439	Buy	1.0609	Sell	No Action
8.0000	196.42	190	52	7.0000	8.4924	-0.4924	Buy	6.440	Buy	1.5604	Sell	No Action
4.5000	196.42	195	52	3.8750	3.5470	0.9530	Sell	1.440	Sell	3.0199	Sell	Sell
2.1250	196.42	200	52	1.7500	0.0000	2.1250	Sell	0.000	Sell	2.1250	Sell	Sell
0.9375	196.42	205	52	0.6875	0.0000	0.9375	Sell	0.000	Sell	0.9375	Sell	Sell
21.2500	195.63	175	50	19.5000	22.4658	-1.2158	Buy	20.647	Buy	0.6030	Sell	No Action
16.3750	195.63	180	50	14.5000	17.5182	-1.1432	Buy	15.647	Buy	0.7275	Sell	No Action
11.7500	195.63	185	50	9.8750	12.5707	-0.8207	Buy	10.648	Buy	1.1020	Sell	No Action
7.0000	195.63	190	50	5.7500	7.6231	-0.6231	Buy	5.648	Buy	1.3515	Sell	No Action
3.8750	195.63	195	50	2.8750	2.6756	1.1994	Sell	0.649	Sell	3.2261	Sell	Sell
1.7500	195.63	200	50	1.1875	0.0000	1.7500	Sell	0.000	Sell	1.7500	Sell	Sell
0.6875	195.63	205	50	0.50000	0.0000	0.6875	Sell	0.000	Sell	0.6875	Sell	Sell

Table 1.5

Closing Premiums	Closing Index	Exercise Price	Days until Expiration	Next trading Day Closing Premiums	Black Scholes Price For Trading Day	Difference Actual - Black Scholes	Likely Action	Black Scholes Price For Next Trading Day	Difference Today's premium Tomorrow's Black Scholes Price	Likely Action	Decision
24.0000	193.68	170	47	27.5000	25.3660	-1.3660	Buy	23.696	0.3039	Sell	No Action
19.5000	193.68	175	47	19.5000	20.4156	-0.9156	Buy	18.697	0.8034	Sell	No Action
14.5000	193.68	180	47	14.5000	15.4652	-0.9652	Buy	13.697	0.8029	Sell	No Action
9.8750	193.68	185	47	10.3750	10.5148	-0.6398	Buy	8.698	1.1774	Sell	No Action
5.7500	193.68	190	47	6.2500	5.5644	0.1856	Sell	3.698	2.0520	Sell	Sell
2.8750	193.68	195	47	3.2500	0.6140	2.2610	Sell	0.000	2.8750	Sell	Sell
1.1875	193.68	200	47	1.3750	0.0000	1.1875	Sell	0.000	1.1875	Sell	Sell
0.5000	193.68	205	47	0.5000	0.0000	0.5000	Sell	0.000	0.5000	Sell	Sell
19.5000	194.13	175	46	20.2500	20.8289	-1.3289	Buy	19.146	0.3537	Sell	No Action
14.5000	194.13	180	46	19.0000	15.874	-1.3374	Buy	14.147	0.3533	Sell	No Action
10.3750	194.13	185	46	14.1250	10.9259	-0.5509	Buy	9.147	1.2278	Sell	No Action
6.2500	194.13	190	46	9.3750	5.9745	0.2755	Sell	4.148	2.1023	Sell	Sell
3.2500	194.13	195	46	5.5000	1.0230	2.2270	Sell	0.000	3.2500	Sell	Sell
1.3750	194.13	200	46	2.8125	0.0000	1.3750	Sell	0.000	1.3750	Sell	Sell
0.5000	194.13	205	46	1.3125	0.0000	0.5000	Sell	0.000	0.5000	Sell	Sell
20.2500	198.06	175	45	22.5000	24.7221	-4.4721	Buy	23.076	-2.8259	Buy	Buy
19.0000	198.06	180	45	20.1250	19.7696	-0.7696	Buy	18.076	0.9236	Sell	No Action
14.1250	198.06	185	45	13.2500	14.8171	-0.6921	Buy	13.077	1.0482	Sell	No Action
9.3750	198.06	190	45	9.0000	9.8646	-0.4896	Buy	8.077	1.2977	Sell	No Action
5.5000	198.06	195	45	5.3750	4.9121	0.5879	Sell	3.078	2.4223	Sell	Sell
2.8125	198.06	200	45	2.6875	0.0104	2.8021	Sell	0.000	2.8125	Sell	Sell
1.3125	198.06	205	45	1.1875	0.0000	1.3125	Sell	0.000	1.3125	Sell	Sell
27.5000	197.58	170	44	38.0000	29.1589	-1.6589	Buy	27.595	-0.0961	Buy	Buy
22.5000	197.58	175	44	23.5000	24.2053	-1.7053	Buy	22.596	-0.0965	Buy	Buy
20.1250	197.58	180	44	18.3750	19.2518	0.8732	Sell	17.596	2.5290	Sell	Sell
13.2500	197.58	185	44	13.5000	14.2982	-1.0482	Buy	12.596	0.6536	Sell	No Action
9.0000	197.58	190	44	8.7500	9.3447	-0.3446	Buy	7.597	1.4031	Sell	No Action
5.3750	197.58	195	44	5.2500	4.3911	0.9839	Sell	2.597	2.7777	Sell	Sell
2.6875	197.58	200	44	2.6875	0.0000	2.6875	Sell	0.000	2.6875	Sell	Sell
1.1875	197.58	205	44	1.3125	0.0000	1.1875	Sell	0.000	1.1875	Sell	Sell
23.5000	196.93	175	43	24.5000	23.5106	-0.0186	Buy	21.944	1.5585	Sell	No Action
18.3750	196.93	180	43	20.1250	18.5640	-0.1889	Buy	16.945	1.4301	Sell	No Action
13.5000	196.93	185	43	14.0750	13.6094	-0.1093	Buy	11.945	1.5547	Sell	No Action
8.7500	196.93	190	43	10.2500	8.6547	0.0953	Sell	6.946	1.8043	Sell	Sell
5.2500	196.93	195	43	6.3750	3.7001	1.5499	Sell	1.946	3.3039	Sell	Sell
2.6875	196.93	200	43	3.5000	0.0000	2.6875	Sell	0.000	2.6875	Sell	Sell
1.3125	196.93	205	43	1.6875	0.0000	1.3125	Sell	0.000	1.3125	Sell	Sell
0.4375	196.93	210	43	0.6875	0.0000	0.4375	Sell	0.000	0.4375	Sell	Sell
24.5000	198.45	175	40	25.0000	24.9282	-0.4282	Buy	23.464	1.0369	Sell	No Action
20.1250	198.45	180	40	20.0000	19.9704	0.1546	Sell	18.465	1.6605	Sell	Sell
14.8750	198.45	185	40	15.2500	15.0127	-0.1377	Buy	13.465	1.4101	Sell	No Action
10.2500	198.45	190	40	10.6250	10.0549	0.1951	Sell	8.465	1.7847	Sell	Sell
6.3750	198.45	195	40	6.5000	5.0971	1.2779	Sell	3.466	2.9093	Sell	Sell
3.5000	198.45	200	40	3.5000	0.1416	3.3584	Sell	0.000	3.0000	Sell	Sell
1.6875	198.45	205	40	1.8125	0.0000	1.6875	Sell	0.000	1.6875	Sell	Sell
0.6875	198.45	210	40	0.7500	0.0000	0.6875	Sell	0.000	0.6875	Sell	Sell

Table 1.6

Closing Premiums	Closing Index	Exercise Price	Days until Expiration	Next trading Day Closing Premiums	Black Scholes Price For Trading Day	Difference Actual - Black Scholes	Likely Action	Black Scholes Price For Next Trading Day	Difference Today's premium Tomorrow's Black Scholes Price	Likely Action	Decision
25.0000	198.72	175	39	27.0000	25.1614	-0.164	Buy	23.734	1.2663	Sell	No Action
20.0000	198.72	180	39	22.5000	20.2826	-0.2026	Buy	10.734	1.2659	Sell	No Action
15.2500	198.72	185	39	17.7500	15.2438	0.0062	Sell	13.735	1.5155	Sell	Sell
10.6250	198.72	190	39	12.6250	10.2849	0.3401	Sell	8.735	1.8901	Sell	Sell
6.5000	198.72	195	39	8.5000	5.3261	1.1739	Sell	3.735	2.7647	Sell	Sell
3.5000	198.72	200	39	5.1250	0.3674	3.1326	Sell	0.000	3.5000	Sell	Sell
1.8125	198.72	205	39	2.7500	0.0000	1.8125	Sell	0.000	1.8125	Sell	Sell
0.7500	198.72	210	39	1.2500	0.0000	0.7500	Sell	0.000	0.7500	Sell	Sell
27.0000	200.74	175	38	25.8750	27.1446	-0.1446	Buy	25.753	1.2466	Sell	No Action
22.5000	200.74	180	38	22.0000	22.1847	0.3153	Sell	20.754	1.7462	Sell	Sell
17.7500	200.74	185	38	17.7500	17.2249	0.5251	Sell	15.754	1.9959	Sell	Sell
12.6250	200.74	190	38	12.7500	12.2650	0.3600	Sell	10.755	1.8705	Sell	Sell
8.5000	200.74	195	38	8.8750	7.3051	1.1949	Sell	5.755	2.7451	Sell	Sell
5.1250	200.74	200	38	5.5000	2.3453	2.7797	Sell	0.755	4.3697	Sell	Sell
2.7500	200.74	205	38	3.1250	0.0000	2.7500	Sell	0.000	2.7500	Sell	Sell
1.2500	200.74	210	38	1.5000	0.0000	1.2500	Sell	0.000	1.2500	Sell	Sell
25.8750	201.26	175	37	29.8750	27.6278	-1.7528	Buy	26.273	-0.3980	Buy	Buy
22.0000	201.26	180	37	26.2500	22.6668	-0.6668	Buy	21.273	0.7266	Sell	No Action
17.7500	201.26	185	37	21.0000	17.7059	0.0441	Sell	16.274	1.4762	Sell	Sell
12.7500	201.26	190	37	16.3750	12.7450	0.0050	Sell	11.274	1.4759	Sell	Sell
8.8750	201.26	195	37	11.6250	7.7841	1.0909	Sell	6.275	2.6005	Sell	Sell
5.5000	201.26	200	37	7.7500	2.8232	2.6768	Sell	1.275	4.2251	Sell	Sell
3.1250	201.26	205	37	4.7500	0.0000	3.1250	Sell	0.000	3.1250	Sell	Sell
1.5000	201.26	210	37	2.7500	0.0000	1.5000	Sell	0.000	1.5000	Sell	Sell
0.5625	201.26	215	37	1.4375	0.0000	0.5625	Sell	0.000	0.5625	Sell	Sell
29.8750	204.62	175	36	34.5000	30.9509	-1.0759	Buy	29.632	0.2431	Sell	No Action
26.2500	204.62	180	36	28.5000	25.9890	0.2610	Sell	24.632	1.6177	Sell	Sell
21.0000	204.62	185	36	23.5000	21.0270	-0.0270	Buy	19.633	1.3674	Sell	No Action
16.3750	204.62	190	36	18.1250	16.0650	0.3100	Sell	14.633	1.7421	Sell	Sell
11.6250	204.62	195	36	13.7500	11.1031	0.5219	Sell	9.633	1.9917	Sell	Sell
7.7500	204.62	200	36	9.3750	6.1411	1.6089	Sell	4.634	3.1164	Sell	Sell
4.7500	204.62	205	36	6.2500	1.1791	3.5709	Sell	0.000	4.7500	Sell	Sell
2.7500	204.62	210	36	3.8750	0.0000	2.7500	Sell	0.000	2.7500	Sell	Sell
1.4375	204.62	215	36	0.0000	0.0000	1.4375	Sell	0.000	1.4375	Sell	Sell
39.2500	207.07	170	33	38.0000	38.2227	1.0273	Sell	37.080	2.1697	Sell	Sell
34.5000	207.07	175	33	33.0000	33.2566	1.2434	Sell	32.081	2.4194	Sell	Sell
28.5000	207.07	180	33	28.5000	28.2905	0.2096	Sell	27.081	1.4190	Sell	Sell
23.5000	207.07	185	33	22.7500	23.3244	0.1756	Sell	22.081	1.4187	Sell	Sell
18.1250	207.07	190	33	17.6250	18.3583	-0.2333	Buy	17.082	1.0434	Sell	No Action
13.7500	207.07	195	33	13.0000	13.3922	0.3578	Sell	12.082	1.6681	Sell	Sell
9.3750	207.07	200	33	9.1250	8.4261	0.9489	Sell	7.082	2.2928	Sell	Sell
6.2500	207.07	205	33	6.0000	3.4600	2.7900	Sell	2.082	4.1675	Sell	Sell
3.8750	207.07	210	33	3.8750	0.0000	3.8750	Sell	0.000	3.8750	Sell	Sell

Table 1.7

Closing Premiums	Closing Index	Exercise Price	Days until Expiration	Next trading Day Closing Premiums	Black Scholes Price For Trading Day	Difference Actual - Black Scholes	Likely Action	Black Scholes Price For Next Trading Day	Difference Today's premium Tomorrow's Black Scholes Price	Likely Action	Decision
38.0000	205.58	170	32	37.5000	36.6978	1.3022	Sell	35.590	2.4100	Sell	Sell
33.0000	205.58	175	32	33.1250	31.7307	1.2693	Sell	30.590	2.4097	Sell	Sell
28.2500	205.58	180	32	24.2500	26.7636	1.4864	Sell	25.591	2.6594	Sell	Sell
22.7500	205.58	185	32	21.7500	21.7965	0.9535	Sell	20.591	2.1591	Sell	Sell
17.6250	205.58	190	32	16.5000	16.8294	0.7956	Sell	15.591	2.0338	Sell	Sell
13.0000	205.58	195	32	11.8750	11.8622	1.1378	Sell	10.591	2.4085	Sell	Sell
9.1250	205.58	200	32	8.1250	6.8951	2.2299	Sell	5.592	3.5332	Sell	Sell
6.0000	205.58	205	32	5.0000	1.9280	4.0720	Sell	0.592	5.4079	Sell	Sell
3.8750	205.58	210	32	3.0000	0.0000	3.8750	Sell	0.000	3.8750	Sell	Sell
2.3125	205.58	215	32	1.6250	0.0000	2.3125	Sell	0.000	2.3125	Sell	Sell
1.1875	205.58	220	32	0.7500	0.0000	1.1875	Sell	0.000	1.1875	Sell	Sell
33.1250	204.66	175	31	32.0000	30.7749	2.3501	Sell	29.670	3.4550	Sell	Sell
24.2500	204.66	180	31	26.3750	25.8067	-1.5567	Buy	24.670	-0.4203	Buy	Buy
21.7500	204.66	185	31	21.2500	20.8386	0.9114	Sell	19.671	2.0794	Sell	Sell
16.5000	204.66	190	31	16.5000	15.8704	0.6296	Sell	14.671	1.8292	Sell	Sell
11.8750	204.66	195	31	12.0000	10.9023	0.9727	Sell	9.671	2.2039	Sell	Sell
8.0000	204.66	200	31	8.0000	5.9341	2.1909	Sell	4.671	3.4536	Sell	Sell
5.0000	204.66	205	31	4.8750	0.9660	4.0340	Sell	0.001	4.9994	Sell	Sell
3.0000	204.66	210	31	2.9375	0.0000	3.0000	Sell	0.000	3.0000	Sell	Sell
1.6250	204.66	215	31	1.5625	0.0000	1.6250	Sell	0.000	1.6250	Sell	Sell
0.7500	204.66	220	31	0.6250	0.0000	0.7500	Sell	0.000	0.7500	Sell	Sell
32.0000	205.06	175	30	31.5000	31.1390	0.8610	Sell	30.070	1.9304	Sell	Sell
26.3750	205.06	180	30	26.5000	26.1698	0.2052	Sell	25.070	1.3051	Sell	Sell
21.2500	205.06	185	30	21.7500	21.2007	0.0494	Sell	20.070	1.1798	Sell	Sell
16.5000	205.06	190	30	16.7500	16.2315	0.2685	Sell	15.070	1.4295	Sell	Sell
12.0000	205.06	195	30	12.0000	11.2623	0.7377	Sell	10.071	1.9292	Sell	Sell
8.0000	205.06	200	30	8.3750	6.2932	1.7068	Sell	5.071	2.9290	Sell	Sell
4.8750	205.06	205	30	5.0000	1.3240	3.5510	Sell	0.095	4.7803	Sell	Sell
2.9375	205.06	210	30	2.8750	0.0000	2.9375	Sell	0.000	2.9375	Sell	Sell
1.5625	205.06	215	30	1.3125	0.0000	1.5625	Sell	0.000	1.5625	Sell	Sell
0.6250	205.06	220	30	0.5625	0.0000	0.6250	Sell	0.000	0.6250	Sell	Sell
37.5000	205.30	170	29	34.0000	36.3133	1.1867	Sell	35.308	2.1916	Sell	Sell
31.5000	205.30	175	29	30.2500	31.3432	0.1568	Sell	30.309	1.1913	Sell	Sell
26.5000	205.30	180	29	24.7500	26.3730	0.1270	Sell	25.309	1.1911	Sell	Sell
21.7500	205.30	185	29	19.7500	21.4028	0.3472	Sell	20.309	1.4409	Sell	Sell
16.7500	205.30	190	29	14.6250	16.4326	0.3174	Sell	15.309	1.4406	Sell	Sell
12.0000	205.30	195	29	9.5000	11.4624	0.5376	Sell	10.310	1.6904	Sell	Sell
8.3750	205.30	200	29	6.0000	6.4922	1.8828	Sell	5.310	3.0651	Sell	Sell
5.0000	205.30	205	29	3.1250	1.5220	3.4700	Sell	0.311	4.6895	Sell	Sell
2.8750	205.30	210	29	1.6250	0.0000	2.8750	Sell	0.000	2.8750	Sell	Sell
1.3125	205.30	215	29	0.6875	0.0000	1.3125	Sell	0.000	1.3125	Sell	Sell
0.5625	205.30	220	29	0.3125	0.0000	0.5625	Sell	0.000	0.5625	Sell	Sell

Table 1.8

Closing Premiums	Closing Index	Exercise Price	Days until Expiration	Next trading Day Closing Premiums	Black Scholes Price For Trading Day	Difference Actual - Black Scholes	Likely Action	Black Scholes Price For Next Trading Day	Likely Action	Difference Today's premium Tomorrow's Black Scholes Price	Likely Action	Decision
30.2500	202.86	175	26	27.0000	28.7981	1.4519	Sell	27.868	Sell	2.3817	Sell	Sell
24.7300	202.86	180	26	22.0000	23.8250	0.9250	Sell	22.869	Sell	1.8815	Sell	Sell
19.7500	202.86	185	26	18.2500	18.8518	0.8982	Sell	17.869	Sell	1.8812	Sell	Sell
14.6280	202.86	190	26	13.1250	13.8786	0.7464	Sell	12.869	Sell	1.7560	Sell	Sell
9.5000	202.86	195	26	8.7500	8.9054	0.5946	Sell	7.869	Sell	1.6307	Sell	Sell
6.0000	202.86	200	26	5.1250	3.9322	2.0678	Sell	2.870	Sell	3.1305	Sell	Sell
3.1250	202.86	205	26	2.5000	0.0000	3.1250	Sell	0.000	Sell	3.1250	Sell	Sell
1.6250	202.86	210	26	1.1875	0.0000	1.6250	Sell	0.000	Sell	1.6250	Sell	Sell
0.6875	202.86	215	26	0.4375	0.0000	0.6875	Sell	0.000	Sell	0.6075	Sell	Sell
0.3125	202.86	220	26	0.1875	0.0000	0.3125	Sell	0.000	Sell	0.3125	Sell	Sell
34.0000	201.41	170	25	37.5000	32.2864	1.7136	Sell	31.417	Sell	2.5826	Sell	No Action
27.0000	201.41	175	25	28.7500	27.3122	-0.3121	Buy	26.418	Sell	0.5824	Sell	No Action
22.0000	201.41	180	25	23.5000	22.3379	-0.3379	Buy	21.418	Sell	0.5821	Sell	Sell
18.2500	201.41	185	25	18.5000	17.3637	0.8863	Sell	16.418	Sell	1.8319	Sell	Sell
13.1250	201.41	190	25	13.7500	12.3895	0.7355	Sell	11.418	Sell	1.7067	Sell	Sell
8.7500	201.41	195	25	9.2500	7.4153	1.3347	Sell	6.419	Sell	2.3335	Sell	Sell
5.1250	201.41	200	25	5.3750	2.4410	2.6840	Sell	1.419	Sell	3.7063	Sell	Sell
2.5000	201.41	205	25	2.5000	0.0000	2.5000	Sell	0.000	Sell	2.5000	Sell	Sell
1.1875	201.41	210	25	1.1875	0.0000	1.1875	Sell	0.000	Sell	1.1875	Sell	Sell
0.4375	201.41	215	25	0.4375	0.0000	0.4375	Sell	0.000	Sell	0.4375	Sell	Sell
0.1875	201.41	220	25	0.1875	0.0000	0.1875	Sell	0.000	Sell	0.1875	Sell	Sell
28.7500	202.35	175	23	30.5000	28.1802	0.5698	Sell	27.357	Sell	1.3927	Sell	Sell
23.5000	202.35	180	23	25.7500	23.2039	0.2961	Sell	22.358	Sell	1.1425	Sell	Sell
18.5000	202.35	185	23	20.7500	18.2276	0.2724	Sell	17.358	Sell	1.1423	Sell	Sell
13.7500	202.35	190	23	15.7500	13.2513	0.4987	Sell	12.358	Sell	1.3920	Sell	Sell
9.2500	202.35	195	23	11.0000	8.2750	0.9750	Sell	7.358	Sell	1.8918	Sell	Sell
5.3750	202.35	200	23	7.0000	3.2988	2.0762	Sell	2.358	Sell	3.0166	Sell	Sell
2.5000	202.35	205	23	3.6250	0.0000	2.5000	Sell	0.000	Sell	2.5000	Sell	Sell
1.1875	202.35	210	23	1.5625	0.0000	1.1875	Sell	0.000	Sell	0.4375	Sell	Sell
0.4375	202.35	215	23	0.5625	0.0000	0.4375	Sell	0.000	Sell	0.4375	Sell	Sell
0.1875	202.35	220	23	0.1875	0.0000	0.1875	Sell	0.000	Sell	0.1875	Sell	Sell
30.5000	204.74	175	22	30.5000	30.5342	-0.0342	Buy	29.746	Buy	0.7537	Sell	No Action
25.7500	204.74	180	22	27.2500	25.5568	0.1932	Sell	24.747	Sell	1.0035	Sell	Sell
20.7500	204.74	185	22	21.5000	20.5795	0.1705	Sell	19.747	Sell	1.0033	Sell	Sell
15.7500	204.74	190	22	17.5000	15.6022	0.1478	Sell	14.747	Sell	1.0031	Sell	Sell
11.0000	204.74	195	22	12.2500	10.6249	0.3751	Sell	9.747	Sell	1.2529	Sell	Sell
7.0000	204.74	200	22	7.4375	5.6476	1.3524	Sell	4.747	Sell	2.2528	Sell	Sell
3.6250	204.74	205	22	4.1250	0.6703	2.9547	Sell	0.000	Sell	3.6250	Sell	Sell
1.5625	204.74	210	22	1.7500	0.0000	1.5625	Sell	0.000	Sell	1.5625	Sell	Sell
0.5625	204.74	215	22	0.5625	0.0000	0.5625	Sell	0.000	Sell	0.5625	Sell	Sell
0.1875	204.74	220	22	0.1875	0.0000	0.1875	Sell	0.000	Sell	0.1875	Sell	Sell

Table 1.9

Closing Premiums	Closing Index	Exercise Price	Days until Expiration	Next trading Day Closing Premiums	Black Scholes Price For Trading Day	Difference Actual - Black Scholes	Likely Action	Black Scholes Price For Next Trading Day	Difference Today's premium Tomorrow's Black Scholes Price	Likely Action	Decision
30.5000	206.23	175	19	32.5000	31.9184	-1.4184	Buy	31.236	-0.7368	Buy	Buy
27.2500	206.23	180	19	26.0000	26.9381	0.3119	Sell	26.236	1.0138	Sell	Sell
21.5000	206.23	185	19	22.0000	21.9577	-0.4577	Buy	21.236	0.2636	Sell	No Action
17.5000	206.23	190	19	16.0000	16.9774	0.5226	Sell	16.237	1.2635	Sell	Sell
12.2500	206.23	195	19	11.1250	11.9971	0.2529	Sell	11.237	1.0133	Sell	Sell
7.4375	206.23	200	19	6.7500	7.0167	0.4208	Sell	6.237	1.2007	Sell	Sell
4.1250	206.23	205	19	3.1250	2.0364	2.0886	Sell	1.237	2.8880	Sell	Sell
1.7500	206.23	210	19	1.1875	0.0000	1.7500	Sell	0.000	1.7500	Sell	Sell
0.5625	206.23	215	19	0.3750	0.0000	0.5625	Sell	0.000	0.5625	Sell	Sell
0.1875	206.23	220	19	0.1875	0.0000	0.1875	Sell	0.000	0.1875	Sell	Sell
37.5000	206.02	170	18	36.0000	36.6536	0.8464	Sell	36.025	1.4748	Sell	Sell
32.5000	206.02	175	18	30.0000	31.6722	0.8278	Sell	31.025	1.4747	Sell	Sell
26.0000	206.02	180	18	24.6250	26.6909	-0.6909	Buy	26.025	-0.0255	Buy	Buy
22.0000	206.02	185	18	19.7500	21.7095	0.2905	Sell	21.026	0.9744	Sell	Sell
16.0000	206.02	190	18	14.7500	16.7281	-0.7281	Buy	16.026	-0.0258	Buy	Buy
11.1250	206.02	195	18	9.7500	11.7468	-0.6218	Buy	11.026	0.0991	Sell	No Action
6.7500	206.02	200	18	5.5000	6.7654	-0.0154	Buy	6.026	0.7239	Sell	No Action
3.1250	206.02	205	18	2.4375	1.7840	1.3410	Sell	1.026	2.0988	Sell	Sell
1.1875	206.02	210	18	0.8125	0.0000	1.1875	Sell	0.000	1.1875	Sell	Sell
0.3750	206.02	215	18	0.2500	0.0000	0.3750	Sell	0.000	0.3750	Sell	Sell
0.1875	206.02	220	18	0.0625	0.0000	0.1875	Sell	0.000	0.1875	Sell	Sell
30.0000	204.19	175	16	30.2500	29.7699	0.2301	Sell	29.195	0.8050	Sell	Sell
24.6250	204.19	180	16	25.7500	24.7865	-0.1640	Buy	24.195	0.4299	Sell	No Action
19.7500	204.19	185	16	20.5000	19.8030	-0.0530	Buy	19.195	0.5547	Sell	No Action
14.7500	204.19	190	16	16.5000	14.8196	-0.0696	Buy	14.195	0.5546	Sell	No Action
9.7500	204.19	195	16	11.3750	9.8362	-0.0862	Buy	9.196	0.5544	Sell	No Action
5.5000	204.19	200	16	6.7500	4.8527	0.6473	Sell	4.196	1.3043	Sell	Sell
2.4375	204.19	205	16	3.0000	0.0004	2.4371	Sell	0.000	2.4375	Sell	Sell
0.8125	204.19	210	16	1.0000	0.0000	0.8125	Sell	0.000	0.8125	Sell	Sell
0.2500	204.19	215	16	0.2500	0.0000	0.2500	Sell	0.000	0.2500	Sell	Sell
0.0625	204.19	220	16	0.0625	0.0000	0.0625	Sell	0.000	0.0625	Sell	Sell
30.2500	205.54	175	15	31.0000	31.0837	-0.8337	Buy	30.544	-0.2940	Buy	Buy
25.7500	205.54	180	15	26.5000	26.0992	-0.3492	Buy	25.544	0.2059	Sell	No Action
20.5000	205.54	185	15	21.1250	21.1148	-0.6148	Buy	20.544	-0.0442	Buy	Buy
16.5000	205.54	190	15	16.7500	16.1303	0.3697	Sell	15.544	0.9557	Sell	Sell
11.3750	205.54	195	15	11.1250	11.1458	0.2292	Sell	10.544	0.8306	Sell	Sell
6.7500	205.54	200	15	7.0000	6.1164	0.5886	Sell	5.545	1.2054	Sell	Sell
3.0000	205.54	205	15	3.2500	1.1769	1.8231	Sell	0.545	2.4553	Sell	Sell
1.0000	205.54	210	15	1.0000	0.0000	1.0000	Sell	0.000	1.0000	Sell	Sell
0.2500	205.54	215	15	0.2500	0.0000	0.2500	Sell	0.000	0.2500	Sell	Sell
0.0625	205.54	220	15	0.0625	0.0000	0.0625	Sell	0.000	0.0625	Sell	Sell

Table 1.10

Closing Premiums	Closing Index	Exercise Price	Days until Expiration	Next trading Day Closing Premiums	Black Scholes Price For Trading Day	Difference Actual - Black Scholes	Likely Action	Black Scholes Price For Next Trading Day	Difference Today's premium Tomorrow's Black Scholes Price	Likely Action	Decision
36.0000	205.58	170	12	31.7500	36.0031	-0.0031	Buy	35.584	0.4164	Sell	No Action
31.0000	205.58	175	12	32.8750	31.0155	-0.0155	Buy	30.584	0.4163	Sell	No Action
26.5000	205.58	180	12	29.3750	26.0280	0.4720	Sell	25.584	0.9162	Sell	Sell
21.1250	205.58	185	12	24.5000	21.0404	0.0846	Sell	20.584	0.5411	Sell	Sell
16.7500	205.58	190	12	19.2500	16.0529	0.6971	Sell	15.584	1.1660	Sell	Sell
11.1250	205.58	195	12	14.2500	11.0653	0.0597	Sell	10.584	0.5409	Sell	Sell
7.0000	205.58	200	12	9.3750	6.0777	0.9223	Sell	5.584	1.4158	Sell	Sell
3.2500	205.58	205	12	4.8750	1.0902	2.1598	Sell	0.584	2.6657	Sell	Sell
1.0000	205.58	210	12	1.8125	0.0000	1.0000	Sell	0.000	1.0000	Sell	Sell
0.2500	205.58	215	12	0.3750	0.0000	0.2500	Sell	0.000	0.2500	Sell	Sell
0.0625	205.58	220	12	0.0625	0.0000	0.0625	Sell	0.000	0.0625	Sell	Sell
32.8750	208.64	175	11	32.5000	34.0393	-1.1643	Buy	33.643	-0.7683	Buy	Buy
29.3750	208.64	180	11	29.3750	29.0507	0.3243	Sell	28.643	0.7316	Sell	Sell
24.5000	208.64	185	11	24.5000	24.0621	0.4379	Sell	23.644	0.8565	Sell	Sell
19.2500	208.64	190	11	17.5000	19.0735	0.1765	Sell	18.644	0.6064	Sell	Sell
14.2500	208.64	195	11	12.5000	14.0849	0.1651	Sell	13.644	0.6063	Sell	Sell
9.3750	208.64	200	11	7.7500	9.0963	0.2787	Sell	8.644	0.7312	Sell	Sell
4.8750	208.64	205	11	3.3750	4.1077	0.7673	Sell	3.644	1.231	Sell	Sell
1.8125	208.64	210	11	1.3750	0.0000	1.8125	Sell	0.000	1.8125	Sell	Sell
0.3750	208.64	215	11	0.2500	0.0000	0.3750	Sell	0.000	0.3750	Sell	Sell
0.0625	208.64	220	11	0.0625	0.0000	0.0625	Sell	0.000	0.0625	Sell	Sell
32.2500	202.52	175	10	26.2500	27.8830	4.3670	Sell	27.523	4.7270	Sell	Sell
22.5000	202.52	180	10	21.2500	22.8934	-0.3934	Buy	22.523	-0.0231	Buy	Buy
17.5000	202.52	185	10	16.2500	17.9038	-0.4038	Buy	17.523	-0.0232	Buy	Buy
12.5000	202.52	190	10	11.5000	12.941	-0.441	Buy	12.523	-0.0233	Buy	Buy
7.7500	202.52	195	10	7.0000	7.9245	-0.1745	Buy	7.523	0.2267	Sell	No Action
3.3750	202.52	200	10	3.1250	2.9349	0.4401	Sell	2.523	0.8516	Sell	Sell
1.3750	202.52	205	10	0.9375	0.0000	1.3750	Sell	0.000	1.3750	Sell	Sell
0.2500	202.52	210	10	0.1875	0.0000	0.2500	Sell	0.000	0.2500	Sell	Sell
0.0625	202.52	215	10	0.0625	0.0000	0.0625	Sell	0.000	0.0625	Sell	Sell
0.0625	202.52	220	10	0.0625	0.0000	0.0625	Sell	0.000	0.0625	Sell	Sell
26.2500	201.26	175	9	26.5000	26.5867	-0.3367	Buy	26.263	-0.0127	Buy	Buy
21.2500	201.26	180	9	21.2500	21.5961	-0.3461	Buy	21.263	-0.0127	Buy	Buy
16.2500	201.26	185	9	15.8750	16.6054	-0.3554	Buy	16.263	-0.0128	Buy	Buy
11.5000	201.26	190	9	10.2500	11.6147	-0.1147	Buy	11.263	0.2371	Sell	No Action
7.0000	201.26	195	9	5.8750	6.6241	0.3759	Sell	6.263	0.7370	Sell	Sell
3.1250	201.26	200	9	2.0625	1.6334	1.4916	Sell	1.263	1.8620	Sell	Sell
0.9375	201.26	205	9	0.4275	0.0000	0.9375	Sell	0.000	0.9375	Sell	Sell
0.1875	201.26	210	9	0.0625	0.0000	0.1875	Sell	0.000	0.1875	Sell	Sell
0.0625	201.26	215	9	0.0625	0.0000	0.0625	Sell	0.000	0.0625	Sell	Sell
0.0625	201.26	220	9	0.0625	0.0000	0.0625	Sell	0.000	0.0625	Sell	Sell

Table 1.11

Closing Premiums	Closing Index	Exercise Price	Days until Expiration	Next trading Day Closing Premiums	Black Scholes Price For Trading Day	Difference Actual - Black Scholes	Likely Action	Black Scholes Price For Next Trading Day	Difference Today's premium Tomorrow's Black Scholes Price	Likely Action	Decision
31.7500	200.16	170	8	29.7500	30.4422	1.3078	Sell	30.162	1.5884	Sell	Sell
26.5000	200.16	175	8	25.5000	25.4505	1.0495	Sell	25.162	1.3383	Sell	Sell
21.2500	200.16	180	8	21.5000	20.4588	0.7912	Sell	20.162	1.0883	Sell	Sell
15.8750	200.16	185	8	16.3750	15.4671	0.4079	Sell	15.162	0.7132	Sell	Sell
10.2500	200.16	190	8	11.5000	10.4754	-0.2254	Buy	10.162	0.0882	Sell	No Action
5.8750	200.16	195	8	6.2500	5.4837	0.3913	Sell	5.162	0.7131	Sell	Sell
2.0625	200.16	200	8	2.1250	0.4920	1.5705	Sell	0.162	1.9006	Sell	Sell
0.4275	200.16	205	8	0.3750	0.0000	0.4275	Sell	0.000	0.4275	Sell	Sell
0.0625	200.16	210	8	0.0625	0.0000	0.0625	Sell	0.000	0.0625	Sell	Sell
0.0625	200.16	215	8	0.0625	0.0000	0.0625	Sell	0.000	0.0625	Sell	Sell
0.0625	200.16	220	8	0.0625	0.0000	0.0625	Sell	0.000	0.0625	Sell	Sell
29.7500	201.42	170	5	31.3750	31.6013	-1.8513	Buy	31.421	-1.6714	Buy	Buy
25.5000	201.42	175	5	26.2500	26.6066	-1.1066	Buy	26.421	-0.9215	Buy	Buy
21.5000	201.42	180	5	21.1250	21.6120	-0.1120	Buy	21.421	0.0785	Sell	No Action
16.3750	201.42	185	5	15.2500	16.6173	-0.2423	Buy	16.422	-0.0465	Buy	Buy
11.5000	201.42	190	5	11.2500	11.6227	-0.1227	Buy	11.422	0.0784	Sell	No Action
6.2500	201.42	195	5	6.2500	6.6280	-0.3780	Buy	6.422	-0.1716	Buy	Buy
2.1250	201.42	200	5	1.3125	1.6333	0.4917	Sell	1.422	0.7033	Sell	Sell
0.3750	201.42	205	5	0.2500	0.0000	0.3750	Sell	0.000	0.3750	Sell	Sell
0.0625	201.42	210	5	0.0625	0.0000	0.0625	Sell	0.000	0.0625	Sell	Sell
0.0625	201.42	215	5	0.0625	0.0000	0.0625	Sell	0.000	0.0625	Sell	Sell
26.2500	201.21	175	4	28.0000	26.3594	-0.1093	Buy	26.211	0.0389	Sell	No Action
21.1250	201.21	180	4	22.8750	21.3636	-0.2386	Buy	21.211	-0.0861	Buy	Buy
15.2500	201.21	185	4	17.7500	16.3679	-1.1179	Buy	16.211	-0.9612	Buy	Buy
11.2500	201.21	190	4	13.0000	11.3722	-0.1221	Buy	11.211	0.0388	Sell	No Action
6.2500	201.21	195	4	8.1250	6.3764	-0.1264	Buy	6.211	0.0389	Sell	No Action
1.3125	201.21	200	4	3.1250	1.3807	-0.0682	Buy	1.211	0.1013	Sell	No Action
0.2500	201.21	205	4	0.3750	0.0000	0.2500	Sell	0.000	0.2500	Sell	Sell
0.0625	201.21	210	4	0.0625	0.0000	0.0625	Sell	0.000	0.0625	Sell	Sell
0.0625	201.21	215	4	0.0625	0.0000	0.0625	Sell	0.000	0.0625	Sell	Sell
28.0000	202.87	175	3	27.3750	27.9820	0.0180	Sell	27.871	0.1293	Sell	Sell
22.8750	202.87	180	3	23.7500	22.9852	-0.1102	Buy	22.871	0.0043	Sell	No Action
17.7500	202.87	185	3	18.8750	17.9804	-0.2384	Buy	17.871	-0.1208	Buy	Buy
13.0000	202.87	190	3	13.7500	12.9916	0.0084	Sell	12.871	0.1292	Sell	Sell
8.1250	202.87	195	3	8.7500	7.9948	0.1302	Sell	7.871	0.2542	Sell	Sell
3.1250	202.87	200	3	3.7500	2.9980	0.1270	Sell	2.871	0.2542	Sell	Sell
0.3750	202.87	205	3	0.3750	0.0000	0.3750	Sell	0.000	0.3750	Sell	Sell
0.0625	202.87	210	3	0.0625	0.0000	0.0625	Sell	0.000	0.0625	Sell	Sell
0.0625	202.87	215	3	0.0625	0.0000	0.0625	Sell	0.000	0.0625	Sell	Sell
0.0625	202.87	220	3	0.0000	0.0000	0.0625	Sell	0.000	0.0625	Sell	Sell

Table 1.12

Closing Premiums	Closing Index	Exercise Price	Days until Expiration	Next trading Day Closing Premiums	Black Scholes Price For Trading Day	Difference Actual - Black Scholes	Likely Action	Black Scholes Price For Next Trading Day	Difference Today's premium Tomorrow's Black Scholes Price	Likely Action	Decision
23.7500	203.74	180	2	21.5000	23.8168	-0.0668	Buy	23.740	0.0096	Sell	No Action
18.8750	203.74	185	2	17.3750	18.8190	0.0560	Sell	18.740	0.1346	Sell	Sell
13.7500	203.74	190	2	12.5000	13.8211	-0.0711	Buy	13.740	0.0096	Sell	No Action
8.7500	203.74	195	2	7.2500	8.8232	-0.0732	Buy	8.740	0.0096	Sell	No Action
3.7500	203.74	200	2	2.3750	3.8254	-0.0754	Buy	3.740	0.0096	Sell	No Action
0.3750	203.74	205	2	0.0625	0.0000	0.3750	Sell	0.000	0.3750	Sell	Sell
0.0625	203.74	210	2	0.0000	0.0000	0.0625	Sell	0.000	0.0625	Sell	Sell
0.0625	203.74	215	2	0.0000	0.0000	0.0625	Sell	0.000	0.0625	Sell	Sell
27.7500	202.35	175	1		27.387	0.363	Buy	27.350	0.4000	Buy	
21.5000	202.35	180	1		22.388	-0.888	Buy	22.350	-0.8500	Sell	
17.3750	202.35	185	1		17.390	-0.015	Sell	17.350	0.0250	Sell	
12.5000	202.35	190	1		12.391	0.091	Sell	12.350	0.1500	Sell	
7.2500	202.35	195	1		7.392	-0.142	Buy	7.350	-0.1000	Buy	
2.3750	202.35	200	1		2.393	-0.018	Buy	2.350	0.0250	Sell	
0.0625	202.35	205	1		0.000	0.063	Sell	0.000	0.0625	Sell	

Table 2.1
Trade Every Day

Decision	Exercise Price	Days Until Expiration	Profits Sell Strategy	Profits Buy Strategy	Difference Today's Premium Tomorrow's Premium
No Action	175	89			0.0000
Sell	180	89	0.5000		-0.5000
Sell	185	89	0.3125		-0.3125
Sell	190	89	0.0625		-0.0625
Buy	170	88		-1.1250	-1.1250
No Action	175	88			-1.0000
No Action	180	88			-0.6250
Sell	185	88	0.3750		-0.3750
Sell	190	88	0.1875		-0.1875
No Action	170	87			0.1250
No Action	175	87			0.1250
No Action	180	87			0.7500
Sell	185	87	-0.4375		0.4375
Sell	190	87	-0.1875		0.1875
No Action	170	86			2.0000
No Action	175	86			1.7500
No Action	180	86			0.7500
Sell	185	86	-0.4375		0.4375
Sell	190	86	-0.1875		0.1875
No Action	170	85			-0.2500
No Action	175	85			-0.3750
No Action	180	85			-0.3750
Sell	185	85			0.0000
Sell	190	85			0.0000
No Action	170	82			-1.7500
No Action	175	82			-1.2500
Sell	180	82	0.6250		-0.6250
Sell	185	82	0.4375		-0.4375
Sell	190	82	0.1875		-0.1875
No Action	170	81			-0.1250
No Action	175	81			0.0000
No Action	180	81			-0.3750
Sell	185	81	0.2500		-0.2500
Sell	190	81	0.1250		-0.1250
Buy	170	80		-0.1250	-0.1250
No Action	175	80			0.1250
No Action	180	80			0.2500
Sell	185	80	-0.1875		0.1875
Sell	190	80	-0.0625		0.0625
No Action	170	79			-1.0000
No Action	175	79			-1.5000
No Action	180	79			-0.8750
Sell	185	79	0.7500		-0.7500
Sell	190	79	0.1875		-0.1875

Table 2.2
Trade Every Day

Decision	Exercise Price	Days Until Expiration	Profits Sell Strategy	Profits Buy Strategy	Difference Today's Premium Tomorrow's Premium
Buy	170	78		-0.1250	-0.1250
No Action	175	78			0.5000
No Action	180	78			0.0000
Sell	185	78	-0.1250		0.1250
Sell	190	78			0.0000
Buy	170	75		-1.1250	-1.1250
Buy	175	75		-0.6250	-0.6250
No Action	180	75			-0.6250
Sell	185	75	0.3750		-0.3750
Sell	190	75	0.1875		-0.1875
Buy	170	74		-0.2500	-0.2500
Buy	175	74		0.1250	0.1250
No Action	180	74			0.0000
No Action	185	74			0.0000
Sell	190	74	-0.0625		0.0625
Sell	195	74	-1.0625		1.0625
Buy	170	73		0.7500	0.7500
Buy	175	73		-0.5000	-0.5000
No Action	180	73			0.1250
No Action	185	73			0.1250
Sell	190	73	-0.0625		0.0625
Sell	195	73	-0.0625		0.0625
Buy	170	72		-1.1250	-1.1250
No Action	175	72			-1.2500
No Action	180	72			-1.3750
Sell	185	72	0.8750		-0.8750
Sell	190	72	0.4375		-0.4375
Sell	195	72	0.2500		-0.2500
Buy	170	71		16.1250	16.1250
No Action	175	71			-2.5000
No Action	180	71			-2.6250
Sell	185	71	2.0000		-2.0000
Sell	190	71	1.2500		-1.2500
Sell	195	71	0.6250		-0.6250
Buy	175	68		-1.5000	-1.5000
No Action	180	68			-1.0000
No Action	185	68			-1.1250
Sell	190	68	1.2500		-1.2500
Sell	195	68	0.7500		-0.7500
Buy	170	67		20.5000	20.5000
No Action	175	67			0.5000
No Action	180	67			1.3750
No Action	185	67			0.7500
Sell	190	67	-0.6250		0.6250
Sell	195	67	-0.2500		0.2500

Table 2.3
Trade Every Day

Decision	Exercise Price	Days Until Expiration	Profits Sell Strategy	Profits Buy Strategy	Difference Today's Premium Tomorrow's Premium
No Action	175	66			-2.0000
No Action	180	66			-2.5000
No Action	185	66			-1.7500
Sell	190	66	1.1250		-1.1250
Sell	195	66	0.7500		-0.7500
Sell	200	66	0.3125		-0.3125
Buy	170	65			0.0000
No Action	175	65			-0.5000
No Action	180	65			0.6250
No Action	185	65			0.7500
Sell	190	65	-0.3750		0.3750
Sell	195	65	-0.3750		0.3750
Sell	200	65	-0.0625		0.0625
No Action	170	64			0.0000
No Action	175	64			1.0000
No Action	180	64			-0.5000
No Action	185	64			-0.6250
Sell	190	64	0.3750		-0.3750
Sell	195	64	0.1250		-0.1250
Sell	200	64	0.0625		-0.0625
Buy	170	61		-0.7500	-0.7500
Buy	175	61			0.0000
No Action	180	61			0.0000
No Action	185	61			0.1250
Sell	190	61	-0.2500		0.2500
Sell	195	61	-0.0625		0.0625
Sell	200	61	-0.1875		0.1875
Sell	205	61			0.0000
No Action	170	60			22.7500
Buy	175	60		-1.2500	-1.2500
No Action	180	60			-0.5000
No Action	185	60			-0.6250
No Action	190	60			-0.5000
Sell	195	60	0.2500		-0.2500
Sell	200	60	0.1250		-0.1250
Sell	205	60	0.0625		-0.0625
No Action	175	59			-1.5000
No Action	180	59			-2.5000
No Action	185	59			-2.2500
No Action	190	59			-1.6250
Sell	195	59	1.1875		-1.1875
Sell	200	59	0.5625		-0.5625
Sell	205	59	0.2500		-0.2500

Table 2.4
Trade Every Day

Decision	Exercise Price	Days Until Expiration	Profits Sell Strategy	Profits Buy Strategy	Difference Today's Premium Tomorrow's Premium
Buy	175	58		-0.6250	-0.6250
No Action	180	58			0.3750
No Action	185	58			0.25001
No Action	190	58			0.1250
Sell	195	58	-0.1250		0.1250
Sell	200	58			0.0000
Sell	205	58			0.0000
No Action	170	57			
No Action	175	57			0.6250
No Action	180	57			0.6250
No Action	185	57			0.8750
No Action	190	57			0.6250
Sell	195	57	-0.5000		0.5000
Sell	200	57	-0.1875		0.1875
Sell	205	57	-0.0625		0.0625
No Action	175	54			-0.2500
No Action	180	54			-0.6250
No Action	185	54			-0.3750
Sell	190	54	0.3750		-0.3750
Sell	195	54	0.2500		-0.2500
Sell	200	54	0.0625		-0.0625
Sell	205	54			0.0000
Buy	170	53		-0.2500	-0.2500
No Action	175	53			-1.7500
No Action	180	53			-2.2500
No Action	185	53			-2.2500
No Action	190	53			-1.7500
Sell	195	53	1.2500		-1.2500
Sell	200	53	0.7500		-0.7500
Sell	205	53	0.4375		-0.4375
Buy	170	52	-0.5000		
No Action	175	52			0.5000
No Action	180	52			1.0000
No Action	185	52			0.7500
No Action	190	52			1.0000
Sell	195	52	-0.6250		0.6250
Sell	200	52	-0.3750		0.3750
Sell	205	52	-0.2500		0.2500
No Action	175	50			1.7500
No Action	180	50			1.8750
No Action	185	50			1.8750
No Action	190	50			1.2500
Sell	195	50	-1.0000		1.0000
Sell	200	50	-0.5625		0.5625
Sell	205	50	-0.1875		0.1875

Table 2.5
Trade Every Day

Decision	Exercise Price	Days Until Expiration	Profits Sell Strategy	Profits Buy Strategy	Difference Today's Premium Tomorrow's Premium
No Action	170	47			
No Action	175	47			0.0000
No Action	180	47			-0.0000
No Action	185	47			-0.5000
Sell	190	47	0.5000		-0.5000
Sell	195	47	0.3750		-0.3750
Sell	200	47	0.1875		-0.1875
Sell	205	47			0.0000
No Action	175	46			-0.7500
No Action	180	46			-4.5000
No Action	185	46			-3.7500
Sell	190	46			3.1250
Sell	195	46	2.2500		-2.2500
Sell	200	46	1.4375		-1.4375
Sell	205	46	0.8125		-0.8125
Buy	175	45		-2.2500	-2.2500
No Action	180	45			-1.1250
No Action	185	45			0.8750
No Action	190	45			0.3750
Sell	195	45	-0.1250		0.1250
Sell	200	45	-0.1250		0.1250
Sell	205	45	-0.1250		0.1250
Buy	170	44		11.5000	27.5000
Buy	175	44		-1.0000	-1.0000
Sell	180	44	-1.7500		1.7500
No Action	185	44			-0.2500
No Action	190	44			0.2500
Sell	195	44	-0.1250		0.1250
Sell	200	44			0.0000
Sell	205	44	0.1250		-0.1250
No Action	175	43			-1.0000
No Action	180	43			-1.7500
No Action	185	43			-1.3750
Sell	190	43	1.5000		-1.5000
Sell	195	43	1.1250		-1.1250
Sell	200	43	0.8125		-0.8125
Sell	205	43	0.3750		-0.3750
Sell	210	43	0.2500		-0.2500
No Action	175	40			-0.5000
Sell	180	40	-0.1250		0.1250
No Action	185	40			-0.3750
Sell	190	40	0.3750		-0.3750
Sell	195	40	0.1250		-0.1250
Sell	200	40			0.0000
Sell	205	40	0.1250		-0.1250
Sell	210	40	0.0625		-0.0625

Table 2.6
Trade Every Day

Decision	Exercise Price	Days Until Expiration	Profits Sell Strategy	Profits Buy Strategy	Difference Today's Premium Tomorrow's Premium
No Action	175	39			-2.0000
No Action	180	39			-2.5000
Sell	185	39	2.5000		-2.5000
Sell	190	39	2.0000		-2.0000
Sell	195	39	2.0000		-2.0000
Sell	200	39	1.6250		-1.6250
Sell	205	39	0.9375		-0.9375
Sell	210	39	0.5000		-0.5000
No Action	175	38			1.1250
Sell	180	38	-0.5000		0.5000
Sell	185	38			0.0000
Sell	190	38	0.1250		-0.1250
Sell	195	38	0.3750		-0.3750
Sell	200	38	0.3750		-0.3750
Sell	205	38	0.3750		-0.3750
Sell	210	38	0.2500		-0.2500
Buy	175	37		-4.0000	-4.0000
No Action	180	37			-4.2500
Sell	185	37	3.2500		-3.2500
Sell	190	37	3.6250		-3.6250
Sell	195	37	2.7500		-2.7500
Sell	200	37	2.2500		-2.2500
Sell	205	37	1.6250		-1.6250
Sell	210	37	1.2500		-1.2500
Sell	215	37	0.8750		-0.8750
No Action	175	36			-4.6250
Sell	180	36	2.2500		-2.2500
No Action	185	36			-2.5000
Sell	190	36	1.7500		-1.7500
Sell	195	36	2.1250		-2.1250
Sell	200	36	1.6250		-1.6250
Sell	205	36	1.5000		-1.5000
Sell	210	36	1.1250		-1.1250
Sell	215	36	-1.4375		1.4375
Sell	170	33	-1.2500		1.2500
Sell	175	33	-1.5000		1.5000
Sell	180	33	-0.2500		0.2500
Sell	185	33	-0.7500		0.7500
No Action	190	33			0.5000
Sell	195	33	-0.7500		0.7500
Sell	200	33	-0.2500		0.2500
Sell	205	33	-0.2500		0.2500
Sell	210	33			0.0000

Table 2.7
Trade Every Day

Decision	Exercise Price	Days Until Expiration	Profits Sell Strategy	Profits Buy Strategy	Difference Today's Premium Tomorrow's Premium
Sell	170	32	0.5000		0.5000
Sell	175	32	0.1250		-0.1250
Sell	180	32	-1.0000		4.0000
Sell	185	32	-1.0000		1.0000
Sell	190	32	-1.1250		1.1250
Sell	195	32	-1.1250		1.1250
Sell	200	32	-1.0000		1.0000
Sell	205	32	-1.0000		1.0000
Sell	210	32	-0.8750		0.8750
Sell	215	32	-0.6875		0.6875
Sell	220	32	-0.4375		0.4375
Sell	175	31	-1.1250		1.1250
Buy	180	31		-2.1250	-2.1250
Sell	185	31	-0.50000		0.5000
Sell	190	31			0.0000
Sell	195	31	0.1250		-0.1250
Sell	200	31	-0.1250		0.1250
Sell	205	31	-0.1250		0.1250
Sell	210	31	-0.0625		0.0625
Sell	215	31	-0.0625		0.0625
Sell	220	31	-0.1250		0.1250
Sell	175	30	-0.5000		0.5000
Sell	180	30	0.1250		-0.1250
Sell	185	30	0.5000		-0.5000
Sell	190	30	0.2500		-0.2500
Sell	195	30			0.0000
Sell	200	30	0.3750		-0.3750
Sell	205	30	0.1250		-0.1250
Sell	210	30	-0.0625		0.0625
Sell	215	30	-0.2500		0.2500
Sell	220	30	-0.0625		0.0625
Sell	170	29	3.5000		3.5000
Sell	175	29	-1.2500		1.2500
Sell	180	29	-1.7500		1.7500
Sell	185	29	-2.0000		2.0000
Sell	190	29	-2.1250		2.1250
Sell	195	29	-2.5000		2.5000
Sell	200	29	-2.3750		2.3750
Sell	205	29	-1.8750		1.8750
Sell	210	29	-1.2500		1.2500
Sell	215	29	-0.6250		0.6250
Sell	220	29	-0.2500		0.2500

Table 2.8
Trade Every Day

Decision	Exercise Price	Days Until Expiration	Profits Sell Strategy	Profits Buy Strategy	Difference Today's Premium Tomorrow's Premium
Sell	175	26	-3.2500		3.2500
Sell	180	26	-2.7500		2.7500
Sell	185	26	-1.5000		1.5000
Sell	190	26	-1.5000		1.5000
Sell	195	26	-0.7500		0.7500
Sell	200	26	-0.8750		0.8750
Sell	205	26	-0.6250		0.6250
Sell	210	26	-0.4375		0.4375
Sell	215	26	-0.2500		0.2500
Sell	220	26	-0.1250		0.1250
Sell	170	25	-3.5000		-3.5000
No Action	175	25			-1.7500
No Action	180	25			-1.5000
Sell	185	25	0.2500		-0.2500
Sell	190	25	0.6250		-0.6250
Sell	195	25	0.5000		-0.5000
Sell	200	25	0.2500		-0.2500
Sell	205	25			0.0000
Sell	210	25			0.0000
Sell	215	25			0.0000
Sell	220	25			0.0000
Sell	175	23	1.7500		-1.7500
Sell	180	23	2.2500		-2.2500
Sell	185	23	2.2500		-2.2500
Sell	190	23	2.0000		-2.0000
Sell	195	23	1.7500		-1.7500
Sell	200	23	1.6250		-1.6250
Sell	205	23	1.1250		-1.1250
Sell	210	23	0.3750		-0.3750
Sell	215	23	0.1250		-0.1250
Sell	220	23			0.0000
No Action	175	22			0.0000
Sell	180	22	1.5000		-1.3000
Sell	185	22	0.7500		-0.7500
Sell	190	22	1.7500		-1.7500
Sell	195	22	1.2500		-1.2500
Sell	200	22	0.4375		-0.4375
Sell	205	22	0.5000		-0.5000
Sell	210	22	0.1875		-0.1875
Sell	215	22			0.0000
Sell	220	22			0.0000

Table 2.9
Trade Every Day

Decision	Exercise Price	Days Until Expiration	Profits Sell Strategy	Profits Buy Strategy	Difference Today's Premium Tomorrow's Premium
Buy	175	19		-2.000	-2.0000
Sell	180	19	-1.2500		1.2500
No Action	185	19			-0.5000
Sell	190	19	-1.5000		1.5000
Sell	195	19	-1.1250		1.1250
Sell	200	19	-0.6875		0.6875
Sell	205	19	-1.0000		1.0000
Sell	210	19	-0.5625		0.5625
Sell	215	19	-0.1875		0.1875
Sell	220	19			0.0000
Sell	170	18	-1.5000		-1.5000
Sell	175	18	-2.5000		2.5000
Buy	180	18		1.3750	1.3750
Sell	185	18	-2.2500		2.2500
Buy	190	18		1.2500	1.2500
No Action	195	18			1.3750
No Action	200	18			1.2500
Sell	205	18	-0.6875		0.6875
Sell	210	18	-0.3750		0.3750
Sell	215	18	-0.1250		0.1250
Sell	220	18	-0.1250		0.1250
Sell	175	16	0.2500		-0.2500
No Action	180	16			-1.1250
No Action	185	16			-0.7500
No Action	190	16			-1.7500
No Action	195	16			-1.6250
Sell	200	16	1.2500		-1.2500
Sell	205	16	0.5625		-0.5625
Sell	210	16	0.1875		-0.1875
Sell	215	16			0.0000
Sell	220	16			0.0000
Buy	175	15		-0.7500	-0.7500
No Action	180	15			-0.7500
Buy	185	15		-0.6250	-0.6250
Sell	190	15	0.2500		-0.2500
Sell	195	15	-0.2500		0.2500
Sell	200	15	0.2500		-0.2500
Sell	205	15	0.2500		-0.2500
Sell	210	15			0.0000
Sell	215	15			0.0000
Sell	220	15			0.0000

Table 2.10
Trade Every Day

Decision	Exercise Price	Days Until Expiration	Profits Sell Strategy	Profits Buy Strategy	Difference Today's Premium Tomorrow's Premium
No Action	170	12			-4.2500
No Action	175	12			-1.8750
Sell	180	12	2.8750		-2.8750
Sell	185	12	3.3750		-3.3750
Sell	190	12	2.5000		-2.5000
Sell	195	12	3.1250		-3.1250
Sell	200	12	2.3750		-2.3750
Sell	205	12	1.6250		-1.6250
Sell	210	12	0.8125		-0.8125
Sell	215	12	0.1250		-0.1250
Sell	220	12			0.0000
Buy	175	11		0.6250	0.6250
Sell	180	11	-6.8750		6.8750
Sell	185	11	-7.0000		7.0000
Sell	190	11	-6.7500		6.7500
Sell	195	11	-6.5000		6.5000
Sell	200	11	-6.0000		6.0000
Sell	205	11	-3.5000		3.5000
Sell	210	11	-1.5625		1.5625
Sell	215	11	-0.3125		0.3125
Sell	220	11			0.0000
Sell	175	10	-6.0000		6.0000
Buy	180	10		1.2500	1.2500
Buy	185	10		1.2500	1.2500
Buy	190	10		1.0000	1.0000
No Action	195	10			0.7500
Sell	200	10	-0.2500		0.2500
Sell	205	10	-0.4375		0.4375
Sell	210	10	-0.0625		0.0625
Sell	215	10			0.0000
Sell	220	10			0.0000
Buy	175	9		-0.2500	-0.2500
Buy	180	9			0.0000
Buy	185	9		0.3750	0.3750
No Action	190	9			1.2500
Sell	195	9	-1.1250		1.1250
Sell	200	9	-1.0625		1.0625
Sell	205	9	-0.5100		0.5100
Sell	210	9	-0.1250		0.1250
Sell	215	9			0.0000
Sell	220	9			0.0000

Table 2.11
Trade Every Day

Decision	Exercise Price	Days Until Expiration	Profits Sell Strategy	Profits Buy Strategy	Difference Today's Premium Tomorrow's Premium
Sell	170	8	-2.0000		2.0000
Sell	175	8	-1.0000		1.0000
Sell	180	8	0.2500		-0.2500
Sell	185	8	0.5000		-0.5000
No Action	190	8			-1.2500
Sell	195	8	0.3750		-0.3750
Sell	200	8	0.0625		-0.0625
Sell	205	8	-0.0525		0.0525
Sell	210	8			0.0000
Sell	215	8			0.0000
Sell	220	8	0.0625		0.0000
Buy	170	5			
Buy	175	5		-0.7500	-0.7500
No Action	180	5			0.3750
Buy	185	5		1.1250	1.1250
No Action	190	5			0.2500
Buy	195	5			0.0000
Sell	200	5	-0.8125		0.8125
Sell	205	5	-0.1250		0.1250
Sell	210	5			0.0000
Sell	215	5			0.0000
No Action	175	4			-1.7500
Buy	180	4		-1.7500	-1.7500
Buy	185	4		-2.5000	-2.5000
No Action	190	4			-1.7500
No Action	195	4			-1.8750
No Action	200	4			-1.8125
Sell	205	4	0.1250		-0.1250
Sell	210	4			0.0000
Sell	215	4			0.0000
Sell	175	3	0.6250		0.6250
No Action	180	3			-0.8750
Buy	185	3		-1.1250	-1.1250
Sell	190	3	0.7500		-0.7500
Sell	195	3	0.6250		-0.6250
Sell	200	3	0.6250		-0.6250
Sell	205	3			0.0000
Sell	210	3			0.0000
Sell	215	3			0.0000
Sell	220	3	-0.0625		0.0625

Table 2.12
Trade Every Day

Decision	Exercise Price	Days Until Expiration	Profits Sell Strategy	Profits Buy Strategy	Difference Today's Premium Tomorrow's Premium
No Action	180	2			2.2500
Sell	185	2	-1.5000		1.5000
No Action	190	2			1.2500
No Action	195	2			1.5000
No Action	200	2			1.3750
Sell	205	2	-0.3125		0.3125
Sell	210	2	-0.0625		0.0625
Sell	215	2	-0.0625		0.0625
	175	1			
	180	1			
	185	1			
	190	1			
	195	1			
	200	1			
	205	1			
			-11.125	28.750	13.875
			17.625		

Table 3.1
Trade Every Day Except Friday

Decision	Exercise Price	Days Until Expiration	Profits Sell Strategy	Profits Buy Strategy	Difference Today's Premium Tomorrow's Premium
No Action	175	89			0.0000
Sell	180	89	0.5000		-0.5000
Sell	185	89	0.3125		-0.3125
Sell	190	89	0.0625		-0.0625
Buy	170	88		-1.1250	-1.1250
No Action	175	88			-1.0000
No Action	180	88			-0.6250
Sell	185	88	0.3750		-0.3750
Sell	190	88	0.1875		-0.1875
No Action	170	87			0.1250
No Action	175	87			0.1250
No Action	180	87			0.7500
Sell	185	87	-0.4375		0.4375
Sell	190	87	-0.1875		0.1875
No Action	170	86			2.0000
No Action	175	86			1.7500
No Action	180	86			0.7500
Sell	185	86	-0.4375		0.4375
Sell	190	86	-0.1875		0.1875
No Action	170	85			
No Action	175	85			
No Action	180	85			
Sell	185	85			
Sell	190	85			
No Action	170	82			-1.7500
No Action	175	82			-1.2500
Sell	180	82	0.6250		-0.6250
Sell	185	82	0.4375		-0.4375
Sell	190	82	0.1875		-0.1875
No Action	170	81			-0.1250
No Action	175	81			0.0000
No Action	180	81			-0.3750
Sell	185	81	0.2500		-0.2500
Sell	190	81	0.1250		-0.1250
Buy	170	80		-0.1250	-0.1250
No Action	175	80			0.1250
No Action	180	80			0.2500
Sell	185	80	-0.1875		0.1875
Sell	190	80	-0.0625		0.0625
No Action	170	79			-1.0000
No Action	175	79			-1.5000
No Action	180	79			-0.8750
Sell	185	79	0.7500		-0.7500
Sell	190	79	0.1875		-0.1875

Table 3.2
Trade Every Day Except Friday

Decision	Exercise Price	Days Until Expiration	Profits Sell Strategy	Profits Buy Strategy	Difference Today's Premium Tomorrow's Premium
Buy	170	78			
No Action	175	78			
No Action	180	78			
Sell	185	78			
Sell	190	78			
Buy	170	75		-1.1250	-1.1250
Buy	175	75		-0.6250	-0.6250
No Action	180	75			-0.6250
Sell	185	75	0.3750		-0.3750
Sell	190	75	0.1875		-0.1875
Buy	170	74		-0.2500	-0.2500
Buy	175	74		0.1250	0.1250
No Action	180	74			0.0000
No Action	185	74			0.0000
Sell	190	74	-0.0625		0.0625
Sell	195	74	-1.0625		1.0625
Buy	170	73		0.7500	0.7500
Buy	175	73		-0.5000	-0.5000
No Action	180	73			0.1250
No Action	185	73			0.1250
Sell	190	73	-0.0625		0.0625
Sell	195	73	-0.0625		0.0625
Buy	170	72		-1.1250	-1.1250
No Action	175	72			-1.2500
No Action	180	72			-1.3750
Sell	185	72	0.8750		-0.8750
Sell	190	72	0.4375		-0.4375
Sell	195	72	0.2500		-0.2500
Buy	170	71			
No Action	175	71			
No Action	180	71			
Sell	185	71			
Sell	190	71			
Sell	195	71			
Buy	175	68		-1.5000	-1.5000
No Action	180	68			-1.0000
No Action	185	68			-1.1250
Sell	190	68	1.2500		-1.2500
Sell	195	68	0.7500		-0.7500
Buy	170	67		20.5000	20.5000
No Action	175	67			0.5000
No Action	180	67			1.3750
No Action	185	67			0.7500
Sell	190	67	-0.6250		0.6250
Sell	195	67	-0.2500		0.2500

Table 3.3
Trade Every Day Except Friday

Decision	Exercise Price	Days Until Expiration	Profits Sell Strategy	Profits Buy Strategy	Difference Today's Premium Tomorrow's Premium
No Action	175	66			-2.0000
No Action	180	66			-2.5000
No Action	185	66			-1.7500
Sell	190	66	1.1250		-1.1250
Sell	195	66	0.7500		-0.7500
Sell	200	66	0.3125		-0.3125
Buy	170	65			0.0000
No Action	175	65			-0.5000
No Action •	180	65			0.6250
No Action	185	65			0.7500
Sell	190	65	-0.3750		0.3750
Sell	195	65	-0.3750		0.3750
Sell	200	65	-0.0625		0.0625
No Action	170	64			
No Action	175	64			
No Action	180	64			
No Action	185	64			
Sell	190	64			
Sell	195	64			
Sell	200	64			
Buy	170	61		-0.7500	-0.7500
Buy	175	61			0.0000
No Action	180	61			0.0000
No Action	185	61			0.1250
Sell	190	61	-0.2500		0.2500
Sell	195	61	-0.0625		0.0625
Sell	200	61	-0.1875		0.1875
Sell	205	61			0.0000
No Action	170	60			22.7500
Buy	175	60		-1.2500	-1.2500
No Action	180	60			-0.5000
No Action	185	60			-0.6250
No Action	190	60			-0.5000
Sell	195	60	0.2500		-0.2500
Sell	200	60	0.1250		-0.1250
Sell	205	60	0.0625		-0.0625
No Action	175	59			-1.5000
No Action	180	59			-2.5000
No Action	185	59			-2.2500
No Action	190	59			-1.6250
Sell	195	59	1.1875		-1.1875
Sell	200	59	0.5625		-0.5625
Sell	205	59	0.2500		-0.2500

Table 3.4
Trade Every Day Except Friday

Decision	Exercise Price	Days Until Expiration	Profits Sell Strategy	Profits Buy Strategy	Difference Today's Premium Tomorrow's Premium
Buy	175	58		-0.6250	-0.6250
No Action	180	58			0.3750
No Action	185	58			0.2500
No Action	190	58			0.1250
Sell	195	58	-0.1250		0.1250
Sell	200	58			0.0000
Sell	205	58			0.0000
No Action	170	57			
No Action	175	57			
No Action	180	57			
No Action	185	57			
No Action	190	57			
Sell	195	57			
Sell	200	57			
Sell	205	57			
No Action	175	54			-0.2500
No Action	180	54			-0.6250
No Action	185	54			-0.3750
Sell	190	54	0.3750		-0.3750
Sell	195	54	0.2500		-0.2500
Sell	200	54	0.0625		-0.0625
Sell	205	54			0.0000
Buy	170	53		-0.2500	-0.2500
No Action	175	53			-1.7500
No Action	180	53			-2.2500
No Action	185	53			-2.2500
No Action	190	53			-1.7500
Sell	195	53	1.2500		-1.2500
Sell	200	53	0.7500		-0.7500
Sell	205	53	0.4375		-0.4375
Buy	170	52		24.5000	24.5000
No Action	175	52			0.5000
No Action	180	52			1.0000
No Action	185	52			0.7500
No Action	190	52			1.0000
Sell	195	52	-0.6250		0.6250
Sell	200	52	-0.3750		0.3750
Sell	205	52	-0.2500		0.2500
No Action	175	50			
No Action	180	50			
No Action	185	50			
No Action	190	50			
Sell	195	50			
Sell	200	50			
Sell	205	50			

Table 3.5
Trade Every Day Except Friday

Decision	Exercise Price	Days Until Expiration	Profits Sell Strategy	Profits Buy Strategy	Difference Today's Premium Tomorrow's Premium
No Action	170	47			
No Action	175	47			0.0000
No Action	180	47			0.0000
No Action	185	47			-0.5000
Sell	190	47	0.5000		-0.5000
Sell	195	47	0.3750		-0.3750
Sell	200	47	0.1875		-0.1875
Sell	205	47			0.0000
No Action	175	46			-0.7500
No Action	180	46			-4.5000
No Action	185	46			-3.7500
Sell	190	46	3.1250		-3.1250
Sell	195	46	2.2500		-2.2500
Sell	200	46	1.4375		-1.4375
Sell	205	46	0.8125		-0.8125
Buy	175	45		-2.2500	-2.2500
No Action	180	45			-1.1250
No Action	185	45			0.8750
No Action	190	45			0.3750
Sell	195	45	-0.1250		0.1250
Sell	200	45	-0.1250		0.1250
Sell	205	45	-0.1250		0.1250
Buy	170	44		11.5000	11.5000
Buy	175	44		-1.0000	-1.0000
Sell	180	44	-1.7500		1.7500
No Action	185	44			-0.2500
No Action	190	44			0.2500
Sell	195	44	-0.1250		0.1250
Sell	200	44			0.0000
Sell	205	44	0.1250		-0.1250
No Action	175	43			
No Action	180	43			
No Action	185	43			
Sell	190	43			
Sell	195	43			
Sell	200	43			
Sell	205	43			
Sell	210	43			
No Action	175	40			-0.5000
Sell	180	40	-0.1250		0.1250
No Action	185	40			-0.3750
Sell	190	40	0.3750		-0.3750
Sell	195	40	0.1250		-0.1250
Sell	200	40			0.0000
Sell	205	40	0.1250		-0.1250
Sell	210	40	0.0625		-0.0625

Table 3.6
Trade Every Day Except Friday

Decision	Exercise Price	Days Until Expiration	Profits Sell Strategy	Profits Buy Strategy	Difference Today's Premium Tomorrow's Premium
No Action	175	39			-2.0000
No Action	180	39			-2.5000
Sell	185	39	2.5000		-2.5000
Sell	190	39	2.0000		-2.0000
Sell	195	39	2.0000		-2.0000
Sell	200	39	1.6250		-1.6250
Sell	205	39	0.9375		-0.9375
Sell	210	39	0.5000		-0.5000
No Action	175	38			1.1250
Sell	180	38	-0.5000		0.5000
Sell	185	38			0.0000
Sell	190	38	0.1250		-0.1250
Sell	195	38	0.3750		-0.3750
Sell	200	38	0.3750		-0.3750
Sell	205	38	0.3750		-0.3750
Sell	210	38	0.2500		-0.2500
Buy	175	37		-4.0000	-4.0000
No Action	180	37			-4.2500
Sell	185	37	3.2500		-3.2500
Sell	190	37	3.6250		-3.6250
Sell	195	37	2.7500		-2.7500
Sell	200	37	2.2500		-2.2500
Sell	205	37	1.6250		-1.6250
Sell	210	37	1.2500		-1.2500
Sell	215	37	0.8750		-0.8750
No Action	175	36			
Sell	180	36			
No Action	185	36			
Sell	190	36			
Sell	195	36			
Sell	200	36			
Sell	205	36			
Sell	210	36			
Sell	215	36			
Sell	170	33	-1.2500		1.2500
Sell	175	33	-1.5000		1.5000
Sell	180	33	-0.2500		0.2500
Sell	185	33	-0.7500		0.7500
No Action	190	33			0.5000
Sell	195	33	-0.7500		0.7500
Sell	200	33	-0.2500		0.2500
Sell	205	33	-0.2500		0.2500
Sell	210	33			0.0000

Table 3.7
Trade Every Day Except Friday

Decision	Exercise Price	Days Until Expiration	Profits Sell Strategy	Profits Buy Strategy	Difference Today's Premium Tomorrow's Premium
Sell	170	32	0.5000		0.5000
Sell	175	32	0.1250		-0.1250
Sell	180	32	-4.0000		4.0000
Sell	185	32	-1.0000		1.0000
Sell	190	32	-1.1250		1.1250
Sell	195	32	-1.1250		1.1250
Sell	200	32	-1.0000		1.0000
Sell	205	32	-1.0000		1.0000
Sell	210	32	-0.8750		0.8750
Sell	215	32	-0.6875		0.6875
Sell	220	32	-0.4375		0.4375
Sell	175	31	-1.1250		1.1250
Buy	180	31		-2.1250	-2.1250
Sell	185	31	-0.5000		0.5000
Sell	190	31			0.0000
Sell	195	31	0.1250		-0.1250
Sell	200	31	-0.1250		0.1250
Sell	205	31	-0.1250		0.1250
Sell	210	31	-0.0625		0.0625
Sell	215	31	-0.0625		0.0625
Sell	220	31	-0.1250		0.1250
Sell	175	30	-0.5000		0.5000
Sell	180	30	0.1250		-0.1250
Sell	185	30	0.5000		-0.5000
Sell	190	30	0.2500		-0.2500
Sell	195	30			0.0000
Sell	200	30	0.3750		-0.3750
Sell	205	30	0.1250		-0.1250
Sell	210	30	-0.0625		0.0625
Sell	215	30	-0.2500		0.2500
Sell	220	30	-0.0625		0.0625
Sell	170	29			
Sell	175	29			
Sell	180	29			
Sell	185	29			
Sell	190	29			
Sell	195	29			
Sell	200	29			
Sell	205	29			
Sell	210	29			
Sell	215	29			
Sell	220	29			

Table 3.8
Trade Every Day Except Friday

Decision	Exercise Price	Days Until Expiration	Profits Sell Strategy	Profits Buy Strategy	Difference Today's Premium Tomorrow's Premium
Sell	175	26	-3.2500		3.2500
Sell	180	26	-2.7500		2.7500
Sell	185	26	-1.5000		1.5000
Sell	190	26	-1.5000		1.5000
Sell	195	26	-0.7500		0.7500
Sell	200	26	-0.8750		0.8750
Sell	205	26	-0.6250		0.6250
Sell	210	26	-0.4375		0.4375
Sell	215	26	-0.2500		0.2500
Sell	220	26	-0.1250		0.1250
Sell	170	25	-3.5000		-3.5000
No Action	175	25			
No Action	180	25			
Sell	185	25	0.2500		-0.2500
Sell	190	25	0.6250		-0.6250
Sell	195	25	0.5000		-0.5000
Sell	200	25	0.2500		-0.2500
Sell	205	25			
Sell	210	25			
Sell	215	25			
Sell	220	25			
Sell	175	23	1.7500		-1.7500
Sell	180	23	2.2500		-2.2500
Sell	185	23	2.2500		-2.2500
Sell	190	23	2.0000		-2.0000
Sell	195	23	1.7500		-1.7500
Sell	200	23	1.6250		-1.6250
Sell	205	23	1.1250		-1.1250
Sell	210	23	0.3750		-0.3750
Sell	215	23	0.1250		-0.1250
Sell	220	23			0.0000
No Action	175	22			
Sell	180	22			
Sell	185	22			
Sell	190	22			
Sell	195	22			
Sell	200	22			
Sell	205	22			
Sell	210	22			
Sell	215	22			
Sell	220	22			

Table 3.9
Trade Every Day Except Friday

Decision	Exercise Price	Days Until Expiration	Profits Sell Strategy	Profits Buy Strategy	Difference Today's Premium Tomorrow's Premium
Buy	175	19		-2.0000	-2.0000
Sell	180	19	-1.2500		1.2500
No Action	185	19			-0.5000
Sell	190	19	-1.5000		1.5000
Sell	195	19	-1.1250		1.1250
Sell	200	19	-0.6875		0.6875
Sell	205	19	-1.0000		1.0000
Sell	210	19	-0.5625		0.5625
Sell	215	19	-0.1875		0.1875
Sell	220	19			0.0000
Sell	170	18	-1.5000		-1.5000
Sell	175	18	-2.5000		2.5000
Buy	180	18		1.3750	1.3750
Sell	185	18	-2.2500		2.2500
Buy	190	18		1.2500	1.2500
No Action	195	18			1.3750
No Action	200	18			1.2500
Sell	205	18	-0.6875		0.6875
Sell	210	18	-0.3750		0.3750
Sell	215	18	-0.1250		0.1250
Sell	220	18	-0.1250		0.1250
Sell	175	16	0.2500		-0.2500
No Action	180	16			-1.1250
No Action	185	16			-0.7500
No Action	190	16			-1.7500
No Action	195	16			-1.6250
Sell	200	16	1.2500		-1.2500
Sell	205	16	0.5625		-0.5625
Sell	210	16	0.1875		-0.1875
Sell	215	16			0.0000
Sell	220	16			0.0000
Buy	175	15			
No Action	180	15			
Buy	185	15			
Sell	190	15			
Sell	195	15			
Sell	200	15			
Sell	205	15			
Sell	210	15			
Sell	215	15			
Sell	220	15			

Table 3.10
Trade Every Day Except Friday

Decision	Exercise Price	Days Until Expiration	Profits Sell Strategy	Profits Buy Strategy	Difference Today's Premium Tomorrow's Premium
No Action	170	12			-4.2500
No Action	175	12			-1.8750
Sell	180	12	2.8750		-2.8750
Sell	185	12	3.3750		-3.3750
Sell	190	12	2.5000		-2.5000
Sell	195	12	3.1250		-3.1250
Sell	200	12	2.3750		-2.3750
Sell	205	12	1.6250		-1.6250
Sell	210	12	0.8125		-0.8125
Sell	215	12	0.1250		-0.1250
Sell	220	12			0.0000
Buy	175	11		0.6250	0.6250
Sell	180	11	-6.8750		6.8750
Sell	185	11	-7.0000		7.0000
Sell	190	11	-6.7500		6.7500
Sell	195	11	-6.5000		6.5000
Sell	200	11	-6.0000		6.0000
Sell	205	11	-3.5000		3.5000
Sell	210	11	-1.5625		1.5625
Sell	215	11	-0.3125		0.3125
Sell	220	11			0.0000
Sell	175	10	-6.0000		6.0000
Buy	180	10		1.2500	1.2500
Buy	185	10		1.2500	1.2500
Buy	190	10		1.0000	1.0000
No Action	195	10			0.7500
Sell	200	10	-0.2500		0.2500
Sell	205	10	-0.4375		0.4375
Sell	210	10	-0.0625		0.0625
Sell	215	10			0.0000
Sell	220	10			0.0000
Buy	175	9		-0.2500	-0.2500
Buy	180	9			0.0000
Buy	185	9		0.3750	0.3750
No Action	190	9			1.2500
Sell	195	9	-1.1250		1.1250
Sell	200	9	-1.0625		1.0625
Sell	205	9	-0.5100		0.5100
Sell	210	9	-0.1250		0.1250
Sell	215	9			0.0000
Sell	220	9			0.0000

Table 3.11
Trade Every Day Except Friday

Decision	Exercise Price	Days Until Expiration	Profits Sell Strategy	Profits Buy Strategy	Difference Today's Premium Tomorrow's Premium
Sell	170	8			
Sell	175	8			
Sell	180	8			
Sell	185	8			
No Action	190	8			
Sell	195	8			
Sell	200	8			
Sell	205	8			
Sell	210	8			
Sell	215	8			
Sell	220	8			
Buy	170	5			
Buy	175	5		-0.7500	-0.7500
No Action	180	5			0.3750
Buy	185	5		1.1250	1.1250
No Action	190	5			0.2500
Buy	195	5			0.0000
Sell	200	5	-0.8125		0.8125
Sell	205	5	-0.1250		0.1250
Sell	210	5			0.0000
Sell	215	5			0.0000
No Action	175	4			-1.7500
Buy	180	4		-1.7500	-1.7500
Buy	185	4		-2.5000	-2.5000
No Action	190	4			-1.7500
No Action	195	4			-1.8750
No Action	200	4			-1.8125
Sell	205	4	0.1250		-0.1250
Sell	210	4			0.0000
Sell	215	4			0.0000
Sell	175	3	0.6250		0.6250
No Action	180	3			-0.8750
Buy	185	3		-1.1250	-1.1250
Sell	190	3	0.7500		-0.7500
Sell	195	3	0.6250		-0.6250
Sell	200	3	0.6250		-0.6250
Sell	205	3			0.0000
Sell	210	3			0.0000
Sell	215	3			0.0000
Sell	220	3	-0.0625		0.0625

Table 3.12
Trade Every Day Except Friday

Decision	Exercise Price	Days Until Expiration	Profits Sell Strategy	Profits Buy Strategy	Difference Today's Premium Tomorrow's Premium
No Action	180	2			2.2500
Sell	185	2	-1.5000		1.5000
No Action	190	2			1.2500
No Action	195	2			1.5000
No Action	200	2			1.3750
Sell	205	2	-0.3125		0.3125
Sell	210	2	-0.0625		0.0625
Sell	215	2	-0.0625		0.0625
	175	1			
	180	1			
	185	1			
	190	1			
	195	1			
	200	1			
	205	1			
			-18.010	38.625	20.823
			20.615		

Table 4.1
Trade Only If There Is
A Trading Day Tomorrow

Decision	Exercise Price	Days Until Expiration	Profits Sell Strategy	Profits Buy Strategy	Difference Today's Premium Tomorrow's Premium
No Action	175	89			0.0000
Sell	180	89	0.5000		-0.5000
Sell	185	89	0.3125		-0.3125
Sell	190	89	0.0625		-0.0625
Buy	170	88		-1.1250	-1.1250
No Action	175	88			-1.0000
No Action	180	88			-0.6250
Sell	185	88	0.3750		-0.3750
Sell	190	88	0.1875		-0.1875
No Action	170	87			0.1250
No Action	175	87			0.1250
No Action	180	87			0.7500
Sell	185	87	-0.4375		0.4375
Sell	190	87	-0.1875		0.1875
No Action	170	86			2.0000
No Action	175	86			1.7500
No Action	180	86			0.7500
Sell	185	86	-0.4375		0.4375
Sell	190	86	-0.1875		0.1875
No Action	170	85			
No Action	175	85			
No Action	180	85			
Sell	185	85			
Sell	190	85			
No Action	170	82			-1.7500
No Action	175	82			-1.2500
Sell	180	82	0.6250		-0.6250
Sell	185	82	0.4375		-0.4375
Sell	190	82	0.1875		-0.1875
No Action	170	81			-0.1250
No Action	175	81			0.0000
No Action	180	81			-0.3750
Sell	185	81	0.2500		-0.2500
Sell	190	81	0.1250		-0.1250
Buy	170	80		-0.1250	-0.1250
No Action	175	80			0.1250
No Action	180	80			0.2500
Sell	185	80	-0.1875		0.1875
Sell	190	80	-0.0625		0.0625
No Action	170	79			-1.0000
No Action	175	79			-1.5000
No Action	180	79			-0.8750
Sell	185	79	0.7500		-0.7500
Sell	190	79	0.1875		-0.1875

Table 4.2
Trade Only If There Is
A Trading Day Tomorrow

Decision	Exercise Price	Days Until Expiration	Profits Sell Strategy	Profits Buy Strategy	Difference Today's Premium Tomorrow's Premium
Buy	170	78			
No Action	175	78			
No Action	180	78			
Sell	185	78			
Sell	190	78			
Buy	170	75		-1.1250	-1.1250
Buy	175	75		-0.6250	-0.6250
No Action	180	75			-0.6250
Sell	185	75	0.3750		-0.3750
Sell	190	75	0.1875		-0.1875
Buy	170	74		-0.2500	-0.2500
Buy	175	74		0.1250	0.1250
No Action	180	74			0.0000
No Action	185	74			0.0000
Sell	190	74	-0.0625		0.0625
Sell	195	74	-1.0625		1.0625
Buy	170	73		0.7500	0.7500
Buy	175	73		-0.5000	-0.5000
No Action	180	73			0.1250
No Action	185	73			0.1250
Sell	190	73	-0.0625		0.0625
Sell	195	73	-0.0625		0.0625
Buy	170	72		-1.1250	-1.1250
No Action	175	72			-1.2500
No Action	180	72			-1.3750
Sell	185	72	0.8750		-0.8750
Sell	190	72	0.4375		-0.4375
Sell	195	72	0.2500		-0.2500
Buy	170	71			
No Action	175	71			
No Action	180	71			
Sell	185	71			
Sell	190	71			
Sell	195	71			
Buy	175	68		-1.5000	-1.5000
No Action	180	68			-1.0000
No Action	185	68			-1.1250
Sell	190	68	1.2500		-1.2500
Sell	195	68	0.7500		-0.7500
Buy	170	67		20.5000	20.5000
No Action	175	67			0.5000
No Action	180	67			1.3750
No Action	185	67			0.7500
Sell	190	67	-0.6250		0.6250
Sell	195	67	-0.2500		0.2500

Table 4.3
Trade Only If There Is
A Trading Day Tomorrow

Decision	Exercise Price	Days Until Expiration	Profits Sell Strategy	Profits Buy Strategy	Difference Today's Premium Tomorrow's Premium
No Action	175	66			-2.0000
No Action	180	66			-2.5000
No Action	185	66			-1.7500
Sell	190	66	1.1250		-1.1250
Sell	195	66	0.7500		-0.7500
Sell	200	66	0.3125		-0.3125
Buy	170	65			0.0000
No Action	175	65			-0.5000
No Action	180	65			0.6250
No Action	185	65			0.7500
Sell	190	65	-0.3750		0.3750
Sell	195	65	-0.3750		0.3750
Sell	200	65	-0.0625		0.0625
No Action	170	64			
No Action	175	64			
No Action	180	64			
No Action	185	64			
Sell	190	64			
Sell	195	64			
Sell	200	64			
Buy	170	61		-0.7500	-0.7500
Buy	175	61			0.0000
No Action	180	61			0.0000
No Action	185	61			0.1250
Sell	190	61	-0.2500		0.2500
Sell	195	61	-0.0625		0.0625
Sell	200	61	-0.1875		0.1875
Sell	205	61			0.0000
No Action	170	60			22.7500
Buy	175	60		-1.2500	-1.2500
No Action	180	60			-0.5000
No Action	185	60			-0.6250
No Action	190	60			-0.5000
Sell	195	60	0.2500		-0.2500
Sell	200	60	0.1250		-0.1250
Sell	205	60	0.0625		-0.0625
No Action	175	59			-1.5000
No Action	180	59			-2.5000
No Action	185	59			-2.2500
No Action	190	59			-1.6250
Sell	195	59	1.1875		-1.1875
Sell	200	59	0.5625		-0.5625
Sell	205	59	0.2500		-0.2500

Table 4.4
Trade Only If There Is
A Trading Day Tomorrow

Decision	Exercise Price	Days Until Expiration	Profits Sell Strategy	Profits Buy Strategy	Difference Today's Premium Tomorrow's Premium
Buy	175	58		-0.6250	-0.6250
No Action	180	58			0.3750
No Action	185	58			0.2500
No Action	190	58			0.1250
Sell	195	58	-0.1250		0.1250
Sell	200	58			0.0000
Sell	205	58			0.0000
No Action	170	57			
No Action	175	57			
No Action	180	57			
No Action	185	57			
No Action	190	57			
Sell	195	57			
Sell	200	57			
Sell	205	57			
No Action	175	54			-0.2500
No Action	180	54			-0.6250
No Action	185	54			-0.3750
Sell	190	54	0.3750		-0.3750
Sell	195	54	0.2500		-0.2500
Sell	200	54	0.0625		-0.0625
Sell	205	54			0.0000
Buy	170	53		-0.2500	-0.2500
No Action	175	53			-1.7500
No Action	180	53			-2.2500
No Action	185	53			-2.2500
No Action	190	53			-1.7500
Sell	195	53	1.2500		-1.2500
Sell	200	53	0.7500		-0.7500
Sell	205	53	0.4375		-0.4375
Buy	170	52			
No Action	175	52			
No Action	180	52			
No Action	185	52			
No Action	190	52			
Sell	195	52			
Sell	200	52			
Sell	205	52			
No Action	175	50			
No Action	180	50			
No Action	185	50			
No Action	190	50			
Sell	195	50			
Sell	200	50			
Sell	205	50			

Table 4.5
Trade Only If There Is
A Trading Day Tomorrow

Decision	Exercise Price	Days Until Expiration	Profits Sell Strategy	Profits Buy Strategy	Difference Today's Premium Tomorrow's Premium
No Action	170	47			
No Action	175	47			0.0000
No Action	180	47			0.0000
No Action	185	47			-0.5000
Sell	190	47	0.5000		-0.5000
Sell	195	47	0.3750		-0.3750
Sell	200	47	0.1875		-0.1875
Sell	205	47			0.0000
No Action	175	46			-0.7500
No Action	180	46			-4.5000
No Action	185	46			-3.7500
Sell	190	46	3.1250		-3.1250
Sell	195	46	2.2500		-2.2500
Sell	200	46	1.4375		-1.4375
Sell	205	46	0.8125		-0.8125
Buy	175	45		-2.2500	-2.2500
No Action	180	45			-1.1250
No Action	185	45			0.8750
No Action	190	45			0.3750
Sell	195	45	-0.1250		0.1250
Sell	200	45	-0.1250		0.1250
Sell	205	45	-0.1250		0.1250
Buy	170	44		27.5000	27.5000
Buy	175	44		-1.0000	-1.0000
Sell	180	44	-1.7500		1.7500
No Action	185	44			-0.2500
No Action	190	44			0.2500
Sell	195	44	-0.1250		0.1250
Sell	200	44			0.0000
Sell	205	44	0.1250		-0.1250
No Action	175	43			
No Action	180	43			
No Action	185	43			
Sell	190	43			
Sell	195	43			
Sell	200	43			
Sell	205	43			
Sell	210	43			
No Action	175	40			-0.5000
Sell	180	40	-0.1250		0.1250
No Action	185	40			-0.3750
Sell	190	40	0.3750		-0.3750
Sell	195	40	0.1250		-0.1250
Sell	200	40			0.0000
Sell	205	40	0.1250		-0.1250
Sell	210	40	0.0625		-0.0625

Table 4.6
Trade Only If There Is
A Trading Day Tomorrow

Decision	Exercise Price	Days Until Expiration	Profits Sell Strategy	Profits Buy Strategy	Difference Today's Premium Tomorrow's Premium
No Action	175	39			-2.0000
No Action	180	39			-2.5000
Sell	185	39	2.5000		-2.5000
Sell	190	39	2.0000		-2.0000
Sell	195	39	2.0000		-2.0000
Sell	200	39	1.6250		-1.6250
Sell	205	39	0.9375		-0.9375
Sell	210	39	0.5000		-0.5000
No Action	175	38			1.1250
Sell	180	38	-0.5000		0.5000
Sell	185	38			0.0000
Sell	190	38	0.1250		-0.1250
Sell	195	38	0.3750		-0.3750
Sell	200	38	0.3750		-0.3750
Sell	205	38	0.3750		-0.3750
Sell	210	38	0.2500		-0.2500
Buy	175	37		-4.0000	-4.0000
No Action	180	37			-4.2500
Sell	185	37	3.2500		-3.2500
Sell	190	37	3.6250		-3.6250
Sell	195	37	2.7500		-2.7500
Sell	200	37	2.2500		-2.2500
Sell	205	37	1.6250		-1.6250
Sell	210	37	1.2500		-1.2500
Sell	215	37	0.8750		-0.8750
No Action	175	36			
Sell	180	36			
No Action	185	36			
Sell	190	36			
Sell	195	36			
Sell	200	36			
Sell	205	36			
Sell	210	36			
Sell	215	36			
Sell	170	33	-1.2500		1.2500
Sell	175	33	-1.5000		1.5000
Sell	180	33	-0.2500		0.2500
Sell	185	33	-0.7500		0.7500
No Action	190	33			0.5000
Sell	195	33	-0.7500		0.7500
Sell	200	33	-0.2500		0.2500
Sell	205	33	-0.2500		0.2500
Sell	210	33			0.0000

Table 4.7
Trade Only If There Is
A Trading Day Tomorrow

Decision	Exercise Price	Days Until Expiration	Profits Sell Strategy	Profits Buy Strategy	Difference Today's Premium Tomorrow's Premium
Sell	170	32	0.5000		0.5000
Sell	175	32	0.1250		-0.1250
Sell	180	32	-4.0000		4.0000
Sell	185	32	-1.0000		1.0000
Sell	190	32	-1.1250		1.1250
Sell	195	32	-1.1250		1.1250
Sell	200	32	-1.0000		1.0000
Sell	205	32	-1.0000		1.0000
Sell	210	32	-0.8750		0.8750
Sell	215	32	-0.6875		0.6875
Sell	220	32	-0.4375		0.4375
Sell	175	31	-1.1250		1.1250
Buy	180	31		-2.1250	-2.1250
Sell	185	31	-0.5000		0.5000
Sell	190	31			0.0000
Sell	195	31	0.1250		-0.1250
Sell	200	31	-0.1250		0.1250
Sell	205	31	-0.1250		0.1250
Sell	210	31	-0.0625		0.0625
Sell	215	31	-0.0625		0.0625
Sell	220	31	-0.1250		0.1250
Sell	175	30	-0.5000		0.5000
Sell	180	30	0.1250		-0.1250
Sell	185	30	0.5000		-0.5000
Sell	190	30	0.2500		-0.2500
Sell	195	30			0.0000
Sell	200	30	0.3750		-0.3750
Sell	205	30	0.1250		-0.1250
Sell	210	30	-0.0625		0.0625
Sell	215	30	-0.2500		0.2500
Sell	220	30	-0.0625		0.0625
Sell	170	29			
Sell	175	29			
Sell	180	29			
Sell	185	29			
Sell	190	29			
Sell	195	29			
Sell	200	29			
Sell	205	29			
Sell	210	29			
Sell	215	29			
Sell	220	29			

Table 4.8
Trade Only If There Is
A Trading Day Tomorrow

Decision	Exercise Price	Days Until Expiration	Profits Sell Strategy	Profits Buy Strategy	Difference Today's Premium Tomorrow's Premium
Sell	175	26	-3.2500		3.2500
Sell	180	26	-2.7500		2.7500
Sell	185	26	-1.5000		1.5000
Sell	190	26	-1.5000		1.5000
Sell	195	26	-0.7500		0.7500
Sell	200	26	-0.8750		0.8750
Sell	205	26	-0.6250		0.6250
Sell	210	26	-0.4375		0.4375
Sell	215	26	-0.2500		0.2500
Sell	220	26	-0.1250		0.1250
Sell	170	25			
No Action	175	25			
No Action	180	25			
Sell	185	25			
Sell	190	25			
Sell	195	25			
Sell	200	25			
Sell	205	25			
Sell	210	25			
Sell	215	25			
Sell	220	25			
Sell	175	23	1.7500		-1.7500
Sell	180	23	2.2500		-2.2500
Sell	185	23	2.2500		-2.2500
Sell	190	23	2.0000		-2.0000
Sell	195	23	1.7500		-1.7500
Sell	200	23	1.6250		-1.6250
Sell	205	23	1.1250		-1.1250
Sell	210	23	0.3750		-0.3750
Sell	215	23	0.1250		-0.1250
Sell	220	23			0.0000
No Action	175	22			
Sell	180	22			
Sell	185	22			
Sell	190	22			
Sell	195	22			
Sell	200	22			
Sell	205	22			
Sell	210	22			
Sell	215	22			
Sell	220	22			

Table 4.9
Trade Only If There Is
A Trading Day Tomorrow

Decision	Exercise Price	Days Until Expiration	Profits Sell Strategy	Profits Buy Strategy	Difference Today's Premium Tomorrow's Premium
Buy	175	19		-2.0000	-2.0000
Sell	180	19	-1.2500		1.2500
No Action	185	19			-0.5000
Sell	190	19	-1.5000		1.5000
Sell	195	19	-1.1250		1.1250
Sell	200	19	-0.6875		0.6875
Sell	205	19	-1.0000		1.0000
Sell	210	19	-0.5625		0.5625
Sell	215	19	-0.1875		0.1875
Sell	220	19			0.0000
Sell	170	18			
Sell	175	18			
Buy	180	18			
Sell	185	18			
Buy	190	18			
No Action	195	18			
No Action	200	18			
Sell	205	18			
Sell	210	18			
Sell	215	18			
Sell	220	18			
Sell	175	16	0.2500		-0.2500
No Action	180	16			-1.1250
No Action	185	16			-0.7500
No Action	190	16			-1.7500
No Action	195	16			-1.6250
Sell	200	16	1.2500		-1.2500
Sell	205	16	0.5625		-0.5625
Sell	210	16	0.1875		-0.1875
Sell	215	16			0.0000
Sell	220	16			0.0000
Buy	175	15			
No Action	180	15			
Buy	185	15			
Sell	190	15			
Sell	195	15			
Sell	200	15			
Sell	205	15			
Sell	210	15			
Sell	215	15			
Sell	220	15			

Table 4.10
Trade Only If There Is
A Trading Day Tomorrow

Decision	Exercise Price	Days Until Expiration	Profits Sell Strategy	Profits Buy Strategy	Difference Today's Premium Tomorrow's Premium
No Action	170	12			36.0000
No Action	175	12			-1.8750
Sell	180	12	2.8750		-2.8750
Sell	185	12	3.3750		-3.3750
Sell	190	12	2.5000		-2.5000
Sell	195	12	3.1250		-3.1250
Sell	200	12	2.3750		-2.3750
Sell	205	12	1.6250		-1.6250
Sell	210	12	0.8125		-0.8125
Sell	215	12	0.1250		-0.1250
Sell	220	12			0.0000
Buy	175	11		0.6250	0.6250
Sell	180	11	-6.8750		6.8750
Sell	185	11	-7.0000		7.0000
Sell	190	11	-6.7500		6.7500
Sell	195	11	-6.5000		6.5000
Sell	200	11	-6.0000		6.0000
Sell	205	11	-3.5000		3.5000
Sell	210	11	-1.5625		1.5625
Sell	215	11	-0.3125		0.3125
Sell	220	11			0.0000
Sell	175	10	-6.0000		6.0000
Buy	180	10		1.2500	1.2500
Buy	185	10		1.2500	1.2500
Buy	190	10		1.0000	1.0000
No Action	195	10			0.7500
Sell	200	10	-0.2500		0.2500
Sell	205	10	-0.4375		0.4375
Sell	210	10	-0.0625		0.0625
Sell	215	10			0.0000
Sell	220	10			0.0000
Buy	175	9		-0.2500	-0.2500
Buy	180	9			0.0000
Buy	185	9		0.3750	0.3750
No Action	190	9			1.2500
Sell	195	9	-1.1250		1.1250
Sell	200	9	-1.0625		1.0625
Sell	205	9	-0.5100		0.5100
Sell	210	9	-0.1250		0.1250
Sell	215	9			0.0000
Sell	220	9			0.0000

Table 4.11
Trade Only If There Is
A Trading Day Tomorrow

Decision	Exercise Price	Days Until Expiration	Profits Sell Strategy	Profits Buy Strategy	Difference Today's Premium Tomorrow's Premium
Sell	170	8			
Sell	175	8			
Sell	180	8			
Sell	185	8			
No Action	190	8			
Sell	195	8			
Sell	200	8			
Sell	205	8			
Sell	210	8			
Sell	215	8			
Sell	220	8			
Buy	170	5			
Buy	175	5		-0.7500	-0.7500
No Action	180	5			0.3750
Buy	185	5		1.1250	1.1250
No Action	190	5			0.2500
Buy	195	5			0.0000
Sell	200	5	-0.8125		0.8125
Sell	205	5	-0.1250		0.1250
Sell	210	5			0.0000
Sell	215	5			0.0000
No Action	175	4			-1.7500
Buy	180	4		-1.7500	-1.7500
Buy	185	4		-2.5000	-2.5000
No Action	190	4			-1.7500
No Action	195	4			-1.8750
No Action	200	4			-1.8125
Sell	205	4	0.1250		-0.1250
Sell	210	4			0.0000
Sell	215	4			0.0000
Sell	175	3	0.6250		0.6250
No Action	180	3			-0.8750
Buy	185	3		-1.1250	-1.1250
Sell	190	3	0.7500		-0.7500
Sell	195	3	0.6250		-0.6250
Sell	200	3	0.6250		-0.6250
Sell	205	3			0.0000
Sell	210	3			0.0000
Sell	215	3			0.0000
Sell	220	3	-0.0625		0.0625

Table 4.12
Trade Only If There Is
A Trading Day Tomorrow

Decision	Exercise Price	Days Until Expiration	Profits Sell Strategy	Profits Buy Strategy	Difference Today's Premium Tomorrow's Premium
No Action	180	2			2.2500
Sell	185	2	-1.5000		1.5000
No Action	190	2			1.2500
No Action	195	2			1.5000
No Action	200	2			1.3750
Sell	205	2	-0.3125		0.3125
Sell	210	2	-0.0625		0.0625
Sel	215	2	-0.0625		0.0625
	175	1			
	180	1			
	185	1			
	190	1			
	195	1			
	200	1			
	205	1			
			-7.323	27.500	43.385
			20.1775		

Business Ethics Beyond the Year 2000: Right Questions and Wrong Questions

Kenneth M. Bond, Ph.D.
Professor of Management
Humboldt State University
Arcata, California

I

In our collective history the study of ethics has typically centered around issues of exchange between two individuals (or an individual and some other third party, such as a community). Frequently, illustrations were developed around one individual doing something to another individual and the second party reacting and doing something in response. The fundamental question was then one of "just exchange" between the two parties. Historically, Hammurabi's Code (eye-for-an-eye) and the numerous version of the Golden Rule would all classify under this broad system of exchange. Traditionally, questions of this kind were not particularly affected by technology.

We are clearly entering into a new era in many ways. Alvin Toffler describes the phenomena as an information society in his book *3rd Wave*. His first wave is the agrarian culture; his second wave is the manufacturing environment; and his third wave is the information society in which the rate of change in technology will uniquely change the nature of the relationships between individuals and other entities with which they interact. The same mentality can be found in John Naisbitt's arguments about overall trends affecting our society. In *Megatrends* he talks about the impacts of an information society. Again, concepts such as world economy, collapse of the information float due to communication satellites, etc., are chronicled in some detail. Several other futuristic writers have echoed similar arguments and insights.

Our technology is providing options for whole new fields of business not available in the past. Nowhere is this more evident than in the area of markets for human body parts. A recent issue of *Business Week* (Dec. 5, 1988) has a short article about a West German firm which was buying kidneys from healthy individuals for $45,000 each and selling them (i.e., open-market system) for $85,000 each. The article went on to note a competitor had sprung up which offered an alternative option of flying the person in need of a kidney to a third world environment for the procedure at less cost. In previous times arguments over concepts such as ownership of body parts were seldom debated. People retained body parts during life and after death because there was no effective alternative uses for them. Now technology has allowed us to ask some very interesting "business" questions about which products we want distributed by a free-market model and which ones we would prefer not be allowed to be part of a free-market model. Our technologically driven society is not simply a better modification of our present society, but in may ways it is significantly different.

II

However unlikely it might seem, technology is a driving force in numerous ethical discussions which currently face business managers. In the years to come many technologically driven ethical questions will surface in greater clarity and concern than ever before. As an *illustration* of this area, consider the following sequence of technological advancement.

In the area of drug testing of employees (alcohol will be considered a drug for this entire analysis) we have had a dramatic change of technology in recent years and will continue to have an advancement in techniques in the future. "In the olden days" drug testing typically called for taking a blood sample. As new equipment was perfected, breathalizers became useful for certain types of drugs, and urine analysis technology provides a wide spectrum methodology for the identification of drugs. However, blood samples and urine analysis are cumbersome and in some cases go against social mores. As technology continued to develop in this area, hair analysis was next developed and is being used in some applications at this time. A single strand of hair contains an accurate record of substances used by an individual. Clearly, asking an individual for a strand of hair is less abusive to various mores than options such as taking blood or obtaining certified urine samples. The next step is just around the corner. Recently, a U.S. university, under government contract, has developed a body scanner which will allow someone operating the scanner to check for life signs of an individual from up to six feet away. While this scanner has nothing to do with drugs itself, the logical growth in technology is apparent. The day is close at hand when Mr. Spock's and Dr. McCoy's small body scanners (*Star Trek* fame) will be able to detect and categorize the substances an individual has in his or her body—*without* ever touching the individual.

Airports are now starting to deploy a new series of detectors which can "smell" the presence of various types of explosives. It would not be a particularly difficult step to reprogram such explosive "smelling" machines to similar machines which would be sensitive to the various types of exhaled gasses which contain different types of drug particles. Do you remember the first "metal detectors" installed at airports? Consider for a moment how "advanced" such a technology would have been considered just 20 or 25 years ago. In the near future an organization could have such a scanner built into a door frame, and it could scan all employees as they pass through the door on their way to work. Such a scanner could detect drug levels of employees through numerous means.

In area after area the same type of advancement is being made. We now have an accurate five minute AIDS test which can be administered without laboratory instruments, using a drop of blood from a finger. Polygraphs are under substantially greater restriction as of the beginning of 1989 due to recently enacted laws in the U.S. However, at the same time substantial progress has been made in effective "paper and pencil" honesty tests.

In all of these areas there is growing confusion about the *technique* used to find out something about an employee (or other individual). The more accurate starting point is not to discuss the pros and cons of a specific technique but rather to ask the more fundamental question, "Am I [as manager] entitled to know?" If the answer is yes, *then and only then* are questions concerning a specific technique appropriate. *The unfortunate reality is that as techniques become faster, cheaper, more accurate, and less intrusive, the trend on the part of uninformed management will be to use such methods simply because they are available.*

Notice the unique change in the nature of the questions as we move from our current (and past) environment to a more technologically driven environment. In a very real sense, the value questions change from "What *can* I know about my employees?" to questions of "What am I *entitled* to know?" In area after area in the foreseeable future management will not be technologically constrained in areas such as information about employees. If management is going to be constrained in any sense, then those constraints will be morally driven. The value questions for managers to ask is "what *should* I know about my employees?" Further, these questions will need to be asked in a world in which the technology is such that management is capable of knowing substantially more than is legitimately required.

The question is *not* a legal one. At best, the law describes the minimum level of acceptable behavior. It is never proactive. For example, in the simplest sense the law requires that one not steal. However, it says little about higher levels of honesty. As a business illustration, consider the reality if one establishes a rule that indicates the minimum acceptable level of production on the part of your assembly line workers to be 20 units per hour. By the very nature of rules of this sort, you have not only defined the minimum acceptable level of performance but you have also established the maximum level of performance. Your rule (law) also states that you never need produce 21 units per hour. In this same sense, to infer that the "law" will protect employees and other legitimate stakeholder groups within an organizational context is clearly not acceptable. There may, or may not, ever be a law regarding the futuristic doorway body scanner. That is not the point. Having or not having a law is clearly not a logic of justice; it is only a logic of the minimum acceptable level of behavior.

Enlightened management of the future will need to go beyond simple precepts such as asking "What is legal?" Granted, what is legal is, and will continue to be, important. However, the issues of value conflict for the manager of tomorrow will far outstrip the mechanics of the law.

The moral dilemma proposed by these technological advancements will pervade a whole new spectrum of issues for future managers. Relationships with customers, employees, independent contractors, city, state, federal, and international governments can all be potentially affected. A logical question naturally evolves from the above stated reflections. Namely, "By what model(s) of analysis might managers determine appropriate behavior when faced with such technologically driven options." Please note, the intuitive response is *not* necessarily to limit the use of such techniques. The goal is to use them *justly*. For example, when an effective body scanner is developed which could be placed in a doorway to drug test employees as they come to work, such a device would effectively deal with one of today's criticism of drug testing. The systems in use today are frequently criticized because they test for past use of substances—*not* the state of the employee at the time. If an employee used marijuana over the weekend, then a test on Monday would show positive. (Please note, the author considers the fundamental logic of such arguments flawed. Numerous studies have effectively shown long run effects of all drug sources. The idea of a weekend user not being impacted during the week simply is not an accurate nor effective argument.)

In the body scanner illustration management could test for drug levels *at the time of going to work*. Clearly, testing at such a time would have at least one additional factor in its favor. However, in *no* sense does such a factor morally justify the use of the technique in and of itself. The use of such a body scanner is a violation of the employee's right to privacy. Use of such a piece of technology is a clear violation. However, that is not the proper question. The proper question is to ask if such a violation of privacy is just. It would probably be fair to say that *all* techniques (past, present, and future) are violations of an employee's right to privacy. It would be fairly easy to argue that everything from application forms to background checks to polygraphs and drug tests *are* violations of the right to privacy. However, in numerous cases when the rights of the organization are also considered, the judgment is made that this or that particular action is a *just violation* of an individual's right to privacy. Clearly, when discussing ethical arguments in organizational settings, the rights of *both sides* must be taken into account and balanced. Thus, proper critical analysis must focus on *just* violations, not simply the issue of violation. The drug testing body scanner is a violation. However, there are in all likelihood numerous situations where such a scanner would be a just violation.

III

What constitutes a "just violation" of the rights of one party to an exchange? Again, it is important to re-emphasize that the drug testing analysis and the arguments about privacy are simply illustrations of numerous areas in which technology will impact in the future.

In cases of exchange the typical starting point is to determine the just rights of both sides to an exchange and then to work through some type of analysis to determine if the rights of one side outweigh the rights of the other. In the development of the models which follow it is important to remember that the models themselves are applicable to numerous issues. This analysis is not just about employee privacy. The methodology presented will provide insight for future managers across a wide array of ethical dilemmas which will be faced in light of our advancing technology.

The right of privacy, like many other rights in the corporate world, is not a fixed commodity. In reality the right to privacy is on a sliding scale which effectively takes into account *both* the rights of the individual and the legitimate needs of the organization. A visual illustration of a possible trade-off system is shown in Figure 1.

Figure 1

Basic Trade-Off of Rights Model

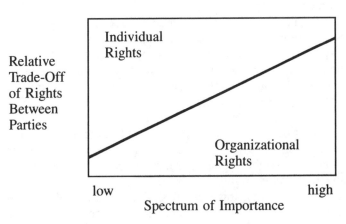

It should be noted that Figure 1 is a generalized model which may be of use in various organizational areas. For the present illustration, the horizontal axis of Figure 1 highlights the concept of organizational importance. The scale moves from low to high and might be interpreted in various ways. Importance might be related to safety of others or corporate reputation or financial stability, etc. On the vertical axis for this illustration is the concept of privacy. As a general observation *the model shows that as an individual's ability to impact the organization increases, then the organization's right to know more about him or her also increases.* Please note that there is a good bit of specific detail which could be developed at this point. Individual rights to privacy are frequently broken into categories such as social privacy, physical privacy, and psychological privacy. Organizational rights can also be developed in substantially greater detail. However, the point of the present analysis is to illustrate a methodology which would be effective across numerous issues, not to concentrate on an extended analysis of privacy rights.

The sliding scale of rights can be illustrated by looking at examples at the extremes. Most literature in the area of privacy would argue that if there is not a legitimate need for the organization to know something about an individual, then the individual should retain as much of his or her privacy as possible. For the lower end of the spectrum in Figure 1, assume any of hundreds of jobs in a typical large organization from operators of copy machines to janitors. The issue here is *not* organizational status, but the ability to impact the organization along some particular concept of importance (such as physical safety of others). In the present illustration the ability of individuals in these types of job classifications to affect the organization is very small. Figure 1 illustrates this position at the far left side of the model and is a position where the individual retains almost all of his or her right to privacy, and the organization's legitimate right to know very much about him or her is severely limited.

At the other end of the spectrum in Figure 1 a good illustration would be a commercial airline pilot. This individual may have the ability to affect the lives of 400 or more people. Further, he or she also controls a multimillion dollar asset of the organization. Logically, one might ask "Is the organization *entitled* to know any more about him or her than about individuals at the other end of the spectrum?" Concerning the concept of safety (not organizational status), the pilot's importance to the organization is much higher, and the model developed in Figure 1 would indicate that there is a *just* trade-off of individual rights in favor of the organization's need-to-know.

Please note that the model developed does *not* converge directly at the intersect points at either the lower left or upper right. The fact that the model does not bisect the axis indicates that there are no organizational environments where the individual has *no* rights (upper right), and there are *no* environments where the organization has *no* rights (lower left).

Beyond the issue of safety, this type of sliding scale model has many alternative uses. The horizontal axis can be changed to represent other issues within an organization. Further, the vertical axis can be changed to show the trade-offs between individual and the organization or between the organization and society, etc. A vast array of ethical issues in organizations are not fixed issues but more effectively belong on a sliding scale. Such a sliding scale means that different levels of an organization will have different equilibrium points of proper balance between the rights of the individual and the organization. This type of sliding scale analysis would lead to different levels of responsibility and obligation for many employees. For example, if an assembly line worker has an opinion on a company policy, that individual's ability to affect the organization is substantially less than if a senior vice-president has the same opinion. Notice that this type of model would lead to different types of organizational consequences for exactly the same behavior on the part of individuals at different levels of an organization. If the assembly line worker engages in behavior which is deemed socially unacceptable (e.g., breaking the law), the consequences to the organization would in all likelihood be less than if a senior vice-president engaged in the exact same behavior. The ability of the one worker to damage the legitimate reputation of the organization is less.

The model developed in Figure 1 has several intuitive appealing properties, not the least of which is its simplicity. Unfortunately, simplicity frequently does not allow for sufficient realism or analytical rigor. The privacy argument is being presented as an *illustration* of the use of such a thinking process which has application in various organization areas. An expansion of Figure 1 is possible which breaks this sliding-scale trade-off analysis into more organizationally specific parts. The organizational concerns of both today's and tomorrow's management can be viewed from a two-variable matrix. The first variable concerns behavior of employees being either job related or not job related. The second variable is if the behavior takes place on-the-job or off-the-job. As a starting point for the analysis of such a matrix, relative terms of importance such as high concern and low concern might be effectively entered into the various quadrants of the matrix. Figure 2 presents a visual representation of such a model.

Figure 2

Orgnaizational Concern
About Employees' Activity

	Job Related	Not-Job Related
On-the-Job Behavior	High Concern	Medium Concern
Off-the-Job Behavior	Medium Concern	Low Concern

Clearly, on-the-job behavior which is also job related is the area of greatest *legitimate* concern for management. Since all on-the-job behavior is of some concern to management, it would be appropriate to label on-the-job but not-job-related behavior (e.g., private phone call home) as of medium concern. The logical extension of this model would also have a medium level of concern as appropriate for job-related but off-the-job activity, and clearly the lowest level of legitimate organization concern would be found for off-the-job and not-job-related activity. For reasons already developed, please note that this final quadrant is *not* listed as "none" but as "low."

The next step in a decision-modeling process to assist future managers with asking the right questions is to combine Models 1 and 2. Figure 3 presents such a model.

Figure 3

Legitimate Privacy Trade-Offs
in Various Organizational Settings

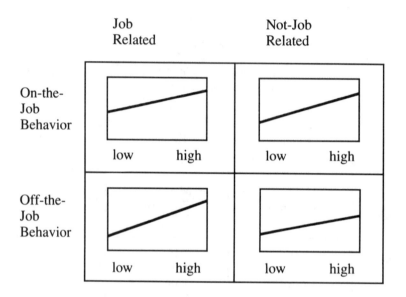

Notice that the *rate of change in the trade-off line is different in the various quadrants*. To explore a couple of the quadrants in this model, consider the upper left quadrant. This quadrant represents on-the-job behavior which is job-related. As can be seen, the intercept point provides organizations with more rights *for all levels of employees* due to the nature of the quadrant. This quadrant can be compared with off-the-job behavior which is not-job-related, the lower right quadrant. In this quadrant the intercept point provides organizations with less rights *for all levels of employees*.

As a final comment, there is nothing which conceptually would dictate that the above cited relationships are necessarily linear. As a simple exercise in exploration, Figure 4 is presented in which the relationships are curvilinear.

Figure 4

Legitimate Privacy Trade-Offs
in Various Organizational Settings

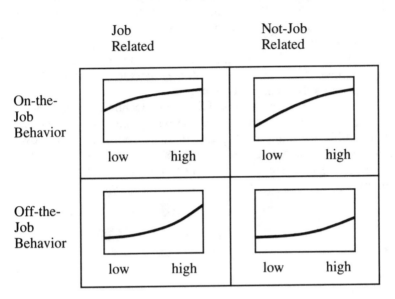

The illustrations in Figure 4 may very well more effectively reflect how many organizations need to deal with the conflicts which will arise between organizational rights and employees' rights. In Figure 4 the two quadrants of "medium concern" are shown with different rates of increase in the trade-off line. Clearly, without evaluating the specifics of a given organization and its unique environment, it is impossible to determine which line more justly reflects proper trade-offs. The point of the illustration is to recognize that many organizations have unique environments and that each individual firm must work to determine just trade-offs with its various stakeholders.

IV

The purpose of this analysis is to illustrate for both present and future managers a *method* of looking at a wide range of conflicts which will arise as technology continues to develop and expand. As was shown in Figure 4, not all the trade-offs are necessarily linear in nature. However, if the appropriate rights of both sides to an organizational relationship are to be justly recognized and taken into account, managers of present and future organizations will need to have a new sensitivity. The modeling process discussed in this paper is a first step in such a process.

Future organizational environments will raise questions which have simply not been asked in the past. For example, what are just means of monitoring employees working in electronic cottages? How often during their day should management "drop-in" (electronically)? Just relationships in the area of parental leave are just starting to be discussed. What about genetic testing? Technology will continue to put increased pressure on managers for higher and higher levels of profit performance. As technology continues to collapse the information float, the results of managerial decision will be known in shorter and shorter time horizons. Such internal pressures will certainly continue to create pressures on managers to find expedient, if not ethical, means to solve many problems.

In the organizational environments of the future, technology will provide numerous options for the solution of numerous problems. The ethical dilemma which will face many managers will stem from a confusion over asking the wrong questions about one technique or another. With multiple options available, the problem of "right" questions and "wrong" questions will become ever greater.

Is Good Ethics Good Business?

Robert E. Frederick, Ph.D.
Center for Business Ethics
Bentley College
Waltham, Massachusetts

◆

Recently a most unusual new way to rehabilitate the American economy has been enthusiastically proposed by a number of people. It is not a tired rehash of the old fiddle with (don't fiddle with) taxes-spending-trade economic policies but something unexpected, trendy, and a little bizarre. It is not an economic policy at all but a management technique or tool that supposedly can be used to right all the things wrong with American business. Yes, it is business ethics. If we can just be ethical in our business dealings, so the story goes, we will help restore profitability, competitiveness, and our preeminent place in the global marketplace that we always knew was ours by moral right anyway. Good ethics, in other words, is good business.

Advocates of the new ethical approach to business are suddenly everywhere. For instance, Kenneth Blanchard and Norman Vincent Peale have just published *The Power of Ethical Management*, which announces on the jacket that "INTEGRITY PAYS." The blurb inside the jacket promises that the book "gives hard-hitting, practical, *ethical* strategies that build profits, productivity, and long term success" (Blanchard and Peale 1988). Somewhat less breathless but decidedly more intense is this statement from the Chairman and CEO of Allied-Signal, Edward L. Hennessy:

> More and more executives have begun to realize that in today's increasingly competitive and complex business environment, ethical conduct plays a vital role in the success of any business. Indeed, it is essential to economic freedom. (Hennessy 1986, 19)

Perhaps the clearest statement of all is from the report "Corporate Ethics: A Prime Business Asset," published in February 1988 by the *Business Roundtable*.

> The corporate community should continue to refine and renew efforts to improve performance and manage change effectively through programs of corporate ethics.... It may come as a surprise to some that...corporate ethics programs are not mounted primarily to improve the reputation of business. Instead many executives believe that a culture in which ethical concern permeates the whole organization is necessary to the self-interest of the company. This is required if the company is to be able to maintain profitability and develop the necessary competitiveness for effective performance.... Effective leadership by management of corporations is the best way to support and advance the cause of private enterprise. Basic to such leadership is the insight that corporate

ethics is a strategic key to survival and profitability in this area
of fierce competitiveness in a global economy. (1988, 9-10)

What are we to make of these rather astounding claims? Is it true, as
many may have suspected in their heart of hearts, that our economic failures
are really moral failures? That all we need to do to gain our just reward both
here and in the hereafter is to be ethical? Or is business ethics just another
fad that, like so many other management fads, will have its day in the sun
before gently receding into those mental mists that so conveniently conceal
our mistakes and misconceptions?

These are difficult questions. Since I believe they are also important ones,
in the remainder of this essay I will try to answer them as best I can. The
short answer is this: business necessarily has an ethical component that
cannot be ignored or set aside, but it is an egregious error to regard ethics
solely as a management tool that will eventually assist in increasing profits
and productivity. Let me try to explain.

It may be best to begin with something we all know but sometimes
forget. Business is not merely a matter of finding the right financial or
marketing or accounting program or of installing the latest machinery or the
most efficient inventory system. At its core, its very heart, business is a
complex web of human relationships—relationships between manufacturers
and consumers, employers and employees, managers and stockholders, members of corporations and members of communities in which corporations
operate. To be sure, these are economic relationships, created by the exchange
of goods and services or the contract of employment. But they are also
moral or ethical relationships. In fact, I believe anything that can be even
remotely considered a mutual human relationship, whether business or otherwise, inevitably has a moral or ethical dimension. The reason for this is
pretty straightforward. To have a relationship with someone else is to interact
with him or her in some way, to act toward him or her or to respond to him
or her in one way rather than another. Now ethics is just the study of how
people *ought* to treat each other, of what is good and right about human
action. It does not merely describe what people actually do; rather it tries
to understand what they *should* do. And I suggest it always makes sense to
ask in our relations with others whether we are acting toward them in the
way that we ought or should act. If this is right, if it does make sense, then
all of our relationships with others have an ethical component, including
our business relationships.

But what does it mean, exactly, to say that our relationships with others
have an ethical component? Philosophers have tried to understand and answer
this question for the last 2500 years. They haven't succeeded in doing so
yet, but they have managed to agree on a few things. One of them is that
being ethical may on occasion require that we place the interests of others
ahead of or at least on a par with our own interests. This implies that the
ethical thing to do, the morally right thing to do, may not be in our own
self-interest.

Let me give you a famous example, slightly updated, that illustrates this point. Suppose you meet a powerful being from another planet. The being makes you the following proposal: if you press the button I hold in my hand then I guarantee you that the following things will happen. First, pushing the button will cause you to be the sole winner of the $20 million lottery drawing tomorrow. Second, pushing the button will cause a 90-year-old man in the remote regions of Asia to die tomorrow of an apparent heart attack. He would not otherwise have died tomorrow, but you do not know him and no harm will ever come to you as a result of his death. Moreover, no one but you and I will ever know that you caused his death.

Would you push the button? It is certainly in your economic self-interest to do so, but I believe it would be completely unethical to do it. You have no right, no moral ground whatever, to cause the old man's death, even though pushing the button would be to your benefit. If this is correct, then the moral thing to do is not always the self-interested thing to do.

This poses a major problem for the idea that good ethics is good business—namely, assuming our own economic interests are closely tied to the interests of the firm we work for, what should be done if the ethical thing to do is not the best thing for the firm? What happens if being ethical actually causes economic harm to the firm?

One way to respond to the question is this. It may be true, someone might concede, that in some circumstances being ethical will cause harm, but in the long run it will be economically beneficial. So, in order to serve our long-term economic interests best, we should be ethical.

There is no doubt it would be convenient if in the long term it would always be in the economic interest of our firm for us to act ethically in our business dealings. Unfortunately, the world doesn't necessarily work that way. For one thing, there may be no long term. There is the possibility of bankruptcy. And in today's frenzied climate of mergers and takeovers, the corporation we work for could well vanish while we are on a lunch break. For another, surely if there is anything we can learn from 10,000 years of human history it is that it is simply not true that things always work out for the best. Sometimes, many times, they don't. So we may as well face it. There may be occasions when it is not in the best interest of our firm, either short term or long term, to do the morally right thing. What happens then?

That's a tough question, one I believe many of the advocates of ethics in corporations simply have not faced or perhaps have refused to face. And I suggest that when the crunch comes, when ethics does conflict with the interests of the firm, any program of corporate ethics that has not already faced up to this possibility is doomed to failure. If ethics is regarded merely as a means to profits, then if and when it harms rather than enhances profits, ethics will be the loser.

But there is another approach that some people seem to take to business ethics, one that apparently avoids the problem of what to do when ethics conflicts with the bottom line. Oddly enough, it begins with a denial that there is any connection between business and ethics at all. The argument goes something like this. Business transactions are essentially *amoral*; that is, the world of business cannot be said to be either moral or immoral. It simply makes no sense to apply words like "morally right" or "morally wrong" to business activities, just as it makes no sense to apply such words to the activities of social insects like ants or bees.

But why doesn't it make sense? Well, the reason it makes no sense to apply "right" and "wrong" to the actions of an ant is that ants are incapable of acting any way other than the way they do. They are not free to choose to do one thing rather than another, and since free choice is a necessary condition of moral behavior, it is pointless to say of an ant that what it did was morally right or wrong. It is a fact of nature that it couldn't have acted otherwise. For precisely the same sort of reason, the argument continues, it makes no sense to apply moral categories to human beings when they are engaged in business transactions. It is the nature of humans always to maximize their economic self-interest. We can't help it. It is our nature to be economically selfish. Thus when we see selfishness in the business world, we shouldn't be surprised. Nor should we say that it is either right or wrong. It is a fact of nature that we are totally self-interested in our business dealings just as it is a fact of nature that water freezes at 32°F or light travels at 186,000 miles per second.

This argument does not imply that we act only out of self-interest in all our relations with others; it only implies that we do so in our economic relations. But if it is true, it completely eliminates the problem of what we ought to do in cases where it seems that good ethics is not good business. The reason is simply that there is no such thing as ethics in business. There is only selfish human nature. Human beings act in their own economic self-interest, and that is all there is to it. So where there is a conflict between ethics in a business relationship and self-interest, self-interest will automatically win out.

Now there may seem to be a kind of contradiction here. I said earlier that some people seem to use the above sort of argument as an *approach* to business ethics. But if there isn't any connection between business and ethics at all, how is this possible?

Perhaps someone who accepted the argument would respond like this. When I say there is no such thing as ethics in our business relationships, that there is only self-interested business behavior, I don't mean to imply there are no generally accepted ethical rules that are used in business. Certainly there are ethical rules in business, but they are nothing other than a series of rules of thumb or guides for behavior that people have found usually serve their economic interests over the long term. For instance, there is the rule "it is wrong to tell a lie." What this rule means, once we understand it correctly within a business context, is that in general it is not in our economic self-interest to tell a lie. Understood this way it is obviously true. We live in a society in which it is usually in our economic interest to tell the truth. Consequently we have a rule that prohibits lying in business because it codifies behavior we have found useful. But we shouldn't take the rule to mean, as some people mistakenly do, that we absolutely should never tell a lie regardless of whether it is in our economic self-interest or not. So the solution to the problem is simple. The conflict between ethics and economic self-interest is not a real conflict; it is only an apparent one. Once we see that ethical rules as they apply in business are only guidelines that are generally but not always in our interest to follow, the conflict disappears.

Let us suppose for a moment that the view just described really is the one that underlies the "good ethics is good business" movement in the corporate world. If so, why are so many corporations initiating various kinds of ethics training programs? After all, if self-interest reigns in business, there doesn't seem to be much point to it. What, then, are corporations really trying to accomplish when they start ethics training programs for their employees? Could they be trying to convey a message like this? "You, the employees of the corporation, should follow generally accepted ethical rules since in the main it will be in the best interest of the corporation if you do so. Any exception to this is an upper-level management decision. That is, any decision to act in a way that is in the interests of the corporation but is contrary to ethical rules should be made, not by lower-level employees who may lack the knowledge and experience to truly gauge the best interests of the corporation, but the upper-level management."

Understood in this way the "good ethics is good business" movement is yet another version of an old, old story—management manipulation and control of employee behavior. It is just another way of making sure that the real power in the organization stays at the top. Notice that it also requires that employees identify their own interests with the interests of the corporation. When acting unethically would benefit the employee but possibly harm the corporation, the employee is told to act ethically. Thus these types of corporate ethics programs are manipulative since they try to get employees to act in ways contrary to what is thought to be the employees' own nature.

This, you might be thinking, is a very cynical view of ethics programs in business. Perhaps it is. Yet it may help explain some of the things that go on in the corporate world. One of them is the curious one-way direction of corporate ethics programs. Frequently they are directed almost entirely toward mid- and lower-level managers. These managers are instructed to behave ethically toward their peers, upper management, and people outside the corporation. But what the programs lack is a corresponding commitment from upper management to behave ethically toward their employees and other stakeholders in the corporation. This makes sense if upper-level managers do not consider themselves bound by ethical rules or not so strictly bound as lower-level employees. As we all know, upper management sometimes treats employees and other stakeholders in ways that many would consider unethical and then tries to explain away their actions by appealing to the interests of the firm. What they are implicitly saying in these cases is that the self-interest of the corporation takes precedence over the rights and interests of employees and other corporate stakeholders and that they, senior management, have the prerogative of setting aside such rights and interests in the name of corporate self-interest. But of course, if self-interest governs our economic behavior, what these managers are really doing is looking out for themselves.

An example of this sort of attitude toward ethics is the harsh treatment given people who blow the whistle on upper management. Even in corporations that have ethics programs whistle blowers are almost always hounded from the corporation, and their lives and reputations are systematically destroyed. If we understand ethics programs as another way for upper management to keep control, then it is easy to see the intention underlying these unfortunate events. It is management's way of reiterating that ethics applies only to lower-level employees and that upper management should not be measured by the same standards.

One problem with corporate ethics programs aimed primarily at controlling employee behavior is that they are, in my judgment, based on a false theory of human nature. There are no compelling reasons, either from economics or biology or psychology, to think that human beings really are like ants and that in their business dealings they really do act only out of self-interest. Human motivation is much more complex than this view of human nature would have us believe. However, even an ethics program based on a false theory may be of use to upper management. It might persuade some people to act in accordance with corporate policy who would not otherwise have done so. But I very much doubt that ethics programs intended to control the behavior of mid- and lower-level managers while exempting upper-level managers will be successful in the long term. Employees of a firm where such an ethics program is in place will soon realize that it is a hypocritical attempt by upper management to use ethical principles to its own advantage. And I suspect the employees will respond in exactly the way people have traditionally responded to these kinds of programs. They will try to subvert it every chance they get, if not by direct action, then by the sort of desultory and grudging compliance that sounds the death knell for almost all management programs that employees perceive as a form of exploitation.

So where does this leave us? Should we abandon ethics programs and proceed with business as usual? I believe that we should not do so, not because good ethics is good business but because we are morally required to adopt the moral point of view in *all* our dealings with other people. Now, to adopt the moral point of view is to acknowledge the relevance of moral considerations and accept the force of moral reasoning. And the moral point of view applies as much in business as in our other human relationships. We cannot justifiably set it aside simply because a relationship is a business one. Business does not confer any special grant of immunity from ethical behavior. It does not and cannot relieve us of our responsibilities as ethical beings.

My justification, then, for ethics in business is not business or economic justification since I do not believe that such a justification can successfully be defended. It is instead unabashedly an ethical one. The reason we should be concerned about ethics in business and the reason corporate ethics programs should be initiated is not because ethics is a means to some other end. It is because if we accept the moral point of view, as I believe we must, then ethics is a part of our lives that we cannot ignore or pretend to abandon without abandoning the very thing that differentiates us from the ants.

I do not mean to imply that all corporate ethics programs either suffer from a juvenile optimism about the beneficial economic effects of ethics or are simply a different way of making sure employees toe the corporate line. Many ethics programs have been carefully thought out and have support from managers who are genuinely concerned about ethical behavior. But I also believe there is disturbing tendency for corporations to adopt ethics programs for the mistaken reasons I discussed above and even worse, for no reason at all other than the fact that others are doing it. We should not assume, in fact it is dangerous to assume, that the ethical thing to do will always or even frequently coincide with the most profitable or competitive thing to do. Nor should we regard ethics as the newest method of controlling behavior. This does not mean that we can ignore ethics in the business world, but it does mean that ethics is not the quick fix that so many seem to believe it is.

References

Blanchard, Kenneth, and Norman Vincent Peale. 1988. *The Power of Ethical Management*. New York: William Morrow.

"Corporate Ethics: A Prime Business Asset." 1988. *Business Roundtable* Feb: 9-10.

Hennessy, Edward, L., Jr. 1986. "Business Ethics: Is it a Priority for Corporate America?" *The Magazine for Financial Executives* October: 19.

My thanks to W. Michael Hoffman, Ellen Hurley, Frank Reeves, Cheryl Ricci, and Wayne Wasserman for their comments on an earlier draft of this paper.

Who Are My Neighbors, and What Do I Owe Them?

Robert A. Eberle, M.B.A, M.S.I.A.
Associate Professor of Management
Hagan School of Business
Iona College
New Rochelle, New York
♦

The first part of a 10-part series, *Ethics in America*, was recently shown on PBS and deservedly attracted considerable interest and comment. The first program was introduced by Fred W. Friendly of Columbia University as an exploration of the fundamental question which faces each one of us, "Who are my neighbors, and what do I owe them?" It was titled "Do Unto Others." Essentially an attempt to understand "the personal relationships that bind us all together, parent and child, husband and wife, friend to friend, and friend to stranger," it proceeded to address admirably why we have "lost our sense of community."

The moderator, Professor Charles Ogletree of the Harvard Law School, was able to elicit widely divergent opinions from a distinguished panel on the extent to which each would voluntarily involve or disengage himself/herself in a series of situations that were superbly presented and role-played by Mr. Ogletree. A critical variable that influenced the amount of involvement, in terms of advice given, help extended, and sense of responsibility, was the overall demographics of the aid-seeker (age, sex, status, member of family, etc.), all of which tended to reduce or enhance the possible perceived relationship of "fellow human being." In management terminology the bottom line was that Emory S. Bogardus and the concept of a "social-distance scale" is as relevant today as it was when he introduced it in 1925.

The question of whether bystanders to a crime will become involved and go to the aid of the victim received an ugly answer in the case of Kitty Genovese more than a generation ago. The nation was shocked to learn that she had been attacked and murdered in a densely populated, middle-class neighborhood in Queens, New York, in the late evening. A subsequent investigation determined that her screams for help had lasted for nearly a half-hour and had been heard by approximately 25 apartment dwellers, none of whom felt personally responsible and all of whom assumed that someone else would become involved.

The issue of the individual versus the group ethic was more recently addressed by Bowen H. McCoy in "The Parable of the Sadhu" (1983). As the first recipient of the Morgan Stanley sabbatical program, he had elected to scale the Himalayas in Nepal. In Mr. McCoy's words:

> During the Nepal hike, something occurred that has had a powerful impact on my thinking about corporate ethics....

Just after daybreak, while we rested at 15,500 feet, one of the New Zealanders, who had gone ahead, came staggering down toward us with a body slung across his shoulders. He dumped the almost naked barefoot body of an Indian holy man—a sadhu— at my feet. He had found the pilgrim lying on the ice, shivering and suffering from hypothermia. I cradled the sadhu's head and laid him out on the rocks. The New Zealander was angry. He wanted to get across the pass before the bright sun melted the snow. He said, "Look I've done what I can. You have porters and sherpa guides. You care for him. We're going on!"

Briefly, the responsibility of caring for the sadhu was passed from one group of climbers to the next, as each group, after providing some aid, pushed on for the summit. Only after reconstructing the decision-making process that had occurred did they realize with great individual guilt that the sadhu had probably been left to die.

In his *Harvard Business Review* article Mr. McCoy drew parallels between what had happened and life in the corporate world. Needless to say, his insights provoked great attention and discussion at the time:

Had we mountaineers been free of physical and mental stress caused by the effort and high altitude, we might have treated the sadhu differently. Yet, isn't stress the real test of personal and corporate values? The instant decisions executives make under pressure reveal the most about personal and corporate character.

Among the many questions that occur to me when pondering my experience are: What are the practical limits of moral imagination and vision? Is there a collective or institutional ethic beyond the ethics of the individual? At what level of effort or commitment can one discharge one's ethical responsibilities?

In December 1988 an article appeared in the *New York Times* that was appropriately titled, "Not My Problem." The author, Michael Lazar, a vice president of a medium-sized industrial firm in Connecticut, was knocked unconscious as he left a pharmacy by a falling iron security gate. It was broad daylight in a moderately affluent town in Westchester County, New York, and Mr. Lazar described himself as having been "well dressed, shaven, clean with no suggestion of drunkenness, or addiction." His cries for help, since he was unable to get up, went unheeded by the proprietor of the pharmacy and his helper. In addition, 15 to 20 passersby briefly looked at him with curiosity before moving on. Finally, someone called the 911 number and summoned help. His questions are as disturbing as those raised by the previous two cases:

Could it be that people are afraid to become involved in a potential lawsuit? What is behind this don't-bother-me disease that is spreading from the Bowery to the small towns of our country? How pervasive is it? Will it eventually spread to farms and rural areas? Has it already?

In the fall of 1988, after retiring from IBM and 20 years of teaching MBA management courses at Iona, I welcomed the opportunity to interact with undergraduate juniors, aged 19 to 23, in the course *Human Factors*. Midway through the term the text contained an exercise that was similar to ones that I had used during my years as a trainer in IBM's management development function (Schermerhorn, et al. 1988, 94-95). To stimulate class involvement, I asked the students to read the case and rank each of the protagonists on a most-least scale with respect to the individual being "Objectionable/Reprehensible/Offensive." Before examining the values and attitudes of the students, the reader may wish to examine his/her own reactions in order to be able to draw a comparison with those of the subjects.

The Alligator River Story

Purpose: To help you realize the different perceptions, values, and attitudes that people have on common, everyday happenings.

There lived a woman named Abigail who was in love with a man named Gregory. Gregory lived on the shore of a river. Abigail lived on the opposite shore of the same river. The river that separated the two lovers was teeming with man-eating alligators. Abigail wanted to cross the river to be with Gregory. Unfortunately, the bridge had been washed out by a flood the previous week. So she went to ask Sinbad, a riverboat captain, to take her across. He said he would be glad to if she would consent to go to bed with him prior to the voyage. She promptly refused and went to a friend named Ivan to explain her plight. Ivan did not want to get involved at all in the situation. Abigail felt her only alternative was to accept Sinbad's terms. Sinbad fulfilled his promise to Abigail and delivered her into the arms of Gregory.

When Abigail told Gregory about her amorous escapade in order to cross the river, Gregory cast her aside with disdain. Heartsick and rejected, Abigail turned to Slug with her tale of woe. Slug, feeling compassion for Abigail, sought out Gregory and beat him brutally. Abigail was overjoyed at the sight of Gregory getting his due. As the sun set on the horizon, people heard Abigail laughing at Gregory.

Table I contains the results of the total student sample (n = 23). In Table II the replies for the female students are similarly shown (n = 9); and in Table

III the responses of the male students are indicated (n =). The number that appears in the cell of a given matrix indicates the number of students who selected the character named on that row as most culpable, the students who considered the character second most culpable of the five characters appears in the second column, etc. For example, in Table I, the "14" which appears in the first row, first column indicates that 14 students selected Sinbad as most reprehensible.

Most Objectionable/Reprehensible/Offensive Rankings						
Character	First(5)	Second(4)	Third(3)	Fourth(2)	Fifth(1)	Mean
Sinbad	14	3	4	1	1	4.2
Abigail	7	8	5	3	-	3.8
Gregory	1	7	5	9	1	2.9
Slug	1	2	8	6	6	2.4
Ivan	-	1	4	3	15	1.6

TABLE I. Total Student Responses (N = 23)

Most Objectionable/Reprehensible/Offensive Rankings						
Character	First(5)	Second(4)	Third(3)	Fourth(2)	Fifth(1)	Mean
Abigail	5	3	1	-	-	4.4
Sinbad	4	1	3	1	-	3.9
Gregory	-	3	3	3	-	3.0
Slug	-	-	4	4	1	1.9
Ivan	-	-	1	-	8	1.2

TABLE II. Female Student Responses (N = 9)

Most Objectionable/Reprehensible/Offensive Rankings						
Character	First(5)	Second(4)	Third(3)	Fourth(2)	Fifth(1)	Mean
Sinbad	10	2	1	-	1	4.4
Abigail	2	5	4	3	-	3.4
Gregory	1	4	2	6	1	2.9
Slug	1	2	4	2	5	2.4
Ivan	-	1	3	3	7	1.9

TABLE III. Male Student Responses (N = 14)

The results indicate that male students and female students differ on which character they hold most reprehensible; the females select Abigail while the males select Sinbad. The remaining characters are rank ordered identically by male and female students.

The most striking statistic, and most troubling one in view of the above discussion and previous cases, is the degree of unanimity in exonerating Ivan from any guilt for not becoming involved. In the context of the exercise it can be viewed as particularly disturbing since he was specifically asked for help, in the form of advice, and elected to disengage himself from the situation.

Some representative comments shed light on how the students view the responsibilities, perhaps duties, of involvement versus the wisdom of "keeping one's distance":

Ivan was wrong, but at least he didn't hurt anyone.

Ivan was smart and did not get involved.

Ivan is least reprehensible since he didn't do anything wrong—he just didn't want to get involved.

He is the least offensive because he just simply did not get involved.

Least because he didn't get involved and didn't actually *do* anything.

Ivan did absolutely nothing but stand on the sideline, so he can't be faulted for his actions because he didn't take any.

Smart man...stayed out of the situation.

In fairness, a handful of subjects did fault Ivan, though slightly, as "being a bad friend" and "for not trying to help." The overall attitudes and values, however, are quite clearly portrayed by the data.

When I reviewed these results with my students, I chose not to engage in polemics (to avoid the risk of becoming too involved?) but did raise the issue that Ivan had the potential power to influence and alter the chain of events, if he had decided to become involved. A few weeks after that discussion, the article by Mr. Lazar appeared in the *New York Times* and I shared that with them, as we had done with "The Parable of the Sadhu."

In a few years they will graduate, enter the corporate world, begin to raise families, and become members of their communities. As a member of "the nothing generation" which graduated from the universities during the 1950s, I find it impossible to hold up to them as examples how we handled "the individual, agonizing decisions" (as a panelist on the *Ethics in America* program termed it) that we faced.

I am sure that they will do no worse than we did, and I apologize to them for passing on the deterioration of values that began long before they were born. We wish them well.

References

Bogardus, E. S. 1925. "Measuring Social Distances." *Journal of Applied Sociology* 9:299-308.

Lazar, Michael. 1988. "Not My Problem." *New York Times* Sept. 30, 1988.

McCoy, Bowen H. 1983. "The Parable of the Sadhu." *Harvard Business Review* 5:103.

Schermerhorn, John R., et al. 1988. *Managing Organizational Behavior.* 3rd ed. New York: John Wiley and Sons.

Performance Appraisal:
Between Scylla and Charybdis

Charles P. Duffy, C.F.C., Ed.D.
Assistant Professor of Management
Hagan School of Business
Iona College
New Rochelle, New York

Kenneth M. Frawley, B.S.
Corporate Director of Training and Development
Nynex Corporation
New York, New York

◆

Scylla is the name of a rock on the Italian side of the Strait of Messina, opposite the whirlpool Charybdis, personified by Homer as a sea monster who devours sailors. "Between Scylla and Charybdis" is to be in a spot where avoidance of one danger exposes one to destruction by the other.

The evaluation of individual performance in the work place is a function the importance of which management has long recognized. The periodic and effective review of one's subordinates has long been regarded as a significant factor in contributing to individual satisfaction and organizational effectiveness. Ideally, it presents both challenge and opportunity, but in reality it too often offers headache as well. For many managers it offers the proverbial position between the rock and the hard place. This review proposes to analyze the practice of performance appraisal, what bears criticism and what holds promise. Leadership in business continues to seek a greater understanding of performance appraisal as it attempts to steer between the Scylla of a process too often poorly done and the Charybdis of a process not always achieving its purpose and promise.

THE ROLE OF APPRAISAL

Productivity improvement is of major concern to all organizations as they seek to increase productivity through improving the performance of their human resources. Managers have long been aware of the fact that of all the resources available to them, the human resource is the one that is the least predictable, the one used much less effectively or efficiently than the other resources, and the only one that over time can experience significant growth. In large part the management literature and practice tend to focus on people, the only resource capable of innovation, creativity, and adaptation and certainly the most difficult element to manage. It is this complex, variable and dynamic element that continues to challenge organizational efforts to purposefully appraise performance.

Performance appraisal serves at least five important organizational functions (Cherrington 1987, 237). The first role of performance appraisal is to "guide personnel actions," such as hiring, firing, and promoting. Good performance data are needed not only to make personnel decisions but also to defend them. Without such data, personnel decisions have to be made randomly, subjectively, and often politically, actions which present concern for both legality and ethics. The second role of performance appraisal is to "reward" employees. Reinforcements such as money, promotion, and recognition should be based on performance. Without performance data, everyone has to be rewarded equally, or rewards have to be distributed subjectively—conditions readily perceived as inequitable. A third role is to provide individuals with information for their own "personal development." Accurate and timely performance feedback facilitates the learning of new behavior, and most individuals want to know how well they are doing and where they need to improve. The fourth role of performance appraisal is to "identify training needs" for the organization. This form of management development provides information regarding which individuals could benefit from training for increased responsibilities. The fifth role of performance appraisal is to "integrate human resource planning." The appraisals form the foundation for an orderly development of a human-resource planning system that integrates information regarding new positions to be created within an organization, the skills of present employees, their potential for development, and the developmental experiences they need. To these five functions we add purposes of motivation and communication, and the universe of performance appraisal begins to show its complexity and the problems posed and the criticism it encounters in attempting to satisfy the multitude of purposes effectively.

These collective purposes of performance appraisal are readily subsumed under three general categories: *reward, development,* and *planning.* It is the ability of performance appraisal systems to serve these several purposes effectively that generates much of the criticism that surrounds the practice. Appraisal systems are based on a philosophy that individual performance can be measured and can be improved, that the process of effective assessment does serve to motivate individuals, and that in consequence the organization is more productive and better served. In truth a single approach to performance appraisal does not easily serve the variety of intended purposes. Using appraisals to develop and to reward and to plan interchangeably does not separate the issues. When we say we have a developmental approach and we use it to reward, we have made them interchangeable. It is difficult even to get one's mind to separate these factors, so concern persists that considerable distance remains between promise and practice.

CONFLICT SURROUNDING APPRAISAL

Most organizations of significant size have some sort of formal appraisal process. In organizations of every size managers do make judgments regarding the performance of their subordinates, if not through formal process, then through some informal approach. This review of performance appraisal relates to practices in organizations which observe some formal and regular system in evaluating the performance of personnel. Such a system provides information on organizational needs as a basis for personnel decisions relating to wage and salary adjustments, individual development, selection of personnel for training, and manpower planning. Over time a variety of performance-appraisal approaches have been developed to meet these organizational and individual needs. Like the perfect vacuum, no one system or approach does exist, or perhaps can exist, that entirely satisfies all situations and serves all purposes. With the intent of making an existing appraisal process more functional or because of widespread dissatisfaction with a current approach, many organizations regularly engage in efforts at fine-tuning or radically changing their formal appraisal process. Unfortunately, changes frequently amount to little more than new packaging, labeling, and instrumentation with no essential changes in the substance, approach, or use of the process. There persists a considerable amount of disenchantment with the entire performance-appraisal process.

A discussion of performance-appraisal systems is prone to generate a degree of confusion without some clear definitions of terminology. The terms "appraisal," "assessment," and "audit" are distinct in both purpose and process. Baker (1988, 3) states that "performance appraisal" involves the comparison of the observed performance of an employee with a performance standard which describes what the employee is expected to do in terms of behaviors and results. Such a system involves a series of actions that include planning what the employees are to do, insuring an understanding of these expectations, assisting employees to perform up to standard, and providing information to assist and support management decisions. The system generally includes a formal performance review between a supervisor and an employee about the level of the employee's performance. "Assessment" refers to the process of judging the potential of an employee or job applicant for future job assignments or established range of responsibilities. The assessment of potential is not considered to be a part of the appraisal system, but it is a part of the selection process for other management systems such as the promotion system, the career-development system, and the hiring of new employees. "Audit" is the term used to describe the process of determining whether the system as designed is implemented and adheres to established organizational policies and procedures. An audit is regarded as a part of the control subsystem that seeks to determine the effectiveness of the appraisal process.

A basic conflict in performance appraisal revolves around the different purposes that the system is required to serve. Frequently, a single approach or even one instrument is intended to satisfy distinct goals of rewarding and developing individuals and personnel planning. Such conflict is at the cutting edge of the continuing challenge that management experiences in attempting to integrate productivity goals and expectations of the formal organization with the individual goals and need dispositions of the informal organizations.

Individuals generally are concerned with receiving information on how they are doing. It is of personal interest and career significance to obtain feedback indicating where one stands with one's superiors and the organization and to learn how to improve one's performance in order to obtain important rewards in the organization, such as pay and promotions. This is the ideal of the situation which often differs from reality and practice. What an individual does not welcome is negative feedback that does not affirm one's self image as being competent. Because of the discomfort that surrounds both the offering and receiving of negative feedback, such communication is frequently either avoided or tempered so as to avoid confrontation. Supervisors are in a position to evaluate their subordinates' performance all day and every day. If appropriate positive and negative feedback are not shared on a regular basis, it becomes no easier to share both on the occasion of an annual performance review. Regarding negative feedback, it may constitute sufficient surprise to heighten defensiveness and lessen the relationship. This feeling is intensified when managers lack the confidence that can come from training in giving feedback. The problem is further compounded if the organizational culture supports a norm of conflict avoidance to avoid the risk of openness concerning negative feedback.

Such concern for conflict avoidance is responsible for much of the criticism that surrounds the performance-appraisal process and which has adversely affected its use. These criticisms refer to what are classified as the common errors in performance appraisals and which make it difficult if not impossible to separate the good performers from the poor performers or compare ratings from different raters. These errors constitute problems that significantly reduce the effectiveness of the process, if not render it useless.

Cherrington (1987) describes these criticisms which represent legitimate problems that need to be addressed. Appraisals can pose an individual threat. Many people, especially low performers, are uncomfortable being evaluated. Some supervisors do not like to evaluate their subordinates and feel threatened to have to explain their evaluations. Supervisors argue that evaluating their subordinates places them in a position of role conflict by forcing them to be judge, coach, and friend at the same time. In many instances "performance" is difficult to define, especially for jobs that do not produce a quantifiable product. These conditions contribute to several effects.

The leniency effect is the grouping of ratings at the positive end of the performance scale regardless of actual levels of performance. Its opposite, the strictness effect, tends to evaluate the same performance levels much more unfavorably. Some evaluators create the central-tendency effect by giving all average ratings to avoid "sticking their necks out" by identifying marginal or outstanding performance. The halo effect occurs when one positive or negative characteristic about a person strongly influences all other attitudes about the person. The sequencing effect is present when one individual's performance may be influenced by the relative performance of the preceding individual. An individual might receive a favorable evaluation

when following a poor performer and an unfavorable evaluation when following an outstanding performer. The recency effect occurs when the rater is
unduly influenced by the employee's most recent positive or negative behavior. Additional criticism relates to interrater reliability where two
evaluators observing the same behavior may disagree and give different
ratings.

In some performance-appraisal systems the number of above-average
ratings has to be balanced by an equal number of below-average ratings.
Such a policy creates a zero-sum problem since some individuals are forced
to receive low ratings in spite of how well they actually performed
(Cherrington 1987). Organizations understandably do control monies allocated for pay increases, and managers often are held to a salary budget that
doesn't accommodate increases generated by all employees achieving all
their goals. Gamesmanship comes into play, and managers are forced to
reduce the goal achievements to fit the budget allocation. Such a practice
of forced distribution of ratings to insure compliance with budgetary alloca-
tions erodes the credibility of the performance-appraisal system and causes
employees to lose the motivation to complete their goals.

There is no provision to accommodate the possibility of all workers
performing at the "superior" level. Instead, managers are forced to make
person-to-person comparisons and rank people in the same organizational
unit with respect to one another's performance. The practice produces rank-
ings of "above-average," "average," and "below average" that do not accurately reflect individual performance or degree of commitment to organizational objectives. In such instances cooperative approaches such as MBO
become charades, and appraisals are neither equitable nor personally
gratifying.

When evaluations are largely subjective and rest almost entirely on the im-
pressions of supervisory personnel, there is the additional potential for bias. Subjective evaluations are prone to discrimination, a practice devoid of ethical,
moral, or legal defense. Performance evaluations or ratings as those mentioned
above have always been susceptible to subjective variables that do not relate to
actual job performance evaluation. An empirical study by Gallagher (1978)
tested the hypothesis that the stated purpose for which performance evaluations
are to be used is an additional nonperformance variable that can significantly
affect the evaluation of on-the-job performance. A single performance should not
be used for different purposes since the stated purpose of the evaluation can affect
the actual performance rating. The problem is more acute when appraisals are
used to serve several purposes that are not compatible with one another. If the
rater knows that an individual is being evaluated for a salary increase, he or she
may decide the individual should receive the salary increase and adjust the
performance evaluation accordingly. If this biased evaluation then is used for
some other purpose, such as determining whether the individual should be laid
off or given additional training, the person who was evaluated may not be laid
off or receive the additional training since he or she was given a high performance
rating. On the other hand, if an appraisal is made to determine who should

receive additional training in a particular area, the rater may emphasize an individual's weaknesses in that area. If the same evaluation is then used as a criterion in a promotion or salary-increase decision, the individual may receive less than equitable treatment. Conducting different kinds of performance evaluations for different purposes would begin to address this dimension of the problem of bias.

A major purpose of performance appraisal is to help the employee "develop." The appraisal instrument used generally includes two or three areas requiring the manager to identify the employee's development needs, write a plan for the development, and comment further on the employee's career interests and potential. These steps are not easily addressed and therefore, are often poorly addressed. Managers experience difficulty in defining development needs in skill-specific terms, and diagnosis often ends up being statements about employee character or attitude. The plans recommended to address these development needs can be equally as imprecise, with broad suggestions for "training programs" as the remedy or statements like "time in the field would help." Development planning needs to be handled separately from work planning, compensation review, and manpower planning. It has its own dynamic and requires a different appraisal instrument, one that is skills oriented and not results oriented. Quite literally, the form follows the function. The development discussion engages the self-interest of the employee for his or her own growth and development. The interaction is more inclined to be cooperative than confrontational.

Avoidance in one form or other is a common abuse of performance appraisal. In some instances managers simply ignore all or part of the appraisal process (King 1984, 139). The appraisal form may be neglected and not sent in or some variation of this theme. Some fill it out but never talk to the employee about it. Some fill it out, discuss it, and send it in but never really appraise the employee's performance. They just make sure to say mostly positive things so there is no pain involved for the manager or the employee, and everyone is "satisfied." Some simply give the form to the employee and say, "Here, you fill it out, and I'll sign it and send it in."

In some instances the process of performance appraisal becomes an end in itself. Managers are told they must appraise their employees, complete the required paper work, and offer recommendations about job actions. When recommendations are not acted upon, the signal sent to managers is that the appraisal system isn't worth the effort they have put into it. If the completed forms are not reviewed but simply filed in the employee's personnel folder and that is the end of it, then mangers question the value of taking careful time in filling out the forms.

It is evident that the potential for error is great. The perfect appraisal system has not been developed, largely because no one yet knows how to factor out human error. Some errors substantially reduce the effectiveness of the performance-appraisal system and expose it to charges of discrimination. While these criticisms represent legitimate problems, they need to be regarded as problems that can be solved.

TOWARD IMPROVING THE APPRAISAL PROCESS

Effective performance appraisal can be one of the most powerful tools that managers have for improving the performance of individual employees and revitalizing productivity. Because of this potential, every performance-appraisal system should be subject to periodic review. The evaluation of the system is an appropriate control measure when the system is regarded to be functioning effectively and even more so when the system is adjudged ineffective and its weaknesses tolerated. Many methods have been developed to evaluate complex systems. The general intent is to see whether the system as designed has been implemented and to ascertain its degree of effectiveness in achieving the stated objectives. This review frequently results in minor adjustments to fine tune the system. Major changes in the system design or a decision to adopt a new system generally occur only when there has been significant dissatisfaction with the existing system at the outset of the review process.

Baker (1988) recommends a comprehensive appraisal system in preference to methods that evaluate only a small portion of the system at one time, and he identifies discrepancy evaluation (Provus 1971) as a model particularly well suited for use in evaluating appraisal systems. Provus sees evaluation as the comparison of performance against standard, and he divides the process into stages: 1) document and evaluate the system design; 2) determine if the system is being implemented according to the design; 3) determine if the objectives of each part of the system are being achieved; and 4) determine if the system is producing usable interim and terminal outputs that meet the needs of the organization. Baker (1988) states that while organizations regularly evaluate other types of management systems, they have generally neglected the evaluation of performance-appraisal systems. The primary reason for this neglect has been the lack of a suitable method of evaluation.

Management commitment is vital to an effective performance-appraisal program. All members of the management team need to understand appraisal's purposes and should agree that it is critical for management to participate in and support the system (Regel and Hollmann 1987, 78). In fact it would be helpful for managers themselves to be evaluated on how capably they carry out their performance appraisal responsibilities. The manager might be asked what he or she has done toward the development of staff through performance appraisal and be rewarded accordingly. If nothing has been done, this would then reflect on his or her own performance review.

Since most performance-appraisal systems in current use have multiple objectives, managers are forced to assume dual roles—one of a judge and one of a counselor. It is difficult if not impossible for any one system to address multiple objectives effectively and for any one person to play two different roles simultaneously. The effectiveness of the performance-appraisal process could be increased if the process were to be divided into three distinct processes to meet three very different sets of objectives (Truell 1983,

19). One objective is counseling. This would be an ongoing system to communicate to employees how they are doing on the job and to help employees improve their performance in the future. A second objective is salary determination. This is a periodic system to meet the organization's need to keep salary levels abreast of changes in the worth of jobs in the labor market and to reward employees for performance. A third objective is manpower planning. This is a periodic system to meet the organization's need to assess the overall strengths and weaknesses of its human resources to meet future requirements.

Comprehensive annual performance appraisals are of questionable value. While managers must conform to an appraisal system over which they have little or no control, this should not preclude any modification of the format of annual or semiannual evaluations which lead to a low probability of behavior change. The practice of conducting more frequent appraisals lends itself to a variety of structures. One approach might have appraisals conducted three times a year, twice "not for real" and a final review that would go into the employee's personnel folder. On the occasion of the first and second interim reviews, managers might be more inclined to include critical comment on performance where such is warranted. The objective would be to improve performance in specific areas, and the approach is decidedly developmental. Managers might be more willing to tell the employee what they hesitate to put into the employee's file. The follow-up reviews would examine the degree of improved performance. With respect to the positive aspects of such review and when the exchange is entirely positive, the communication serves to support behavior. A procedure that would include more frequent appraisals would lessen the onus that annual performance appraisal places on managers, considerably lessen the elements of surprise and anxiety that characterize the review process for subordinates, and might result in more honest and effective appraisals.

Rater training can have a positive impact upon the appraisal system. All managers require training in performance appraisal. Newly appointed managers should receive basic appraisal training that is skill oriented and which provides a sound conceptual foundation for the practices involved. The training should extend beyond the more traditional approach to performance-appraisal training in which attention is directed toward how to use the appraisal form, how to address possible rating errors such as "halo" or "central tendency," and how to conduct appraisal interviews (Shneier, Beatty, and Baird 1986, 78). A required, formal training program of perhaps two full days duration would also focus on procedures for setting and measuring objectives and on approaches for developing subordinates through work assignments. Even experienced managers can benefit from periodic retraining and updating whenever major parts of the appraisal system are changed. Such training signals the importance the organization attributes to the function and might substantially improve the reliability of interrater appraisals.

Performance appraisal is indeed a complex, difficult, time-consuming, often discomforting, but exceedingly valuable management tool. It is an exercise that can have substantial impact on productivity and individual satisfaction. To realize its rich promise, organizations need to steer carefully between its Scylla and its Charybdis.

References

Baker, Joe, Jr. 1988. *Causes of Failure in Performance Appraisal.* New York: Quorum Books.

Cherrington, David J. 1987. *Personnel Management.* Dubuque: William C. Brown.

Gallagher, Michael C. 1978. "More Bias in Performance Evaluation?" *Personnel* 55.4: 35-50.

King, Patricia. 1984. *Performance Planning & Appraisal.* New York: McGraw-Hill.

Provus, Malcolm. 1971. *Discrepancy Evaluation for Education Program Improvement and Assessment.* Berkeley: McCutchen.

Regel, Roy W., and Robert W. Hollmann. 1987. "Gauging Performance Objectively." *Personnel Administrator* 32.6: 75-78.

Schneier, Craig Eric, Richard W. Beatty, and Lloyd S. Baird. 1986. "Creating a Performance Management System." *Training and Development Journal* 40.5: 74-79.

Truell, George F. 1983. *Performance Appraisal: Current Issues and New Directions.* Buffalo: PAT.

How Do Corporate Managers Shape Public Policy Issues?

Norman Bowie, Ph.D.
Center for the Study of Values
University of Delaware
Newark, Delaware

◆

Public policy is too important to be left up to government or interest groups alone. Many of the adverse consequences of government regulation formulated in the 1960s and 1970s might have been avoided if business had been more active in its formulation. Business has a responsibility to participate in the public policy process and help solve the nation's economic and social problems.

Rogene A. Buchholz
Essentials of Public Policy for Management

I

Business is probably more involved in the formation of public policy than any other profession. Business interests in Washington are represented by the National Association of Manufacturers (NAM), the Chamber of Commerce of the United States, and by the various trade associations, e.g., the American Petroleum Institute, the National Automobile Dealers Association, and the U.S. Brewers Association. To give some idea of the size and power of these organizations, consider the following statistics. The NAM's member firms account for 75% of the nation's industrial capacity. The United States Chamber of Commerce has a membership of 154,000, most of which are corporations. The nation's capital is now the headquarters for 1,500 trade associations and the number is likely to grow. Business also affects public policy through its extensive lobbying activities, both individual and through Political Action Committees (PACs) (Buchholz 1985, 233, 236).

Perhaps the organization most concerned with general matters of public policy is the Business Roundtable. Although the Business Roundtable is fairly new (established in 1972) and fairly small (membership of 200 chief executive officers), its influence is substantial. Many of the acknowledged leaders of American business are or have been members of the Roundtable. The bulk of the work done by the Roundtable is accomplished in task forces. The broad range of issues concerned by the task forces is seen in Table I.

TABLE I
THE BUSINESS ROUNDTABLE TASK FORCES
1983

Accounting Principles	Government Regulation
Antitrust	International Trade and Investment
Construction Cost Effectiveness	National Health
Corporate Responsibility	Product Liability
Employment Policy	Social Security and Pensions
Energy Users	Taxation
Environment	Tort Liability Issues
Federal Budget	(Buchholz 1985, 236)

II

But surely there is a difference between affecting public policy so that public policy will be favorable to business interests and affecting public policy so that the general interest will be served. While everyone will concede that business tries to affect public policy so that business interests will be enhanced, many believe that business does little if anything to promote the public good or the general welfare. To put the matter more crudely, many believe that attempts by business to affect public policy are inherently selfish.

Before assessing that charge, a distinction must be drawn between attempts to use public policy to support specific industries and attempts to improve the business climate in general. While the former is clearly self-interested and often opposed by competing industries, the latter policy, business persons argue, is not simply self-interested. What is good for business (a good business climate) is good for the public. Moreover, business persons are not alone in their assessment. The public apparently believes that a favorable economic climate is the most important goal of public policy. After all, the most important determinant of election outcomes seems to be the economic climate. When the economy is good, incumbents do well; when the economy is not good, incumbents are usually in trouble. The remainder of this paper will consider only attempts by business to influence public policy by improving the business climate in general or by achieving some other public good. Attempts to influence public policy for the benefit of specific industries will be ignored.

III

There are two competing philosophies as to how business contributes to the public good. The classical view contends that the public good is enhanced when goods and services are produced which turn a profit for stockholders. Hence public policy which allows business to be profitable is in the public good. The less government interferes with business the better. Moreover, since attempts by business to solve social problems or to do good in other ways interfere with its profit-making function, it is better for society if business sticks to its job of making a profit and leaves concern for the broader social good to others. In other words, since the pursuit of profit leads to a social good, profit making is an inherently moral activity.

The scholarly statement of this position is best expressed in the following quotation.

> Frequently when it is suggested that business has moral duties and obligations in addition to or even in potential competition with making a profit, spokespersons for business respond that the pursuit of profit legitimately takes priority over such external and idealistic moral expectations. But if one attends carefully to the tone of such assertions, their seriousness and intensity, one begins to suspect that making a profit is itself seen as a moral obligation, that it is being suggested that for a business knowingly to compromise its capacity to make a profit even in the pursuit of supposedly higher goals such as social responsibility would be immoral. This would be seen as a betrayal of the investors who entrusted their wealth to the business precisely to make a profit, and/or as a culpable weakening of the force which drives the entire economic system, the pursuit of profit. Thus it may be that the persistent and conscientious pursuit of profit is perceived as and so should be treated as one element in business' actual morality. (Camenish 1983, 72)

But this quotation by a scholar does not capture the intensity of the business person's view that the pursuit of profit for stockholders is an essential moral activity.

> Business is the most responsible institution by far. I resent Ralph Nader calling his organization a public service organization. My company is a public service institution.

> The American free enterprise system is not perfect, yet it has produced more benefits than any other system in history. We are the healthiest, wealthiest, best educated, most generous nation in the history of the world.

> The objectives of business and the achievement of social goals are the same. Without business, there is no money, no resources, no environmental protection.

> We believe our goals are compatible with the best interests in society.

Our role is what it has always been: to meet material needs. That is our special area of competence. We are not responsible for establishing society's goals or values or for changing social behavior. By providing a right product in a right manner, business fulfills its responsibility for society. (qtd. in Silk and Vogel 1976, 129,131,132,136)

But is it always true that what is good for business in general is good for the public? Does the power of business bring with it special responsibilities to help resolve social ills? The posing of these questions has led several business persons and academics to adopt an alternative theory of business's responsibility for the public good. That theory, which I shall call the broad theory of corporate responsibility for the public good, states: in addition to seeking profits for stockholders, corporations have additional responsibilities to society and a broader constituency to serve than that of stockholders alone.

Although the broad view is short on specific suggestions as to how society should be helped, its negative thesis is strong and clear. Maximization of stockholder wealth is not sufficient for meeting corporate responsibility to the public good; indeed, on occasion emphasizing stockholder wealth at the expense of other duties is irresponsible.

There are other important contrasts between the two theories as well. At the center of professional ethics is the professional-client relationship, e.g., the doctor-patient relationship. In the classical view the one and only client is the stockholder. In the broader view any corporate stakeholder is a client. A stakeholder is a member of any group without whose support the organization would cease to exist. The traditional stakeholders include stockholders, employees, customers, suppliers, lenders. (The local community is often added as another stakeholder.) There are many more clients under the broad view.

Adherents to the two views often have different motives for moral conduct (conduct in behalf of the public interest). Adherents to the classical view are motivated to do well—well for themselves and well for the company. All business people are similarly motivated, and by the invisible hand, the self-interested behavior of individual firms is coordinated by market forces to produce the good for all. Doing good is achieved by doing well.

Adherents to the broad view are motivated to do good. If a manager emphasizes the production and distribution of *quality* products that customers *need* and if she maintains a *good working environment* for those who manufacture the product and if she is *honest* and *fair* with suppliers and lenders, then both the manager and the firm will be profitable. Doing well results from acting on the motive to do good. To the extent that managers are motivated by a desire to serve others, that service motive is found in adherents to the broad philosophy. The service motive is most apparent in a business person's relationship to customers. However, in serving others, the business person expects to do well.

Although these two positions differ on the relationship between doing good and doing well, they share the assumption that the two are related. Neither position considers in depth the situation where a firm can do well by not doing good or even by doing harm. Both views have been criticized for having an inadequate conception of the public good. Adherents to the broad management philosophy are criticized for having a merely instrumental view of the public good. They do good only because it helps them do well. There is nothing intrinsically valuable about service. Adherents to the classical view are often criticized as either intellectually dishonest or intellectually naive. An appeal to an invisible hand which produces public good from self-interested action is nothing more than an elaborate justification for selfish behavior. Certainly adherents to the classical view are not motivated to do good. It may be worth noting that many other professionals who allegedly put service to clients first have been criticized for being hypocritical. The general public clearly believes lawyers and doctors are in it for the money rather than to serve clients, and the general public's attitude has spread and is spreading to the other professions.

Another difference between the two views is that subscribers to the classical view are more likely to believe that following the law is sufficient for socially responsible conduct. A general rule of thumb is that if conduct is not illegal, it is morally permissible. Under the broad view, adherence to law is only the first step in socially responsible conduct. If economic conditions are bad, laying employees off is legally permitted, but for IBM, at least so far, it is not morally permitted. Many firms advertise products that "exceed government standards," whereas Ford's true claim that the Pinto met government standards fell on deaf ears. Ford's failure to go beyond the legal minimum and its use of cost-benefit analysis to accept cost savings at the expense of human lives were found morally wanting and were punished in the marketplace.

Although managers in the classical view do accept law as the proper conduct for corporations, many go far beyond what is legally required as individuals. There is a long tradition of volunteerism among supporters of the classical tradition. Charitable contributions have long been recognized, but there is a philanthropic tradition among classically oriented business executives. A contemporary scholar and foundation executive, Robert Payton, defines philanthropy "as an umbrella term to cover all types of private giving for public purposes" (Payton 1985, 2). Payton distinguishes philanthropy from charity by pointing out that philanthropy is designed to improve the life of the community through generally large, carefully rationalized, impersonal, and spontaneous gifts directed to the future. Classicists believe philanthropic gifts should come from individuals and most do. Broad-view managers believe that corporations as corporations have philanthropic obligations. In 1983 corporations did give $3.1 billion (Payton 1985, 2). Since classicists believe the obligation of a manager is to the stockholder, the manager's primary client, they believe that corporations as corporations do not have charitable or philanthropic obligations. Those corporate funds belong to the stockholder. Adherents to the broad view do accept *corporate* philanthropic obligations, in part because they believe philanthropy helps the corporations do well and because they recognize a moral obligation to improve the public good of the local community—a corporate stakeholder.

This discussion of the contrast between the two management philosophies helps us see the dichotomy between the two views—a dichotomy which is sharper in discussion of management than it is in actual practice.

Classical view: The purpose of the firm is to increase stock-holder wealth and in so doing society benefits. Business should seek to affect public policy in ways that are favorable to a good business climate; i.e., one that promotes opportunities to increase stockholder wealth.

Broad view: The purpose of the firm is multifaceted; increasing stock-holder wealth is but one of its responsibilities. Actually business has responsibilities to all corporate stakeholders and has positive responsibilities to society as well. Business must work with government and other interested parties in a cooperative effort to meet these responsibilities. Business, in this view, actively participates in setting the public policy agenda.

IV

Which of the competing theories is more adequate? This section sets out some of the standard arguments offered on behalf of each theory.

Until at least the 1930s, the classical theory represented the consensus of the implicit contract between society and business. It is buttressed by law and presupposed in charters of incorporation. In other words, society at least gave permission for corporations to increase stockholders' wealth; the law transformed that permission into a legal obligation. In 1919 the Michigan Supreme Court found the broad based stakeholder philosophy of Henry Ford to be illegal. Ford discovered that his Model T Ford was too profitable. His solution was to lower prices and raise employee salaries. Some of his stockholders argued that Ford had no right to use their money for charitable purposes. They sued and the court agreed with the stockholders. The language of the court is instructive.

> The record, and especially the testimony of Mr. Ford, convinces that he has to some extent the attitude towards shareholders of one who has dispensed and distributed to them large gains and that they should be content to take what he chooses to give. His testimony creates the impression, also, that he thinks the Ford Motor Company has made too much money, has had too large profits, and that, although large profits might be still earned, a sharing of them with the public, by reducing the price of the output of the company, ought to be undertaken. We have no doubt that certain sentiments, philanthropic and altruistic, creditable to

> Mr. Ford, had large influence in determining the policy to be pursued by the Ford Motor Company.... There should be no confusion (of which there is evidence) of the duties which Mr. Ford conceives that he and the stockholders owe to the general public and the duties which in law he and his codirectors owe to protesting, minority stockholders. A business corporation is organized and carried on primarily for the profit of the stockholders. The powers of the directors are to be employed for that end. (*Dodge v. Ford Motor Company*)

But why did society make that choice? One answer is utilitarian. Society believed that corporations which sought to increase shareholder wealth would produce great wealth for all and hence, in utilitarian ethical theory, be morally justified. Adam Smith's doctrine of the invisible hand as well as elaborate mathematical models by economists have been invoked to show that profit-maximizing firms in a free market do maximize the production of goods and services. Another argument rests on property rights. The owners of a firm are entitled to the profits of the firm, and hence the stockholders as the owner have rights the other stakeholders don't have.

Still another argument, most commonly associated with Milton Friedman, contends that profit-making firms support our democratic freedoms. If a firm in a competitive situation focuses on profit, it can ill afford to be concerned with the color of the skin, the political beliefs, or any other irrelevant factor (factor which is not causally linked to producing profit) of any employee, supplier, or customer. A competitive profit-seeking economic system is thus protective of political liberty.

The competitive profit-seeking economic system is supportive of our democratic traditions in another way as well. What democrats most have to fear is the concentration of power. So long as there are competing centers of power, e.g., business, labor, and government, there is less need to be concerned with a concentration of power. But suppose business took the broad view seriously and cooperated with labor and government to solve social problems. In such circumstances there is a danger that a governing elite would form to "solve" social problems. Such a powerful elite is antithetical and down right dangerous to our democratic traditions. This argument has been well formulated by Theodore Levitt—the current editor of the *Harvard Business Review.*

Yet a final argument is a practical analogue to the argument above. Business leaders do not have the expertise to solve social problems. To think otherwise is presumptuous. Just because one is a good CEO at GM does not mean that he or she should be the president of Harvard University.

Hence, the classical theory is the traditional theory; it has the law on its side. Adherents to the classical view argue that the profit-seeking firm in a competitive situation is supportive of our democratic traditions and political liberties, that it honors the property rights of corporate owners, that it recognizes the limited expertise of corporate management, and that it maximizes consumer wealth. In this way business provides for the public interest.

What can be said on behalf of the broad view? Much of the argument is negative in the sense that it represents an attack on the classical view. The defense of the classical view ignores the negative externalities of the practices of the classical firm and it totally ignores effects on the distribution of income. Air and water pollution, noise pollution, and unemployment are but a few of the problems which have caused citizens to doubt that firms seeking to increase shareholder wealth actually do produce the greatest good for the greatest number.

Similarly, the classical profit-seeking firm unjustly treats labor as any other factor of production; i.e., capital, machines, and land. When it pays to substitute machines for people, the profit-seeking firm should simply do it, and that is the end of the matter. If the firm can hold down wages by threatening to move to another region or another country, it should do so. In fact, if it pays to move a plant from one part of the country to another, the firm should do so whatever the reason. If the going wage in an industry is $4.00 an hour and if it is extremely difficult for workers to live on $160 a week (40 hrs x $4), that is not the concern of the employer. In fact, he should seek to lower wages if he can. Even if an economic system with profit-making firms maximizes total income, that does not establish the justice of such a system. Hence, critics argue that the higher average wealth comes at the expense of the poor. And in any case, treating employees on a par with capital, land, and machines violates a fundamental moral maxim; i.e., that people cannot be treated like objects but are uniquely worthy of respect.

Moreover, even if Friedman is right in his analysis of the support that profit-making firms give to political liberties, he ignores the fact that the employee has few liberties within the corporation. As one commentator notes, the corporation is the black hole in the Bill of Rights (Ewing 1977). The Constitution simply does not apply. Moreover, the employment at will doctrine still predominates. In the absence of a contract to the contrary an employee can be fired for any reason, be it a good reason, immoral reason, or indeed no reason at all. Since most people are far more involved with their jobs than they are with public affairs, it is not unreasonable to believe that many employees would trade some political freedom for more freedom on the job or would trade political liberties for job security. The classical view has a rather poor record protecting the liberties many people most want.

In response to the contention that stockholders have rights employees do not have because stockholders are the owners of the corporation, the critic of the classical view points out that property rights are not absolute. No individual can do what she wants with her property and neither can a firm. Moreover, the products of a business do not resemble the products of a family-owned firm. Consider the following disanalogy between home-owners and stockowners. A homeowner who works on her home and perhaps improves it beyond what the improvements could return in resale is not judged to be irrational. A stockholder who treats his stock in that way is considered to be irrational. Which type of property ownership is most in need of restrictions? By the way, the manager and the employer usually have the most reason to treat the company as a homeowner treats her home. If the company does poorly, the costs fall more heavily on the managers and employees. They can lose their entire livelihood. Far less often does the collapse of a company means that the stockholders lose their livelihood. Besides, analyses since the 1930s and 40s have shown that most stockholders do not identify with the corporation in which they own stock. At this point in our history, the "big players" are the pension fund managers, and hence much of the outstanding stock is not even directly chosen by the individuals who own it. Therefore, if restrictions on personal property are legitimate for homeowners, they are even more legitimate for stockholders.

But the arguments for the broad view need not be limited to critical attacks on the classical position. First, adherents of the broad view argue that there is a moral minimum to which all institutions and individuals in society ought to adhere. We created corporations and they ought to follow the fundamental rules of our society. Society would not give any institution the right to lie, steal, cheat, deceive, or cause physical injury to members of society. As we know more, the number of activities which cause physical injury expands. That is why air and water pollution are concerns now. Of course, as members of society, business interests should have a voice in determining moral standards as these standards evolve.

As for these negative externalities like air and water pollution, the following moral principle applies: those who contribute to social harms should contribute to their resolution. If business activity is to be in the public good, some way should be found to compensate society for the harm it creates. To say that this should be done is one thing; to specify how it is to be done is quite another. But on the principle that with great social power comes great responsibility, society has a right to expect a heavy commitment of resources by business to help resolve social problems. The notion of "trustee" is well established in business practice. Business has been granted extraordinary power over the economic resources of the nation and should act as a trustee with respect to those resources.

A final argument for the broad view rests on the claim that businesses, like all citizens, have duties of citizenship to the larger society. This is especially true given the benefits that society bestows on corporations—not the least of which is that we permit them to exist. What the classical view overlooks are the vast external economies society provides business. Who benefits from family and institutional training that instills the attitudes of cleanliness, promptness, hard work, etc.? The corporation. Who benefits from the infrastructure of sewer lines, highways, etc.? The corporation. The corporation is a free rider with respect to these goods, and hence corporations owe society something. The argument based on gratitude which applies to the individual citizen applies even more forcefully to the corporation.

In essence these arguments all tie together: society did not create corporations for the sole purpose of increasing shareholder wealth. Society assumes that profit making will be constrained by the moral minimum. What has created such difficulties is the discovery that duties under the moral minimum can be far reaching indeed. Moreover, society assumes that some stockholders' profits should be sacrificed in order that businesses meet their obligations to alleviate the social harms they have caused as well as their obligations as citizens and trustees.

V

Some might argue that the contrast between the broad view and the classical view is not as sharply distinguished as I have made out. Even the most hard nosed classicists recognize both legal and limited moral constraints on profit making. Friedman says "there is one and only one social responsibility of business—to use its resources and engage in activities designed to increase its profits so long as it stays within the rules of the game, which is to say, engages in open and free competition, without deception or fraud" (1962, 15-16). And Theodore Levitt says, "In the end business has only two responsibilities—to obey the elementary canons of everyday face to face civility (honesty, good faith, and so on) and to seek material gain" (1958). Traditionally, the emphasis has been on material gain rather than on spelling out the rules of the game. Hence there seems to be a great gulf between the position of the classicists and the adherents to the broad view. However, the only reason such a gulf seems to appear is because the classicists ignore the socially beneficial activities which lead to long-term profitability and ignore the fact that the corporate behavior recommended by the broad view would in fact be profitable. If the classicist manager could remove these blind spots, the management decisions made under either philosophy would be very similar. Business would adopt the perspective of the broad view in order to achieve the results consistent with classical goals. Concern with *all* corporate stakeholders and with the public good is the most dependable way to make a profit.

In theory such a unification of the two views is possible. However, business practice prevents such a unification from taking place. The most common complaint of corporate managers is that all the pressures conspire to emphasize *short-run* profits. Investors are not interested in what a company did one year ago or what the company will do in five years. They are interested in what the company did in the most recent quarter. Moreover, to put corporate funds into research and development, employee development, or social programs does take profits away from the stockholders in the short run. Other countries have an advantage in this respect. In Japan investment has a public dimension absent in the U.S. Long-term investment decisions are often made cooperatively between business and government. If the perspective of the broad theory is to be a realistic management style, ways must be found to direct stockholder attention to long-term profits from short-term profits. However, the widespread success of corporate raiders has made it far more difficult for management to take the long-term perspective. So has the law. As indicated, the classical model, even after *A.P. Smith v. Barlow*, is still the paradigm for legal analysis. Moreover, as ethicists know, moral conduct is much less likely when there is heavy pressure for short-term results which if not achieved have a severe adverse impact on the individuals involved. In those situations moral short cuts and other questionable corner cutting becomes almost irresistible.

VI

Suppose all corporations agreed that the proper way for business to affect public policy was for them to adopt the broad view rather than the classical view of the function of the firm. How could that goal be accomplished? What is required is a new framework that would involve changes in the attitude of chief executives, changes in how MBAs are educated, changes in our beliefs about the power of individuals within corporations to bring about this change, and finally changes in what one philosopher has called the corporate internal decision-making structure (CIDS) (French 1984).

Among the required changes in attitude is business's attitude toward government. Business people should see activity in the political process as a legitimate activity and even as activity required by morality. Citizens in a democracy should be active, not passive; living in a democracy brings civic responsibilities as well as benefits. Although the notion of civic responsibilities is severely weakened in our culture, a limited notion of civic responsibility is strongly held by some corporate leaders. For example, business leaders usually chair the United Way and the boards of local artistic and educational institutions. Some companies like IBM actually allow employees to work for extended periods for charitable organizations. However, some of this civic concern must now be shifted toward broader and more abstract questions of public policy—a realm where corporate leaders do not frequently dwell.

To expand the sense of civic responsibility to broader questions of public policy will require a further change in the attitude of many corporate officials. First, they will have to give up any pretenses to expertise in these matters. One of the reasons a corporate executive is chosen to head the United Way is because the executive has expertise as an efficient leader. However, the reason an executive should assist in the formulation of public policy is because business persons have an obligation to participate as equals in the political process. In this activity cooperative partners, not efficient managers, are what is required (although the manager's perspective on efficiency is valuable as input in the process). In this wider debate corporate leaders must acknowledge their own lack of expertise as to what is ultimately in the public good.

But what about the dangers associated with the abuse of power. Business activity faces a potential dilemma. On the one hand, it has a moral obligation to assist in the determination of public policy. On the other hand, the very exercise of this obligation may itself be immoral.

> On one side, executives are in virtually unanimous agreement that business must more forcefully present its point of view to the government officials whose decisions play such a decisive role in shaping their corporate welfare, and must participate more actively in the formation of public policy; on the other side, they are fearful that as they do, public opposition to their political role will intensify, together with public measures to hamstring their corporations. (Silk and Vogel 1976, 154-55)

Some thought has been given to this problem, particularly by public affairs professionals. Indeed, the profession has adopted a statement of ethical guidelines which speak directly to the concern of abuse of corporate power.

A STATEMENT OF ETHICAL GUIDELINES
FOR BUSINESS PUBLIC AFFAIRS PROFESSIONALS

A. The *Public Affairs Proffessional* maintains professional relationships based on honesty and reliable information, and
   therefore:...
   3. Recognizes diverse viewpoints within the public policy
      process, knowing that disagreement on issues is both in-
      evitable and healthy.

B. The *Public Affairs Professional* seeks to protect the integrity
   of the public policy process and the political system...

C. The *Public Affairs Professional* understands the interrelation
   of business interests with the larger public interests, and therefore:
   1. Endeavors to ensure that responsible and diverse external
      interests and views concerning the needs of society are
      considered within the corporate decision-making process.
   2. Bears the responsibility for management review of public
      policies which may bring corporate interests into conflict
      with other interests.
   3. Acknowledges dual obligations—to advocate the interests
      of his or her employer, and to preserve the openness and
      integrity of the democratic process.
   4. Presents to his or her employer an accurate assessment of
      the political and social realities that may affect corporate
      operations. (Mack 1980, 28)

Of course, it is one thing to adopt a set of guidelines and quite another to live by them—particularly when the guidelines are as general as these. However, the tone of the document is certainly in the spirit of partnership that I have been advocating.

There must also be changes in the education of MBAs. The change in attitude described above must occur in professors of business administration as well as in corporate managers. Moreover, these changes must be reflected in the courses taught. The Harvard Business School has as its motto, "To Make Business a Profession." But what does it mean to be a professional? The practitioner of a profession exercises a special technical skill on behalf of a client— a skill that the client needs but does not possess. MBAs bring highly developed quantitative skills to the firms that employ them (their clients). But traditionally, the professional skill is a service skill, specifically a skill that benefits human kind. Doctors, lawyers, teachers, and the clergy exercise skill *for the benefit of human beings.* The making of money is secondary. If the MBA is to be a professional in the traditional sense, the MBA must make providing a service primary and making money secondary. That set of priorities is certainly closer to the broad view of the function of the firm.

Recently business education has received much criticism in the popular business press on the grounds that MBAs lack "people skills," lack a developed sense of business ethics, and are generally deficient in liberal arts training. If these criticisms are based on an accurate assessment of MBA education, these gaps in MBA education should be filled.

But they cannot be filled simply by making individuals more moral. Much of the discussion is individualist based. The focus of the discussion in professional ethics is on the relationship between the individual lawyer or doctor and her client. Should confidential information be revealed and if so, how much, when, and to whom? Often the ethical dilemma is presented as one between the good of the individual client and the good of society. In the realm of business ethics the problem of when to blow the whistle would represent a problem of this type.

Business persons often accuse ethicists of being naive because they do not understand the competitive nature of business. And some ethicists stand guilty as charged. As I indicated previously, the fatal flaw in the broad view is that its concerns cannot be addressed if the emphasis is on short-term profits. And the problem of overcoming the emphasis on short-term profits is a collective not an individual one. What do I mean by that? I mean the problem rests in a deficiency of the competitive system; it does not rest primarily with deficiencies in individual character. Indeed, even when individuals are charged with acts of misconduct, those individuals are often victimized by the system. In the market economy it is very difficult to overcome free-rider problems. A rational individual, in situations that require cooperation, knows that she does best when everyone else cooperates and she does not; she then free rides on the cooperative activity of others. But if everyone reasons this way, then the cooperative activity will not occur or will occur at a level below optimum. Since morality is essentially a cooperative activity, it easily falls victim to free-rider problems. This argument has been brilliantly made in Fred Hirsch's, *Social Limits to Growth*, Part Three, "The Depleting Moral Legacy." Morality is particularly vulnerable when the pressure is on corporations to produce short-term gains. Truth, trust, acceptance, and restraint—"canons of everyday face to face civility"— recognized by the classicist Theodore Levitt, are required for the conduct of business, yet the very practice of business undermines them. As Hirsch argued, "The point is that conventional, mutual standards of honesty and trust are public goods that are necessary inputs for much of economic output (1976, 141). However, since they are public goods, their value cannot be fully captured in the market. If business is to conduct its activities in the public good, attention should not be directed to individuals. The emphasis on individualism is part of the problem. Rather the emphasis must be on collective action and that emphasis would require changes in business practice and corporate structure.

These remarks bring us to our last set of changes. Cooperation must be emphasized over competition because cooperation is necessary to provide the cohesiveness necessary for the practice of morality. It is harder to be a free rider if you see your associates as colleagues or teammates rather than as competitors. Much is now being written in decision theory on ways to avoid zero-sum games and prisoner dilemma situations. This research needs to be made accessible to managers and then applied to the business context.

One change in corporate practice might be the introduction of a notion of group merit to replace or supplement individual merit. A profit-sharing system should supplement the traditional wage structure. When an economic down turn occurs, everyone could be put on a reduced work week rather than placing the entire burden on the few who are laid off. Although these specific suggestions may have flaws, they capture the flavor of the more cooperative collective approach.

More important than specific recommendations of the sort suggested above is a change in perspective on how the corporation is viewed. Rather than emphasizing the goals of the individual CEO, we must speak of corporate goals and organizational decisions. If we have better corporations we will have better individual corporate persons. Professor Kenneth Andrews's (1987) notion of a corporate strategy is extremely valuable in providing a focus for the ideas I have in mind.

However, the classical theory which emphasizes individualism and competition is not a useful management perspective in this new framework. Only the broad view with its emphasis on *all* corporate stakeholders can work in an environment of cooperation. The traditional Protestant ethic has as one of its tenets the value of deferred gratification. The necessity to provide an ever growing array of consumer products has created an internal conflict with the ethics of deferred gratification (Bell 1976). That contradiction is survivable. However, it is absolutely necessary that practicing capitalists recognize the duty of delayed profit gratification. But such exhortations to duty will fall on deaf ears unless structural reforms are made that reward long-term profits. To identify and implement such reforms is the greatest challenge facing contemporary managers. I have described some of the changes that are necessary to encourage the activities described by the broad view of corporate responsibility as well as the kind of civic responsibility recommended here.

References

Andrews, Kenneth R. 1987. *The Concept of Corporate Strategy*. 3rd. ed. Homewood: Dow Jones-Irwin.

Bell, Daniel. 1976. *The Cultural Contradictions of Capitalism*. New York: Basic Books.

Buchholz, Rogene A. 1985. *Essentials of Public Policy Management*. Englewood Cliffs: Prentice-Hall.

Camenish, Paul. 1983. *Grounding Professional Ethics in a Pluralistic Society*. New York: Haven.

Dodge v. Ford Motor Company 204 Mich. 459, 170 N.W. 668 3 A.L.R. 413.

Ewing, David. 1977. *Freedom Inside the Corporation*. New York: E.P. Dutton.

French, Peter. 1984. *Collective and Corporate Responsibility*. New York: Cambridge UP.

Friedman, Milton. 1962. *Capitalism and Freedom*. Chicago: U of Chicago P.

Hirsch, Fred. 1976. *Social Limits to Growth*. Cambridge: Harvard UP.

Levitt, Theodore. 1958. "The Dangers of Social Responsibility." *Harvard Business Review* 36 (Sept.-Oct.): 41-50.

Mack, Charles S. 1980. "Ethics and Business Public Affairs." *Public Affairs Review* 1:28.

Payton, Robert L. 1985. *Philanthopy as a Right*. Bowling Green: Social Philosophy and Policy Center.

Silk, Leonard, and David Vogel. 1976. *Ethics and Profits*. New York: Simon and Schuster.

*This paper was originally prepared in conjunction with a Hastings Center Project on Professional Ethics and the Public Role of the Professions under a grant from the Walter and Elise Haas Fund.

A Framework for the Establishment of Applied Ethics in the Exercise of Management Activities

Sebastian A. Sora, D.P.S.
Manager of Educational Services
Latin American Headquarters
IBM Corporation
Mt. Pleasant, New York

◆

The intent of this article is to establish a framework in which management can apply ethics from a situational perspective. Its purpose is to explore some of the implications that arise when management exercises it prerogatives in the business context specifically as it relates to decision making and people management in a free enterprise system.

THE NEED

Whenever management acts in a concerted manner to affect the actions of individuals, management must understand both the long- and short-term effect that those directed actions have on individuals and systems. The effect must be understood beyond the immediate requirement for that action. In understanding the effect of their actions, they (managers) must make judgments that are normative in nature. Such judgments indicate a manager's or corporation's favorable or unfavorable attitude toward some state of affairs (Velasquez 1982). Information technologists have a special burden for they are the custodians of a very powerful technology (Emery 1982). It is the very pervasiveness of this technology in modern society that makes it so powerful and effective. How they use this technology can have the widest effect on all members of the work place and society. Deciding what personal information ought to be collected or acquired—the privacy question—is the broadest challenge to management or organizational authority (Westin 1972). This increasing vulnerability to the employees' right to privacy (Velasquez 1988) and the rights of workers versus the rights of a corporation becomes a key issue for management.

In order to apply an ethical context for management action, we must first identify what is meant by the business ethic. The relation of business to morality is based on the fact that business is a human activity. Like most social activities, business presupposes a background of morality. Morality consists of rules for human behavior which specify actions as right or wrong. Businesses do not expect their employees to steal as a general rule, contracts are expected to be honored, advertisements should have some truth in them, and so on. If everyone acted immorally or amorally, business would soon grind to a halt. Morality is the glue and the oil of society and business (DeGeorge 1982).

Business ethics concentrates on how moral standards apply particularly to business policies, institutions, and behaviors (Valesquez 1982). Given that definition, I will advocate that a type of utilitarianism be used to form a judgment on the ethical base (Bayles 1968) of management actions. The basis of utilitarianism is to supply the greatest benefits with the least harm (Sedgwick 1962). It is efficient and from a business perspective, at least, causes management to understand why it is attempting to control. Clearly control is a function of leadership. Leadership's most important action is the vigilant stewardship of its human resources, with the resulting development and promotion of those who support its values and the correction or removal of those who do not (Kelly 1988). Management must judge the good it is accomplishing as well as the bad for all of its actions in a situational or contextual basis. A systematic ethic is impossible, because we deal with moral fractals, a linked set of events (Goodpaster 1988). Thus, from a contextual point of view and a utilitarian perspective, I shall set up key areas in which to judge the ethical context for management control.

Today, industry is greatly worried by the intensity of the conflict between management and workers and is increasingly becoming interested in the possibilities for reducing work alienation and increasing job satisfaction (Mumford and Weir 1979). Although significant progress has been made on worker alienation in the last decade, much debate remains on whether the problem is part of the capitalistic system, as Marxists charge (DeGeorge 1982). Alienation is morally wrong because it separates human beings into antagonistic groups. Management must be aware that the solutions it advocates can work in closed environments to achieve desired ends but must be tested if they can; for if misused, they increase alienation. These solutions will decrease job satisfaction through the perceived curtailment of employee freedom. They could stultify the workers, since they can be construed to involve domination, and then lead to conflict. However, conflict can be thought of as positive if it results in constructive behavior such as participation in discussion groups, mutual problem solving, and other forms for constructive criticism. Confrontation should emphasize a sense of community; the basis for the sense of community (Kelly 1988) in the work place is clearly the job.

JOB SATISFACTION

Maslow (1954) argues that a worker must be motivated in order to seek satisfaction in any job. Clearly, multiple levels of satisfaction can exist within a job for the same person; however, management must understand the effect that working solutions might have on employee motivation. Motivation is complex and the way people are supervised affects motivations (Likert 1967). The values that management holds towards employees affect motivation, and it is believed that employees' behavior is somewhat affected by what management expects (Crozier 1964).

The question then is do the actions proposed by any solution enhance or limit job satisfaction or are they neutral? Would the solution enable management to abridge personal freedom? What are the appropriate parameters of personal freedom and organizationally appropriate requirements for abridgement, given the society in which the corporation is found? Clearly, the environment management creates must be extremely wary of political abuses of personal liberty (Emery 1982) that could result. This abuse of personal liberty will be a demotivator to satisfaction and establishes what I shall term management context 1: *How is job satisfaction affected?*

MOTIVATION

Serious management action must always be concerned with ways to motivate staff to achieve and grow, both professionally and as human beings. Professional growth is tied to the improvement of skills and position; human growth is tied to our ability to become better people through growth of all of our positive attributes. Thus, in the implementation of any solution the question of effect on motivation and individual respect must be addressed.

As a result of Frederick W. Taylor's pioneering time studies in the 1900s, work became fractionalized in order to improve efficiency. This concern with parts of a system to determine what drives the entire system led research to consider the sources of motivation (Golembiewski 1965). Those sources identified were:

a. Deficiency
b. Growth
c. Paternalism.

The methods for management action presented can be enforced via any of the three sources. Deficiency motivation would accentuate threat and punishments; paternalism would accentuate hygiene factors (Herzberg 1959); and growth would accentuate job-related factors.

Any management techniques used must be understood in the context of motivational sources which are supported by the corporation and are in some manner encapsulated and operationalized in an explicit corporate code of ethics. Thus a second management context is created: *All management actions must be measured against an explicit corporate code of ethics.*

Abraham Maslow in 1954 proposed that individuals strive to satisfy a hierarchy of needs. Those needs were psychological well-being, safety, belonging, self-esteem, status, and self-actualization (Maslow 1954). Management actions should not disable an individual's attempt to self-actualize, except in situations that are short run and emergency in nature. Any management action that enables self-actualization then can be a force for good. Thus a third management context is: *any management action must not frustrate an individual's growth to self-actualization.*

TECHNOLOGY

Harold A. Innis's book *The Bias of Communication* showed how communication media affected social, political, and cultural development through the ages. Abbe Mowshowitz picks this theme up in *The Bias of Computer*

Technology but relates the theme only to computer hardware. Software technology is much more flexible than hardware, so its power to affect cultural development would be at least as powerful. It is the driver to hardware. The dimensions of ethics associated with technology in general are then related to time, mediation, and space.

Thus there exists a functional relationship between values and technology, so we must understand how management values will be affected by technological innovation. Some changes have little effect, but others shake the foundations of value systems. The industrial revolution caused upheavals in management values, and the age of computer will likewise be seen to have had such an effect. What corporate practices will be modified and what will happen to the modes of human interaction is what is meant by mediation. Finally, how information will flow, as a result of technological change, is what is meant by space. Thus management action must be seen as part of a fourth context: *In the implementation of control the results must be acceptable from the perspective of mediation, space, and time.*

MANAGEMENT VALUES

In theory a manager cannot be ethically accountable if he is oblivious to the consequences of his actions (Schoeffler 1982). It is values which have been tested to ensure goodness beyond the act itself that permit accountable courses to be navigated. However, when values are changing due to technology, we must question them until they are tested. S. Schoeffler (1982) of the Strategic Planning Institute has stated that science is intrinsically cross-sectional. This is also true of management; management, when successful, creates a surplus which goes beyond our basic needs and improves the quality of life by using the tools of science. These tools are found in technology, psychology, biology, and mathematics. A manager learns something about his own situation by comparing it to other current or similar (in his judgment) situations. This is what is meant by being inherently cross-sectional. However, the act of comparing takes time, and while values are in flux, every attempt should be made to keep key values relatively stable; a fifth context is thus established. *Values in the short run should be unaffected to allow for testing.*

TESTING MANAGEMENT VALUES

In the intermediate to long-run time intervals values must have been tested if they are to be used. How? I believe a key way is to see how the new or changed values are accommodated into the current work environment. Accommodation can be determined by employee responsiveness and customer responsiveness. It can be determined by effect on efficiency or effectiveness. Clearly these tests should only be done in the longer run and change should be a gradual response. This establishes context six. *Values should change slowly and the change should be measured by some response solicitation.*

PRODUCTIVITY

Few can deny that productivity is a function of the degree of harmony between capital and labor. It is empirically conceded that it is the happy worker who in the long run is productive. Long-run productivity is directly related to self-esteem.

Let us look at productivity in light of a sense of justice. What is this sense of justice? Simply, it is what is inherent in a man to judge appropriateness of action or the difference between good and evil. This sense of justice is bounded by two areas (Mothersill 1965):

    a. To whom is justice owed?

    b. What drives the need to do what is just?

Management action should be a driver to do what is just and should therefore be an aid to productivity. How could this be accomplished? Certainly if such action can be shown to protect individuals from mistakes it would aid productivity. However, individuals must be able to learn from their mistakes and not be entrapped by them. The worker has a right to be treated justly, by management permitting him to learn in a trusting environment and enabling him to have the best equipment available to insure his productivity. It is the duty of the worker to strive for personal productivity and growth as a human being. This is a working definition of the spirit of justice. Thus a seventh context is created: *the effect of management actions on productivity must be understood in light of the spirit of justice.*

HUMAN INTERACTION AND TECHNOLOGY

The key question here is not how people communicate before and after a technological innovation but whether the quality of that interaction is improved. For what value is technology if it does not improve the human condition? Is human interaction enhanced?

Management actions that enhance the strength of a computer system to collect and gather information are of a timely concern. It would be difficult to prove that by gathering this information individualism and autonomy are increased; however, it is important to understand how individualism is enabled on a situational basis to deal with such a collection or structure of information.

Capitalizing on the strength of the computer's ability to analyze should be balanced by the capability of the computer to inform. Human interaction can be enhanced by enabling the machine to be a part of that interaction. Just as in human interaction an individual has the right to say "no," so a computer can be enabled to do just that. This "no" can be generated by an artificial intelligence system that embodies the value system of the society and corporation. The impact of the system can have a positive effect on human values because they can be simulated and explored. So we find an eighth context: *management action should be the logical outcome of a corporate value system which supports improving human interaction.*

INFORMATION FLOW

If we can make all technological innovation part of the human interactive environment, then the space available to the solution can enhance information flow. Electronic global communication is at everybody's finger tips, and its realization can improve human discourse. The counter view that such communication is negative would be supported in a Hobbesian view of man. The outdated notion that "Men have no pleasure, but on the contrary a great deal of grief in keeping company, where there is no power to overawe them" (McGovern 1941) certainly does not reflect the heritage of free enterprise and individualism in a shrinking, interconnected global village. The ninth context: *the flow of information between humans must not be affected negatively.*

THE CODE OF ETHICS

Corporate and business ethics is a topic of increasing concern to the public; thus it is important to understand how a specific business firm supports its positions and actions. This interest in ethics is driven by mistrust. Consumer groups accuse large corporations of inflicting dangerous products on the unsuspecting public, advertising has been shown to manipulate vulnerable groups like children, and the environment has been damaged by corporations for the sake of efficient production (Velasquez 1988). There are four general assumptions that support this perception:

      a. Size equals power and power corrupts.
      b. Size equals social impact as well as economic impact.
      c. Size equals complexity and the impossibility of control.
      d. Size equals political success in disputes.

It is a combination of factors that engenders mistrust; this mistrust is based on uncertainty. The uncertainty leads to the fear of power which is based on the unwarranted conclusion that certain counterproductive behaviors will become normal or acceptable. This in effect becomes an egocentric anti-ethic: an abandonment of idealistic goals, a lack of commitment to the long-term welfare of the organization and society, an emergence of destructive special interest conflicts, and a decreased sense of community in institutions as they grow larger and more complex (Kelly 1988).

Generally corporate ethics are seen at three levels (Berenbeim 1987):

      Corporate mission
      Constituency relations
      Policy and practices

Management issues must be understood as a function of policies and practices as they relate to customers and employees.

Of 223 companies responding to a Conference Board questionnaire on ethics, 90% had such a code for greater than three years. In 80% of those cases top management participated in drafting the codes, and 90% of those codes addressed employees. However, employees were generally unaware of the codes or what value they could put on them.

In the sample of those companies that have codes, far fewer companies have structures to oversee and induce compliance. Further, of those companies that have ethics discussion programs, only 50% invite employees to participate. While in most cases everyone in a corporation receives or can obtain the code of ethics, open skepticism is found among employees (Berenbeim 1987).

It is difficult to understand why any firm would develop a code of ethics but not see to it that it is understood by all employees and enforced by management. It is difficult to understand why it is not a condition of employment. Clearly it cannot be a condition of employment if it is not understood or enforced or if it is looked on with skepticism. Failure to recognize this eliminates the code of ethics (credo) as a driver to evaluate business actions in times of stress or in normal times.

A credo therefore must be a statement of values, expectations, and responsibilities of each member of the corporation. It serves to protect participants who are part of that culture, whether they are employees, managers, customers, or other stakeholders. To be such a culture binder, then, such codes of ethics must speak specifically to each participant:

1. Enterprise   - define its mission in society

2. Society   - define how society benefits from the enterprise

3. Employer   - define its objectives and its organizational structure and major policies and procedures to achieve those objectives

4. Employees   - define their valid expectations and their responsibilities

5. Stakeholders   - define the enterprise's responsibility to them

The code of ethics will be part of the context for all management control actions. It will serve to delimit and bound. It will further define a valid set of expectations and increase general trust. The tenth context: *a vital and dynamic code of ethics will increase the effectiveness of management actions because they would be culturally sanctioned.*

CHANGE

It is ultimately management's responsibility to protect the assets of any business; hence its actions must be beneficial to the corporation. As the environment (internal/external) is generally in flux, so all businesses go through change to survive. Management action is the mechanism to get a business and its constituencies to change in a planned manner. These actions must not be isolated but instead seen as managing the change and fostering growth. This growth will enable changes to take place in work, in relationships, and in productivity. This management control yields planned intervention, and this is generally recognized as a central concern of management (Natale 1983). Change management brings us full circle to motivation. A manager must create a situation in which the implementation of his actions will enable an employee to satisfy personal objectives, e.g., security, while attaining organizational objectives (Natale 1983). Thus we find the eleventh context: *management actions that control must be viewed as an integral part of change management which enable survivability.*

EDUCATION

If all management action is shown as part of an ethical and a change context, then its role must support education. Education supports self-actualization as well as change. Education will enable a consensus on control, and a code of ethics will circumscribe its full potential. To achieve this education, business constituencies must be taught to achieve effective and cognitive goals (Natale 1987).

Given such directed education, the *why* of management control can be understood at the level of logical, critical, analytical thinking; the execution of control can take place in an empathic, open, and accepting environment. The two educational thrusts will enforce and also balance one another. The twelfth and final context is: *management action must be addressed by education, such that it is given at two levels, cognitive and affective.*

SUMMARY

The 12 ethical contexts proposed by this article are meant to form a base for management control. They should be thought of as the axioms for ethical control. On top of these, practices can be developed to enable businesses to survive in a competitive environment. Practices will change through time, but the basic axioms of any system must remain intact. Thus we have an ability to change and grow while maintaining the norms and ethics of any society.

References

Bain, D. 1982. *The Productivity Prescription.* Washington: Library of Congress.

Bayles, M. D., ed. 1968. *Contemporary Utilitarianism.* New York: Doubleday.

Berenbeim, R. E. 1987. *Research Report 900 - Corporate Ethics.* New York: Conference Board.

Caellii, W. J. 1987. "Guidelines for Privacy and Security in Computer Systems." *Australian Computer Journal* 19.4 (December).

Crozier, M. 1964. *The Bureaucratic Phenomenon*. London: Tavistock.

DeGeorge, R. T. 1982. *Business Ethics*. New York: Macmillan.

Emery J. C. 1982. "The Promise and Problems of Computer Technology." *Proceeding of the Fourth National Conference on Business Ethics.* Cambridge: Oelgeschlager, Gunn and Hain.

Golembiewski, R. P. 1965. *Men, Management, and Morality: Towards a New Organizational Ethic*. New York: McGraw-Hill.

Goodpaster, K. 1988. "Business Ethics." Iona Business Seminar. Iona College, New Rochelle, New York. October.

Herzberg, F. 1966. *Work and the Nature of Man*. London: Staples.

Innis, H. A. 1951. *The Bias of Communication*. Toronto: U of Toronto P.

Kelly, C. M. 1988. *The Destructive Achiever: Power and Ethics in the American Corporation*. Reading: Addison-Wesley.

Koontz, H., and H. Weinrich. 1988. *Management*. New York: McGraw-Hill.

Likert, R. 1967. *The Human Organization*. New York: McGraw-Hill.

Maslow, A. H. 1954. *Motivation and Personality*. New York: Harper.

McGovern, W. M. 1941. *From Luther to Hitler*. Cambridge: Riverside Press.

Mowshowitz, A. 1978. "Computers and Ethical Judgment in Organization." *ACM: Proceedings of the 1978 Annual Conference*. Washington.

Mumford, E., and M. Weir. 1979. *Computer Systems in Work Design—The Ethics Method*. New York: John Wiley.

Natale, S. M. 1983. *Ethics and Morals in Business*. Alabama: REP.

————. 1987. *Ethics and Morals in Business*. Alabama: REP.

Sedgwick, H. 1962. *Methods of Ethics*. Illinois: U of Chicago P.

Velasquez, M. G. 1982. *Business Ethics*. Englewood Cliffs: Prentice-Hall.

Economic Development and Values: Life Beyond Gross National Product

Joseph W. Ford, Ph.D.
Associate Professor of Business Economics
Hagan School of Business
Iona College
New Rochelle, New York

◆

Something rather curious has been happening in recent years, something considered momentous and overdue by some but viewed as inappropriate and disastrous by others. The phenomenon of "development" is being removed from the exclusive domain of the technicians and their equations; now a variety of groups and individuals in a pluralistic forum are articulating specific values, priorities, and perspectives as part of the development process. We are specifically concerned with the advocacy of values by selected religious groups and individuals such as Pope John Paul II and the U.S. National Conference of Catholic Bishops (NCCB).

An immediate word of caution as well as a disclaimer: this is not a paper about theology, spirituality, religiosity, or religion as such. It is not a paper dealing with guidelines for belief. It is about the process of value determination in the public policy debate. What perspective is to be used in articulating the dimensions of economic development? Are we to talk about mere quantitative measures, or are there qualitative norms to consider and grapple with as well? It is this paper's basic contention that the latter is true.

The pluralistic public policy forum has indeed seen a substantially more visible role for policy expansions by religious institutions in recent times. Not that this is something new, but it is now more assertive and controversial. The NCCB has issued pastoral letters on war and nuclear deterrence and on the economy. These have had a wide range of response—from almost uncritical acceptance on one end to outright rejection and contempt on the other. Most of the response has been thoughtful, understanding that these statements are proposals for normative guidelines and as such, attempts to persuade the public of their merits. In other words, they are values being articulated and marketed.

In the present context we are concerned with two specific documents and with one major theme. The theme is the increasing interplay of the public policy debate with religious groups and their values. The documents are the papal encyclical of John Paul II *Sollicitudo Rei Socialis* ("On Social Concern"), dated December 30, 1987, and *Economic Justice For All*, the pastoral letter on the American Economy of the National Conference of Catholic Bishops, dated November 1986. Both of these have been recognized as major statements of economic concern and as major proposals for determining values in the setting of policy. That they are highly controversial for many people is also a given, but that's not necessarily a bad thing in the policy forum. We shall therefore look at these documents in the following ways: first, an evaluation of their historical and environmental settings; second, an examination of the novel terminology introduced as an alternative value base to the conventional framework of development.

THE SETTING

Both documents are creatures of the 1980s, and they emerged in their final form reasonably close to each other, about a year and a half apart. *Economic Justice For All*, the third and final draft of the Bishops' letter, appeared in November 1986. Earlier drafts had been published in late 1984 and late 1985. Work on the papal letter began in early 1986, and after some revisions, it was released on February 19, 1988. The "official" date of publication was December 30, 1987 because it was to commemorate the twentieth anniversary of the publication of *Populorum Progressio* (The Progress of Peoples, an encyclical of Pope Paul VI in 1967) (Hebblethwaite 1988, 3).

Work on the Bishops' letter started with the creation of an *ad-hoc* committee in 1980 and was in full gear at the start of 1984. When the committee announced at that time that a first draft would be ready at the end of 1984, a group of conservative lay Catholics, headed by former Secretary of the Treasury William Simon, formed the Lay Commission on Catholic Social Teaching and the U.S. Economy. Their expressed fear was that the Bishops' analysis of the economy and the policy proposals flowing from it would embrace "liberal" values on the issues of government's role in economic development, etc., which they deemed unacceptable. And of course they were correct in their fear. The Bishops did come out with a statement that focused on what the economy does *for* people, what it does *to* people, and how people *participate* in it. It was a document that stresses a "preferential option" for the poor, that talked about economic rights as equal to civil rights, and that recommended cooperative modes of behavior as well as competitive ones. For example, the Bishops said in their second (1985) draft:

> The nation's founders took daring steps to create structures of mutual accountability and widely distributed power to ensure that the political systems would support the rights and freedoms of all. We believe that similar institutional steps are needed today to expand the sharing of economic power and to relate the economic system more accountably to the common good. (paragraph #285)

Examine carefully the provocative power of that statement. Note how the NCCB has artfully linked up a proposal for an adaptation of the system (rather than an extremist junking of it—which, of course, would be self-destructive) with the truly radical formation of the nation's structure at its birth. The notion of the need for evolutionary change is made compatible with hallowed conservative tradition. Very clever and very disturbing, for it suggests change rather than tradition as the benchmark. It sidesteps the issue of contrasting economic systems by focusing on desired end products rather than on specific economic arrangements. It finesses the question of being for or against the market free-enterprise system by presenting forcefully normative guidelines for economic behavior, so that any kind of economic system is brought under the microscope. The letter of the Bishops, and indeed the whole thrust of Catholic social doctrine since Pope Leo XIII in his encyclical *Rerum Novarum* ("About New Things," 1891) has been to keep it separate from any specific economic system, so that ideological tags like "liberal," "conservative," "market-oriented," or "socialist" have been relatively absent. This permits Catholic social thought to focus on normative guidelines, on fundamental moral principles which have broad and solid support. The normative questions which are asked are those of *any* economic scenario so that Catholic social thought remains free to challenge any economic system on any economic issue and to do it without any ideological baggage.

And challenge the American economic system the Bishops' letter does. In focusing on the pattern of U.S. economic development, it raises unsettling questions about our experience and treatment of poverty, unemployment, and the farm sector, among others. It focuses uncomfortably on the reality of the "marginalized," blacks, hispanics, women as single parents, the elderly, etc.—who cannot participate fully and consistently in the rhythm and benefits of economic development. These are the groups that economic growth either does not touch at all or affects only lightly and sporadically. An economic growth process that is principally shaped by technical factors is rarely tailored to particular needs.

The Bishops' policy recommendations are equally disturbing. To some, they are disturbing because they propose an expanded role for government programs and fiscal and monetary policy. For others, they are a tired rehash of unsatisfactory Roosevelt-era programs of long ago and the Great Society programs of the 1960s. Andrew Greeley calls the pastoral an "inept and inadequate document," a timid failure in the stream of Catholic social thought (1985, 25). Nobel Laureate in economics Milton Friedman describes the "collectivist moral strain that pervades the document repellent" (99). Reaction to the Bishops' position covers the whole spectrum, but certainly the paper has not been ignored, and policy debates are beginning to reflect the values proposed.

The setting for the publication of *Sollicitudo Rei Socialis* (hereafter to be called *SRS*) was unique but nevertheless compatible with the Bishops.

> I was quite pleased, but not at all surprised, to see the great congruity between the encyclical's principles and conclusions on the one hand, and those employed and reflected in the U.S. bishops' major public portions in recent years—in particular their Respect Life Program and their pastoral letters on war and peace, and on the economy. (Bernardin 1988, 5)

The encyclical of Pope John Paul II was specifically triggered by a desire to commemorate the twentieth anniversary of the publication of Paul IV in 1967. This had been a major statement on economic development in its time, and some way of noting it was deemed appropriate. Work on the encyclical began in late 1986, and a first draft was completed in August 1987. A second draft was written, it wandered through layers of the Vatican administration, and it was finished in February 1988. As noted above, it was actually dated December 30, 1987 so as to denote the twentieth anniversary (Hebblethwaite 1988, 3).

Populorum Progressio was, indeed, an important statement. Paul VI made the point that the gap between the Northern hemisphere "haves" and the Southern hemisphere "have nots" was far more ominous than the East-West conflict (*Populorum Progressio* #33). "Development," he also noted, "is the new name for peace" (#87). Finally:

> Development cannot be limited to merely economic growth. In order
> to be authentic, it must be complete: integral, that is, it has to
> promote the good of every man and of the whole man. (#14)

The encyclical of 1987-1988 is designed to build on Pope Paul VI's "groundbreaking encyclical on development"—groundbreaking because it took "a different approach by emphasizing the need for a moral vision" (Lernoux 1988, 9).

The encyclical of John Paul II spends a considerable portion of its contents (in fact, two sections out of seven) dwelling on the importance of the encyclical of Paul VI, and much of the rest is involved with extending it and applying it to the present.

> I am convinced that the teachings of the encyclical *Populorum
> Progressio* addressed to the people and the society of the 1960s,
> retain all their force as an appeal to conscience today in the last part
> of the 1980s. (*SRS* #4)

THE VALUE-BASED TERMINOLOGY

> The aim of the present reflection is to emphasize, through a theological investigation of the present world, the need for a *fuller and more
> nuanced concept of development*, according to the suggestions contained in the encyclical. (*SRS* #4, emphasis added)

Section three of the encyclical, entitled "Survey of the Contemporary World," notes that distressingly modest progress has been made in the underdeveloped world over the past 20 years. Burdens of poverty, inadequate production and distribution of food, unsanitary water, disease, and limited life expectancy have not been relieved and have contributed to the widening of the gap between the North and South (*SRS*#12-14). Other dimensions of the failure include illiteracy, lack of accessibility to higher education, social, political, and religious oppression, and all forms of discrimination.

In brief, modern underdevelopment is not only economic, but also cultural, political and simply human.... Hence, at this point we have to ask ourselves if the sad reality of today might not be, at least in part, the result of a too narrow idea of development, that is, a mainly economic one. (*SRS* #15)

This reality of inadequate development also involves the touchy question of different economic systems—capitalism and central planning. The Pope carefully steers a critical course between the two. His important question: How capable are these two systems of changing in order to promote "true and integral development of individuals and peoples in modern society" (#21)? This is the core of the issue, and it is deeper than the notion of the system in question. The Pope received a tremendous amount of flack for the "moral equivalency" from commentators such as William Safire in the *New York Times*, Michael Novak in *Crisis*, and William Buckley in the *National Review* (qtd. in Heuriot 1988, 7). But as Heuriot notes, a careful reading of the encyclical reveals that "nowhere in the encyclical does John Paul morally equate the two systems.... But he does subject both to stinging critiques" (7).

John Kenneth Galbraith, prominent and senior maverick economist, offers another angle of perspective on the issue of systems, a perspective honed by more than three decades of research about the system of American capitalism. (It began with *American Capitalism: The Principle of Countervailing Power* in 1952.) He says that the encyclical is meant to be highly critical of economic and social policy in the United States and the other rich countries with regard to conditions in the poor countries. It condemns "single-minded concentration on the symbols and satisfactions of wealth" especially at the expense of basic needs of health, comfort and well-being" (Galbraith 1988, 13). To alleviate this,

There is only government and the encyclical, accordingly, is a powerful case for government action on behalf of the poor at home and abroad. It is not favorable to Marxist collectivism, but it is especially, or perhaps even more, critical or "liberal (meaning ideological staunch) capitalism" and or refusal to recognize the need for requisite public action. (13)

The next critical step in the letter's analysis is to articulate a "fuller and more nuanced concept of development"; the term used is "authentic human development." In its fourth section the process begins with pessimism. We cannot delude ourselves to think that development is an automatic and straight forward phenomenon of inevitable progress. Two world wars and nuclear danger have ended that naiveté. In addition "the 'economic' concept itself, linked to the word 'development', has entered into crisis" (*SRS* #27, 28). A narrow, mechanistic understanding of development, it is asserted, does not bring happiness. Science and technology benefits have another side to them which can be unpleasant. Medical technology, with its ability not only to sustain life but even to create it in a laboratory beaker, confronts us with exceedingly difficult issues of ethics, value priorities, and policy decisions.

> The experience of recent years shows that unless all the considerable
> body of resources and potential at man's [sic] disposal is guided by
> a moral understanding and by an orientation toward the true good
> of the human race, it easily turns against man to oppress him. (#28)

Another pessimism: the contrast between underdevelopment with what John Paul calls "superdevelopment." This is the easy abundance of material goods for elite special groups, which makes them slaves of material possessions and immediate gratification, while the majority are denied decent living standards. This is the so-called "throw-away" society of wasteful consumption. This is at its core a pattern of development with a relative few possessing much and with many owning almost nothing. "It is the injustice of the poor distribution of the goods and services originally intended for all" (#28).

What is the concept of development advocated by the encyclical in a positive description? All of the values noted so far have been negative, and the value-based proposal of development in the document is strong, clear and detailed. Development is a concept which is to be measured and oriented according to the totality of the person in both the person's interior and exterior dimensions. Material goods are to be seen as a gift from God and to be enjoyed as the fruits of human effort. That there is a danger of misusing them and that there is the reality of engendering artificial and superficial needs should not dissuade us from appreciating new goods and resources.

At this juncture John Paul II describes "authentic human development" in two complementary fashions, in theological and humanistic terms. For some, the former may be terminology that is awkward and uncomfortable, but it meshes rather nicely with the more secular language of the latter. Close inspection of the two approaches confirms this, and it powerfully charges the value base of the development debate. Theologically, since the individual has been created by God in his image and likeness, he or she must remain subject to the will of God; this means subordinating the possession, dominion, and use of the products of human industry to a greater good, a greater social good, and also a transcendent immortality for the person (#29). Formidable words, but they boil down to a simple idea: the individual is a social being and is called upon to improve the lot of his or her fellow creatures.

> The obligation to commit oneself to the development of peoples is
> not just an individual duty.... It is an imperative which obliges each
> and every man and woman as well as societies and nations. (#32)

An interesting aside is that the letter notes that development which did not respect human rights—including economic rights—would not meet the above criteria. The specific mention of and inclusion of "economic rights" appears to be a reflection in 1987-1988 of a controversial idea advocated by the American Bishops in their economic pastoral from 1984 to 1986 in all three drafts (*Economic Justice for All* 1986 #80-84; *SRS* #33). The Bishops propose that the people have a right to employment, to decent food and housing, and these economic rights are to have the same "pride of place" in American culture as political and civil rights. This seems to have crossed the Atlantic and made it to Rome.

Sometimes the language used has a more secular tone, but the conclusions remain the same.

> Today, perhaps more than in the past, the intrinsic contradiction of a development limited only to its economic element is seen more clearly. Such development easily subjects the human person...to the demands of economic planning and selfish profit.

> The intrinsic connection between authentic development and respect for human rights once again reveals the moral character of development. (*SRS* #33)

A common denominator in this part of the encyclical (and one that permeates much of *Economic Justice for All*) is the relentless emphasis on the rights and dignity of every person. Furthermore, it means that those who share responsibility for the developmental process must be especially aware of the individual's rights. Further still, it imposes the need to ensure that everyone has access to the "full use of the benefits offered by science and technology" (#33).

Respect for rights is articulated in some detail. Within a nation it means the right to life at every stage, the rights of the family as the basic unit, the right to fair working conditions, the rights to free political action, and the right to religious beliefs. Internationally it means the right of each people to have complete respect for its own cultural and historical characteristics.

> Both peoples and individuals must enjoy the fundamental equality which is the basis, for example, of the charter of the United Nations: the equality which is the basis of the right of all to share in the process of full development. (*SRS* #33)

The words may seem like standard stuff, but there is more to it than that. Most of the literature on development deals with the technicalities surrounding the process: how scarce resources are to be allocated among competing sectors; how balanced or unbalanced the process is to be; what the trade-offs involved are, etc. The letter doesn't get into any of these, nor should it, but it does say with clarity and firmness that development means people and that development includes ethical dimensions. Just as the Bishops demand that an economy be judged by what it does *to* people and *for* people, so too the Pope says that authentic development must be achieved through freedom and solidarity. The latter is described as a "firm and persevering determination to commit oneself to the common good"; it is not "a feeling of vague compassion or shallow distress" (*SRS* #38).

Solidarity becomes a new term thrown into the political debate. The Pope sees the unity of the world as seriously compromised; this is symbolized by the use of terms like First World, Second World, Third World, and Fourth World. His response is solidarity, and according to Peter Henriot, this is the major emphasis of the encyclical (1988, 8). If political world blocs (North-South, East-West, etc.) are thrown aside in favor of solidarity, then distrust is changed to collaboration.

These are idealistic words, to be sure, and maybe fantasy, but the very daring nature of the approach forces a different focus on the development issue. Peter Henriot argues,

> Solidarity, the political response to the political analysis of John Paul II is in my view the new encyclical's major contribution to the development of the church's social teaching. His discussion of solidarity poses serious challenges to U.S. government stances and policies, not only toward Third World peoples but also toward our domestic population. (1988, 8)

Few people or institutions have the global reach or credibility that the Vatican does, so that documents like *Sollicitudo Rei Socialis* can gain access to the policy forum and trigger discussion. If it succeeds in shifting the angle of debate only a few degrees, that is a formidable start.

To charges that he is naive about how the world operates, consider this wonderful image:

> John Paul II has bravely refused to allow the church to be present in world affairs somewhat like a clergyman at a political dinner, a symbol of domesticated religion invited to ease the consciences and the digestive tracts of the powerful with vague but affable prayers. These diners, looking up from their endless courses are troubled by the Pope's insistence that religion is tested and proven in daily living and that we share the burden and opportunity to make the world a more hospitable community for all people. (Kennedy 1988, 11)

In this role, as portrayed by Kennedy, the Pope shrewdly challenges two major players in the development game. He asks the controllers of wealth to think deeply about their responsibilities. This is important but hardly new. However, he also confronts the utopian-style ideologues who emphasize the "us versus them" mentality in the development process and accentuate divisiveness rather than unity (Kennedy 1988, 11). This is more insightful because the latter wear the guise of reform but in fact often manipulate the process for their own purposes. They frustrate the attainment of solidarity.

Solidarity is linked to interdependence. The moral outrage that all peoples feel at violations of human rights in any part of the world (El Salvador, Nicaragua, and so on) is a stunning example of what is really meant by interdependence. It means more than economic or trade or resource interlinkage;

it is mutual bonding on a moral level as well. It is sensed "as a system determining relationships in the contemporary world, in its economic, cultural, political and religious elements, and accepted as a moral category. When interdependence becomes recognized in this way, the correlative response as a moral and social attitude, as a virtue, is solidarity" (*SRS* #38). Solidarity is a way by which individuals and peoples can place themselves in the position of the "other" and recognize each other as persons.

Solidarity is offered as a contribution to the development policy debate, not as a technical solution—for the Church cannot do that—but as something which affects the dignity of people in the process. The Church presents itself as an "expert in humanity" (*Populorum Progressio* #13 and qtd. in *SRS* #41).

> Following the example of my predecessors I must repeat that whatever affects the dignity of individuals and peoples, such as authentic development, cannot be reduced to a "technical" problem. If reduced in this way, development would be emptied of its true content, and this would be an act of betrayal of the individuals and peoples whom development is meant to serve. (*SRS* #14)

THE SIGNIFICANCE OF ALL THIS

Assessing the impact of documents like the Bishops' pastoral letter on the American economy is always hard, because we are talking about the realm of ideas and discussion rather than gross national product, about conceptual frameworks rather than numbers being crunched. One cannot quantify ideas and values. We have, however, clearly reached a stage of societal development in this country where values and priorities count for much. We talk incessantly about "quality of life," about "quality time," about ethical dimensions of business and personal behavior. On the other hand (the economist's favorite expression!), we have as a society long since grown beyond the view of the 1950s that higher GNP equals more economic well-being. Secretary of Defense during the Eisenhower administration (and a former CEO of General Motors Corp.) Charles Wilson remarked that "what's good for G.M. is good for the country." But this has been relegated to the nostalgia bin as a quaint reminder of what we were in that time.

On the other hand, the emphasis on values and qualitative dimensions is shown in counterpoint against the bald materialism of some of the players in the financial markets. In the financial scandals of recent times the relentless amassing of wealth by prominent individuals sets up not only unsavory role models but seems also to challenge the fundamental economic law of diminishing marginal utility when applied to money.

Economic development as an issue is less publicized than in the past, but is no less important. It is also more deadly in its implications because of the widening gap between the have and have-not nations. Despair, desperation, and economic and political terrorism have surfaced more prominently. In this kind of cauldron countersignals are needed. The documents we have looked at provide just that. They are statements by people who command respect in the domestic and global forums about what the full understanding of economic development is. They are contributing to the debate, influencing the focus of the discussion, and insuring that the non-economic elements are retained and highlighted. They make sure that humanistic criteria are present and that ethical standards are applied to policy proposals. Who else, after all, will do it?

The advanced stage of societal development, with its affluence, material-ism, technological wizardry, and cynicism, is also proving to be an advanced laboratory for concerns about values. If we can do almost anything technologi-cally, then the only real remaining barriers concern what should be done rather than what *can* be done. Many contemporary Americans are less well-fitted to deal with the former, because it can't be reduced to numbers. The Bishops and John Paul II offer guidelines for the development maze, and their suggestions should continue to resonate in the development debate for years to come.

References

Bernardin, Joseph. 1988. "Encyclical Meshes with U.S. Bishops' Pastorals." *National Catholic Reporter* May 27:5.

Friedman, Milton quoted in Thomas N. Gannon, ed. 1987. *The Catholic Challenge to the American Economy.* New York: Macmillan.

Galbraith, John Kenneth. 1988. "Encyclical a Strong Swipe at U.S. Economic Policies." *National Catholic Reporter* May 27:13.

Greeley, Andrew. 1985. "The Bishops and the Economy: A Radical Dissent." *America* Jan. 12:25.

Hebblethwaite, Peter. 1988. "*On Social Concern* Lofts a Few New Concerns." *National Catholic Reporter* May 27:3.

Henriot, Peter. 1988. "Neither East nor West Has Panacea." *National Catholic Reporter* 27:7.

John Paul II. 1987. *Sollicitudo Rei Socialis (On Social Concern).* Washington: U.S. Catholic Conference.

Kennedy, Eugene. 1988. "Pope, Thoroughly Moved, Aims to Disturb Us." *National Catholic Reporter* May 27:11.

Lernoux, Penny. 1988. "Technology Not the Answer, As Brazil Shows." *National Catholic Reporter* May 27:9.

National Conference of Catholic Bishops. 1986. *Economic Justice for All: Pastoral Letter on Catholic Social Teaching and the U.S. Economy.* Washington: U.S. Catholic Conference.

Business Ethics in the Global Workplace

Darlene A. Pienta, Ph.D.
Department of Management
University of San Diego
San Diego, California

♦

A lot of people have principles until it costs them something.
(from the 1984 film, "Word of Honor")

One of the problems plaguing research into personal values and ethics is the reality that a self-report of "I value life" or "I am an ethical manager" may be perception rather than actual behavior. Furthermore, it is often only when values clash that persons can test through observable behavior to what extent they value life or to what degree they will choose right over wrong behavior. In other words, "the proof is in the pudding." Unfortunately, pudding has far more defined boundaries than do values or ethics.

The world of business ethics suffers even further ambiguity because of certain legal devices. The concept of corporation gives a single identity, a form of "personhood" to a business which often includes many persons and personalities. This concept of single entity or identity carries many advantages for the organization, and while it may help clarify its legal accountability and that of its individual members, it complicates the understanding of ethical responsibility. "What then of the ethical dilemma on a personal level? Can the corporation have an ethical dilemma that is not shared by the individual corporation manager? I think not" (Stanley 1986, 504).

Further confusion occurs when reification of the corporation is accepted as not only a legitimate assumption but the basis for theory and hypothesis building. Thus, analyses have appeared that focus on the "sociopathic" firm or the "addictive" organization. While fascinating from a sociopsychological perspective, it mixes levels of analyses and may even minimize or dismiss the significant limitations of aggregation. This approach distracts attention from important preliminary exploration of the complexity of corporate ethical conduct.

Years ago Winston Churchill wrote a book entitled *While England Slept* in which he discussed England's unpreparedness for World War II. Some time after, a young undergraduate Harvard student, John F. Kennedy, wrote a thesis entitled *Why England Slept*. This supposed play on words was an attempt to apply additional data and analysis to understand better the delicate balance between war and peace. Business communities of today are recipients of prodigious amounts of data yet have access to sophisticated systems of analysis. And so simple description of reality has given way to a more refined analysis that accommodates the complexity of "why." This fine tuning of knowledge has also affected humankind's and business's understanding of themselves in relationship not only to other stakeholder groups who share their nation's cultural system but to the foreign groups whose culture results in behavior that is different and, at times, in conflict with their own.

This chapter will consider business ethics within the perspective of a global workplace. It will emphasize the complexity of human behavior and thus the complexity of human business behavior. Value pluralism even domestically is often a quagmire of competing claims. The multinational corporation within its international workplace faces even greater difficulties as ethical issues of nationalism and economic dependency are confronted.

This discussion will first present *assumptions* upon which this paper is based. A second part will examine *problems* associated with an ethical understanding of global business behavior. A last section will offer *practical steps* for businesses of all nationalities to begin to solve each of the problems. While this author is a citizen of the U.S., an attempt is made to present ideas from a nonnational-based perspective; this is the author's understanding of *global* as distinct from international where a more distinct national identity is predicated. An effort is made to step back from assuming that any one philosophical system provides a global standard for ethics. In fact if the bias of nationality is at least acknowledged in deliberations over "right" behavior, false dilemmas are introduced (DeGeorge 1986) and compromise the resolution of the issues. Indeed, there is a distinct effort at suggesting that the world's communities have *just arrived* at the initial phase of simply *recognizing* the difficulties in developing acceptable standards for global business transactions. Historically, difficulties were often resolved by war by virtue of the value "might makes right." In a modern nuclear age the battle field has leveled. And while ancient questions of survival and dominance continue to be asked, answers are today moderated by technological know-how. Infusing this know-how with wisdom is the difficult task of ethical living.

ASSUMPTIONS

Ethics are prescriptive standards of behavior.

Ethics are principles or standards that prescribe what I should do; that is, what is *right* to do in this particular situation. If the principles or standards are rooted in a system of belief or philosophy regarding the nature of person, then these principles might also be regarded as morals. So one speaks of a "Protestant Ethic" or a "Christian Ethic." Behavior, then, that follows ethical principles is called ethical behavior. Behavior that is contrary to ethical principles is deemed unethical.

Values are descriptive standards of behavior.

While values *are* standards, they do not prescribe. They *describe* a desirable state of being or desirable object. They are flexible yet relatively stable hierarchical standards against which and toward which the evaluator measures and/or directs his or her behavior (Pienta 1987). "Values [are] not tied to any specific object or situation. [They] transcendentally guide actions and judgments across specific objectives and situations" (Harrison 1981, 152). Ethical or right behavior is rooted in what is considered desirable; unethical or wrong behavior is rooted in what is considered undesirable.

Society is the final arbitrator of acceptable, ethical behavior.

Who decides what is desirable and ultimately, what behavior is ethical? Society, through socialization and enculturation, determines what is acceptable behavior. Because socialization is a developmental process (some would consider it evolutionary), society moves through a process of increased sophistication in which the understanding of the nature of person and personal relationship is adjusted.

Ethical behavior is developmental.

This movement of "society" is at one and the same time a movement or development of *individuals* within that society. Although individual behavior is moderated by the groups in which the individual has membership, individual insight and charisma through both actual and vicarious experience is able to break the miasma of group consciousness and draw the group or society to new understandings of itself and its relationship to other groups and societies. The impact of society on individual ethical behavior is somewhat similar to the proverbial question about the fallen tree. That is, if a tree falls and no one is there to witness the fall, did the tree make a noise? Likewise, if an individual without another individual observing behaves unacceptably, was it unethical behavior? The point is that individuals exist with other individuals who help define the world about them. Marilyn Vos Savant, in a Q&A newspaper column, was asked, "Is morality universal, or is it relative to the individual?" Her response underscored the mutual dependency of individual and society.

Morality may be relative to the individual, but where there are enough individuals who think alike—for good or bad reasons— they conceive principles of conduct whereby they seek to influence the behavior of all. (1988,7)

Business's understanding of its ethical responsibility within the international workplace is at a very rudimentary level.

Society reflects on differences and either accommodates, assimilates or rejects. It is at this *point of reflection* that global business and aspiring global business finds itself today. The proliferation and extent of international business transactions have caused questions of applied business ethics across national borders to become focal points of concern in company boardrooms and legislative assemblies. Using Erikson's life-cycle model, the issue is somewhat analogous to the first crisis of human development, that of trust vs. mistrust.

Increasingly, corporations face litigation that is mired in the grayness of a behavior-judgment continuum that stretches from very acceptable to grievously mortal and unacceptable. Many business transactions may be placed at any one of several positions on that continuum depending on the value system and subsequently, on the ethical-legal perspective of the business transactors. "All pay-off situations are not straight forward and unambiguous which may make a clear response more difficult" (Lane and Simpson 1984, 36). Thus, this paper confronts the first problem in understanding business in a global workplace, the problem of "when" or "at what point?"

THE PROBLEM OF WHEN

When or at what point is giving a gift a bribe, and when is it simply appreciation (either before or after the fact) for facilitating business? *When* is information, however it is communicated, insider trading, and when is it simply fair dealing with a legitimate stakeholder? Moreover, *who* decides what standards will prescribe behavior? Is there a mistake in perception when a Mexican observes her North American friend slipping a $10 bill into the *maitre d*'s hand, is subsequently guided to a front table, and suggests to her friend that "morida" is a fine reward system for a job well done? Pastin touches on this confusion over definition in a discussion of ethical values as "categorical" or *"prima facie."* Categorical rules allow no exceptions; *prima facie* rules allow no exceptions *when other things are equal.* But as he cautions, "The problem, then, is determining when other things are equal" (1986, 116). Another author refers to the "Kew Gardens principle" which again raises consideration of when. Kew Gardens is a section in New York City where in 1960 a young woman was stabbed to death while many neighbors heard and saw the crime.

> The Kew Gardens principle says that when four conditions hold, and *the more they hold* [italics my own], the more you have an obligation to go to the aid of another. The four conditions are need, proximity, capability, and last resort. (Simon, et al. 1972, 22)

Determining need and deciding that no other alternative exists may assume an understanding of culture that is often not available to international business negotiators or managers. Reports of corporate bungling of less mortal ethical dilemmas faced reveal the paucity of cultural sensitivity within corporate life.

Problems of Language and Custom — A Mythology of International Ethics

Because language is a sophisticated embodiment of a culture, an inability to speak the language is often accompanied by a misunderstanding of the culture's standard operating procedures. It is obvious to those who have struggled through English, Italian, French, or Spanish 101 classes or Berlitztype immersion experiences, that communicating in a second language is difficult without extensive practice. Idioms, when literally translated, often bring uproarious laughter from the native; nuances are less noticeable but are hardly less serious a problem than the idiom. Thus, even discussion aimed at clarifying whose standards and how rigidly they will be observed is complicated by barriers of embarrassment, frustration, and ultimately suspicion raised by nonfamiliarity with the client's native language.

> They [managers of foreign subsidiaries] feel that communication entails a good deal more than mechanical translation; that one cannot really understand another culture without access to the language. They also have found that the trust established when speaking a person's native language is often essential for effective communication. (Korbin 1984, 35)

Consequently a third problem arises, a problem of "mythology."

Various behaviors are symbolic manifestations of a culture's philosophical bases. Thus, a protracted ceremony of food and drink may be a sign of respect in one culture; in another it may represent delay tactics or worse, a disinterest in the deal to be negotiated. Without the facility of language, misperceptions are difficult to clarify and often are communicated back to one's own culture in the form of mythology (Johnson 1985). "All of those officials are corrupt. Bribery is the only language they understand." This misunderstanding sets the stage for developing a certain predisposition on the part of business persons with little foreign experience to believe that Country A is corrupt, with pay-offs as their cultural fact-of-life. Add to this a failure to examine the evidence or its source critically and the sensationalism of some media reporting, and the myth becomes more believed than the reality (Lane and Simpson 1984). Other misconceptions, such as "They aren't worried about pollution and pesticides; they need all the help they can get and we need all the business we can get" leads to a third problem, that of economic vulnerability. "Is it ethical to produce whatever the market wants or should there be some kind of limit?" (Spiller 1986).

THE PROBLEM OF ECONOMIC VULNERABILITY

This problem is perhaps cast best in terms of less developed countries (LDCs) and developed countries (Windsor 1986). The question of economic vulnerability is two sided. One side might be considered from the humanitarian view. As straightforward as this may appear, it is subject to various interpretations. The LDC may reason that a lack of resources entitles it to certain business gratuities and advantages. This notion is based on the assumption that the market mechanism associated with free choice and full information systems is not valid in certain undeveloped economies (Stanley 1986). Ironically, since this market norm does not operate, the *developed* country's multinational enterprise (MNE) seeking transactions with the LDC may reason that other norms which govern their domestic behavior may also be waived and a Bhopal or Nestle baby formula tragedy is judged an unanticipated secondary consequence of an imperfect marketplace.

This dilemma is exacerbated when LDCs resent the implication that they are less safety conscious or less humanitarian than their foreign business partners and demand autonomy from developed countries' system of product or safety norms.

Secondary consequences have also been considered from a positive perspective. A prime example is the use of an international business presence to cajole the host government economically into making ethical decisions that reflect the values of that foreign business's culture. South Africa is a major example of this thinking. On the other hand, economic blockades have been initiated to move beyond cajoling toward ultimatum-type negotiation.

Resource dependency may be on the part of the developed country seeking cost efficient raw materials of labor, minerals, etc., from the "unmined" LDC. In this kind of reverse humanitarianism the developed country considers itself the less fortunate. Here a company's financial position or its need for a contract takes precedence over the possible secondary consequences such as unemployment in the developed country or pollution in the LDC.

Someone has interpreted the Golden Rule to mean, "Them who has the gold, rules." This reference to resource surplus has been used to suggest that large, so-called socially responsible corporations are more sensitive to ethical issues because they can *afford* to be. Obviously, economic vulnerability is a complex issue. It is singled out here as a critical perspective because of the frequency with which the LDC is part of and often the victim in international business scandals in which ethical standards are violated.

It was suggested above that standards of right and wrong are developmental; that as a country satisfies basic needs of safety, housing, and food, *standards* of safety, of adequate housing, and of food can be developed that define *how* safe, *how* adequate the housing, and *how* adequate the food. That is, to what extent can crime, slums, and malnutrition be tolerated before behavior that contributes (or causes) crime, slums, and malnutrition be judged unethical? Can the rather crude maxim be true, that "beggars can't be choosers" and implicitly that those from whom the less developed receive aid, albeit in the form of investment or technology transfer, can choose to follow standards that, while acceptable (ethical) in the LDC society, are unacceptable (unethical) in the industrialized country's society? Perhaps the answer lies in accepting local custom regardless of violating personal or organizational ethics?

WHEN IN ROME...

Finally, we would offer the advice that when in Rome do as the "better" Romans do. But, we would add, do not underestimate the time, effort, and expense it may take to find the better Romans and establish a relationship with them. (Lane and Simpson 1984, 42)

Can it be as simple as finding the "better" Romans? Or perhaps it is *not* simple to find them. Perhaps the cost of time, effort, and other resources demand that the socially minded foreign investor do as the Romans do hoping that the better Romans, as a result of their economic benevolence (and regardless of the Coliseum games), will rise to the top like cream in milk and be the initiators of a more ethical society; i.e., stop the games. Or is there a choice somewhere between finding the Romans and finding the "better" Romans?

It appears that there is a kind of ethical osmosis that has been occurring as international business transactions increase. When values clash, there is a residue of moral uncertainty that lingers after the conflict has been resolved. All transactors in the confrontation are forced to reevaluate personal and organizational hierarchies of values. As a result, questionable business dealings generally identified by under-the-table or covert practice may in time move from a questionable status to openly embraced or patently rejected transactions. This cross fertilization of values and beliefs that occurs through the very process of international business transactions directly affects individual value development. The protest movements of 1815-1848 and the 1960s witnessed this consciousness-raising phenomenon.

This understanding, then, suggests that there may be universal ethics (Vernon and Dillon 1986) that, given conditions of increased international business, can be formulated to the mutual satisfaction of all parties involved. At this relatively introductory stage of truly global business, it would be premature to assume that no such consensus is possible even granting the radical diversity of world communities. If the "thought is parent to the action," then the assumption is parent to the thought. It is important not to limit alternatives too early in the analysis. These universal ethics call for a step beyond what the laws of the land demand (Tuleja 1985). They mean going beyond what the Romans or even the better Romans do.

> Establishing good relationships with the right people requires an
> investment of time, money and energy. An unwillingness of either
> party to make this investment is often interpreted as a lack of
> sincerity or interest. (Lane and Simpson 1984, 41)

Practically speaking, it is a stretching exercise for the foreign country in that it may call for acceptance of a different or nonlegislated ethic and stretching for the home country's business-seeking enterprise in that it may require a cost in time or money that is beyond what is currently profitable practice. How far beyond is again a judgment call of "when" or at what point. For example, at what point "should" foreign countries who denounce apartheid enter into business transactions with South Africa? How much "stretching" is required? Should it be when Pretoria binds itself to observance of the Sullivan Code, or when the system of Homelands is abolished, or—when?

As the U.S. learned, benevolent slave masters did not resolve the basic inequities of human bondage. It would appear that systemic inequities create ethical dilemmas that may not be resolvable by evolutionary development but only through a shock with enough trauma to reconfigure the parts of the system. The extent of the system's pathology or a measure of the amount that members stand to lose through a reconfigured system determines the tenacity of the system to self-perpetuation. Obviously a granite-like resistance to change defies the most optimistic vision of a global ethic as well as proposed models of ethical principles to which the vast majority of countries might aspire.

One of the dilemmas that occupy the minds of philosophers and lawyers is that of moral agency (Noreen 1988). That is, while it is apparent that an individual can be morally responsible for his or her behavior, it is not as apparent that a corporation can be held morally responsible for its behavior. More than one writer has commented on this as an exercise in futility (Manning 1984). It is perhaps of more use to provide individuals and groups of all sizes (families, educational classes, small to large businesses, industry, and societal groups) with opportunities to investigate the values that most affect behavior as well as the values that most affect the behavior of foreign cultures (Paul and Bremer 1986). Various kinds of analytical techniques such as simulation, brainstorming, Delphi, exchange programs, etc., are invaluable in this investigation. In today's business world much effort is spent on determining who is culpable. It would appear that a simultaneous, multilevel, and notably more positive approach to successful business transactions might be taken through intensive educational efforts funded and supported by business. "The process of formulating, implementing, and revising a code [or clarifying values] may be more important than the code itself" (Berenbeim 1988).

BUSINESS ETHICS IN A GLOBAL WORKPLACE:
A STRATEGIC ISSUE
SOME SUGGESTIONS

As in strategic planning, it behooves the organization to identify as many alternatives as possible and choose that one or those alternatives that maximize strengths and opportunities and minimize weaknesses and threats. Several strategic alternatives for *developing* effective business ethics in a global context are offered below. If large and not so large corporations are increasingly being advised to "think international," then there is some urgency for business to begin a proactive management of their ethical position. Generally, these suggestions must be implemented in tandem. That is, they are mutually dependent and most likely must be developed simultaneously.

No place to hide

My theory is that with the information age we are in, with telecommunications expanding and improving all the time, there is little place to hide. Everything you do is apt to be known someday somewhere by somebody; so maybe it is better not to do it, not because you are a believer, but just because you do not want to be caught. I think this may be the reason why the behavior of companies is changing—not because companies are becoming more ethical. (Spiller 1986, 90)

This appears to be a salutory motivation to "do good and avoid evil." And while it has a significant bottom-line appeal, it was placed here for top-line attention to remind us all that we exist and indeed will prosper only through the consent of others. An overriding assumption here is that the reciprocal back-scratching that often accompanies business dealings can be a personally and communally enhancing arrangement. The balance to be struck between the personal and the societal may be very dependent on business's perception of places to hide and society's acquiescence to certain kinds of behavior. A major tenet of this paper has been that this balance changes as societies are confronted with opposing values.

Ethical responsibility is learned: Concentric Diversification

The learning approach suggested here is an inductive one. And while there's a certain linearity implied, the learning system is an open one with continual feedback loops.

The Individual

The individual comes to the organization with personal values in place. This relatively stable hierarchy of standards is subject to adjustment depending on the circumstance. Also, depending on circumstance, there will be more or less discomfort when high-priority values are consistently or temporarily displaced by lesser values.

Since the organization has values which have been developed through the primary influence of founder and top management yet has been chosen as a desirable workplace by the individual, it is likely that there will be some congruencies and some incongruencies between individual and corporate values. Once again, the balance is critical. There is some evidence to suggest that highest performers may be rated as such because of *incongruent* values (Pienta 1987). That is, it appears that a certain dissonance in values is renewing and leads to more success than too similar values. How is this fine tuning to be implemented by the organization?

Values Clarification: A process of values clarification will allow individuals to express what is important to them. If nothing else is gained from sessions where exercises are provided for this purpose, middle and top managers will gain an insight into what motivates their subordinates. More importantly, however, is the opportunity for businesspersons to confront different value systems and to make decisions through a relatively nonthreatening simulation of probable international business dilemmas. Before an international incident actually occurs, the scenario can be "played" with consequences listed and weighed and appropriate action suggested. A "stitch in time" may save the organization millions of dollars in litigation that could arise from unanticipated employee misdemeanors.

The Corporation

There is an assumed hope that a company can be more than the sum of its parts—that each person and each activity contribute synergistically to a successful enterprise. This hope is given a more than even chance for success if the individual members of the organization are committed to its goals and objectives. Personal value clarification not only is able to help individuals define priority values but gives the organization a chance to concentrate its strategy by aligning its goals and goals of the individual member more precisely. As open systems, both the individual and the organization as an entity receive mutual feedback and are in turn modified to face feedback once again with subsequent adjustment and so on. If the organization is to compete successfully in an international workplace, it must carefully consider the impact of its corporate values and the personal values of its managers on successful negotiations with other organizations whose business behavior is likewise shaped by individual and corporate values. This strategic analysis has several steps:

1. Understanding the personal values operating in the home corporate culture as well as the company's competitive strengths and weaknesses.
2. Understanding where opportunities and threats lie within the international market and being able to describe the cultures (as well as the countries) where business might best succeed.
3. Anticipating differences in foreign philosophy, values, and customs.
4. Writing down a corporate Code of Conduct (Ethics) that will capitalize on the value focus that exists within the company by maximizing the similarities that exist with the foreign cultures and minimizing the differences.

This is not a one day, one week, or even one month process. It is more likely to take three to six months in which individual value clarification occurs simultaneously with corporate sessions aimed at developing a cohesive and comprehensive Code. It is also important to recognize that as strategic alliances shift, so too will some of the more detailed sections of the Code. This last point suggests that any Code will include both general and specific prescriptions.

Any Code is only as effective as its ability to direct and monitor behavior. If the Code is so vague that any activity can be construed as acceptable, it is a useless document. A second criteria recommends that each person in the organization be formally given a written copy and secondly, that sanctions be established that will motivate compliance and discourage infraction. A system of periodic and well-defined rewards and swift retaliation for violations will encourage appropriate behavior. There is a self-motivating element already built into the Code insofar as it specifically recognizes values as defined in the values-clarification sessions proposed above.

The International Business Community

This is perhaps the most difficult level to operationalize as it is the most remote and the subject of considerable uncertainty and thus control. Nonetheless, efforts at organizing some type or coordinating system are already occurring. Even though a working International Code of Business Ethics may be currently elusive, it would well serve the world's communities if discussions might begin on mechanisms that might promote the growth and prosperity of all nations as we move toward a world economy. Researchers who today are investigating cross-cultural business values offer a great service to this cause. And while it may be difficult if not impossible to find an "ethical one-size-fits-all," researchers can help identify variations in the sizes.

CONCLUSION

The inconsistency of behavior has historically frustrated the efforts of social scientists to construct rigorous predictive models of human behavior. Nonetheless, there are behavioral consistencies that allow peoples to live in peace and to work together to build a better world. In an era of internationalism it is becoming more evident that the efforts of businesses to build better mousetraps may be more amply rewarded if the mousetrap includes directions for use in Arabic, Spanish, Japanese, English, etc. But just as language uses symbols to express its speaker's essence, hopes, and fears, so too must business develop and express, through concrete behavior, its value of right behavior. And because "right behavior" is determined by society and because our world is a *many* "societied" world, right behavior cannot be viewed as the product of any one society but the collective wisdom of many societies contributing their unique insights into the nature of person. If Dante spoke of the universe present in each person, then consider the excitement of discovery that lay ahead in a truly global community.

References

Berenbeim, R. E. 1988. "An Outbreak of Ethics." *Across the Board* 25: 15-19.

Bowie, H. 1981. *Business Ethics*. Englewood Cliffs: Prentice-Hall.

DeGeorge, R. T. "Ethical Dilemmas for Multinational Enterprise: A Philosophical Overview." Ed. W. M. Hoffman, A. E. Lange, and D. A. Fredo, Lanham: U P of America. 39-57.

Harrison, E. F. 1981. *The Managerial Decision-Making Process*. 2nd ed. Boston: Houghton Mifflin.

Johnson, H. L. 1985. "Bribery in International Markets: Diagnosis, Clarification and Remedy." *Journal of Business Ethics* 4: 447-55.

Kobrin, S. J. 1984. *International Expertise in American Business: How to Learn to Play with the Kids on the Street*. New York: Institute of International Education.

Lane, H. W., and D. G. Simpson. 1984. "Bribery in International Business: Whose Problem Is It?" *Journal of Business Ethics* 3: 35-42.

Manning, R. C. 1984. "Corporate Responsibility and Corporate Person-hood." *Journal of Business Ethics* 3: 77-84.

Noreen, E. 1988. "The Economics of Ethics: A New Perspective on Agency Theory." *Accounting, Organizations and Society* 13.4: 359-69.

Pastin, M. 1986. *The Hard Problems of Management: Gaining the Ethics Edge*. San Francisco: Jossey Bass.

Paul, K., and O. A. Bremer. 1986. "Using Macroeconomic Theory to Anchor Problems: Ethical Issues and Multinationals." *Ethics and the Multinational Enterprise: Proceedings of the Sixth National Conference on Business Ethics* Ed. W. M. Hoffman, A. E. Lange and D. A. Fedo. Lanham: U P of America. 47-57.

Pienta, D. A. 1987. "An Investigation of the Impact of Congruent Managerial Values on Appraisal Behavior." Unpublished doctoral dissertation, University of Southern California.

Spiller, H. J. 1986. "Multinational Corporations: Ethics or Self-Interest?" *Ethics and the Multinational Enterprise: Proceedings of the Sixth National Conference on Business Ethics*. Ed. W. M. Hoffman, A. E. Lange and D. A. Fedo. Lanham U P of America. 87-91.

Stanley, M. T. 1986. "The Foreign Direct Investment Decision and Job Export as an Ethical Dilemma for the Multinational Corporation." *Ethics and the Multinational Enterprise: Proceedings of the Sixth National Conference on Business Ethics*. Ed. W. M. Hoffman, A. E. Lange and D. A. Fedo. Lanham: U P of America. 493-509.

Tuleja, T. 1985. *Beyond the Bottom Line: How Business Leaders Are Turning Principles into Profits*. New York: Facts on File.

Vernon, R., and C. Dillon, 1986. "Ethics and the Multinational Enterprise." *Ethics and the Multinational Enterprise: Proceedings of the Sixth National Conference on Business Ethics*. Ed. W. M. Hoffman, A. E. Lange and D. A. Fedo. Lanham: U P of America. 61-69.

Von Savant, Marilyn. 1988. "Q & A." *Parade* (December 11):7.

Windsor, D. 1986. "Defining the Ethical Obligations of the Multinational Enterprise." *Ethics and the Multinational Enterprise: Proceedings of the Sixth National Conference on Business Ethics*. Ed W. M. Hoffman, A. E. Lange and D. A. Fedo. Lanham: U P of America. 71-85.

Contributors

Kenneth M. Bond is Professor of Management at Humbolt State University. He teaches extensively on the relation between business and society. His *Bibliography of Business Ethics and Business Moral Values* was published in its fourth edition in January of 1988.

Norman Bowie is Director of the Center for the Study of Human Values at the University of Delaware.

Vincent Calluzzo is Assistant Professor at the Hagan School of Business, Iona College, New Rochelle, New York.

Barbara Cowell is a Research Fellow for the Oxford Philosophy Trust, Oxford, England.

Charles P. Duffy is Assistant Professor of Management at the Hagan School of Business, Iona College, New Rochelle, New York specializing in Business Strategy and Organizational Behavior. He is co-founder of the Management Development Institute at Iona College and was the recipient of the Fullbright Fellowship Senior Lecturer Award in 1984-85. During that year he was Guest Professor on the business faculty at the University of Mannheim, West Germany. He has served as consultant on managerial issues for New York Telephone Company, Merrill Lynch, the NYNEX Corporation, the County of Westchester and several other organizations.

Robert A. Eberle is Associate Professor of Management at the Hagan School of Business, Iona College, New Rochelle, New York.

Kenneth M. Frawley is the Corporate Director of Training and Development for the NYNEX Corporation. His areas of specialization include Management Assessment and Executive Development. He serves on the Board of Directors of the American Assembly of Collegiate Schools of Business and is Director of The Leo House.

Robert Frederick teaches in the Philosophy Department at Bentley College, Waltham, Massachusetts. He is also Assistant Director of the Center for Business Ethics at Bentley and is Chairperson of the Center's National Conferences on Business Ethics. He has published and lectured extensively on Business Ethics and served as a consultant to several major corporations.

Joseph W. Ford is Associate Professor of Business Economics at the Hagan School of Business, Iona College, New Rochelle, New York.

Samuel M. Natale is Director of the Institute for Professional and Management Ethics at Iona College and is Professor of Studies in Corporate Values at the Hagan School of Business, Iona College, New Rochelle, New York.

He is the Editor of the *International Journal of Value-Based Management* and is the author of eight books and numerous articles.

Darlene A. Pienta teaches in the Department of Management at the University of San Diego. She is Editor for Management and Public Policy for the *International Journal of Value-Based Management*.

David P. Schmidt is Director of the Trinity Center for Ethics and Corporate Policy in New York. He has worked as a Corporate Relations Officer for the University of Chicago where he also received a Doctorate in Social Ethics. He has appeared on national television as a speaker on corporate ethics.

Arthur Sharplin is Distinguished Professor of Management at McNeese State University, Lake Charles, Louisiana, USA. He formerly taught at Bentley College. He served in the Navy's nuclear submarine program during the 1960s. Before starting his teaching career in 1980, he founded and managed several entrepreneurial businesses, in manufacturing, merchandising, and contracting. Sharplin presently serves as consultant to the Attorney General of Louisiana, the Asbestos Victims of America, and numerous business clients. He is an author of 10 textbooks and over 50 articles. His management cases, including one featuring the Manville Corporation, appear in 40 college textbooks.

Sebastian A. Sora is Manager of Educational Services at the Latin American Headquarters of IBM in Mt. Pleasant, New York. He is editor for Science and Technology for the *International Journal of Value-Based Management*.

John B. Wilson is a Fellow of Mansfield College, University of Oxford. He is European Editor of the *International Journal of Value-Based Management*.